Edward Bartlett

A monograph of the weaver-birds,

Ploceidand arboreal and terrestrial finches, Fringillid

Edward Bartlett

A monograph of the weaver-birds,
Ploceidand arboreal and terrestrial finches, Fringillid

ISBN/EAN: 9783337733285

Printed in Europe, USA, Canada, Australia, Japan

Cover: Foto ©ninafisch / pixelio.de

More available books at **www.hansebooks.com**

A MONOGRAPH

OF THE

WEAVER-BIRDS,

PLOCEIDÆ,

AND

ARBOREAL AND TERRESTRIAL FINCHES,

FRINGILLIDÆ,

BY

EDWARD BARTLETT.

Maidstone:
PUBLISHED BY THE AUTHOR.
1888.

TEXTOR DINEMELLI.
THE GREAT WHITE-HEADED WEAVER.

PLATE I., Fig. 1.

Textor dinemelli, Horsfield.
Textor dinemelli, Gray et Mitch. Gen. of Birds, ii. p. 350 pl. lxxxvii. fig. 2. (1844).
Textor leucocephalus, Rüpp. Syst. Ueber. Vög. Nord-ost-Afrika's, p. 72. (1845).
Textor dinemelli, Rüpp. Syst. Ueber. Vög. Nord-ost-Afrika's, pp. 72, 76. pl. xxx. (1845).
Textor dinemelli, Lefebv. Voy. en Abyssinie, vi. p. 108 (1845-50).
Alecto dinemelli, Bonap. Consp. Gen. Av. p. 438 (1850).
Textor dinemelli, Buvry, Journ. für Ornith. 1855, p. 65.
Alecto dinemelli, J. W. von Müller, Journ. für Ornith. 1855, p. 460.
Textor dinemellii, Heugl. Syst. Übers. Vög. N.-O.-Afr. p. 37 (1856).
Textor dinemelli, Horsf. et Moore, Cat. Birds in Mus. E. I. C. ii. p. 521 (1856-8).
Dinemellia leucocephala, Reich. Singvögel, p. 88. pl. xlv. figs. 327-28 (1861).
Alecto dinemelii, Heugl. Journ. für Ornith. 1862, p. 25.
Alecto dinemelli, Antin. Cat. di Uccelli, p. 63 (1864).
Textor dinemellii, Heugl. Journ. für Ornith. 1867, p. 367.
Textor dinemelli, Heugl. Peterm. Geogr. Mith. 1869, p. 415.
Textor dinemelli, Finsch und Hartl. Vög. Ost-Afrika's, p. 386 (1870).
Textor dinemellii, Gray, Hand-List B. ii. p. 40. No. 6556 (1870).
Textor dinemelli, Heugl. Ornith. Nordost-Afrika's, p. 534. Append. p. cxxviii. (1871).
Textor dinemelli, Sharpe, Cat. of African Birds, p. 58 (1871)
Textor dinemelli, Cab. Journ. für Ornith. 1878, pp. 217, 232.
Textor dinemelli, Fischer und Reichenow, Journ. für Ornith. 1878, pp. 299, 351.
Textor dinemelli, Brehm, Thierl. ii. p. 366 (1879)

Textor dinemelli, Shelley, Proc. Zool. Soc. 1882, p. 307.
Textor dinemelli, Böhm, Journ. für Ornith. 1883, p. 196.
Textor dinemelli, Schalow, Journ. für Ornith. 1883, p. 361.
Textor dinemelli, Salvad. Ann. Mus. Civ. di Genova, 1884, p. 194.
Textor dinemelli, Fischer, Zeitsch. für Gesam. Ornith. 1884, p. 333.
Textor dinemelli, Fischer, Journ. für Ornith. 1885, p. 132.
Limoneres dinemelli, Reichenow, Journ. für Ornith. 1885, p. 372.
Textor dinemelli, Shelley, Ibis, 1885, pp. 390, 392, 409.
Textor dinemelli, Shelley, Ibis, 1887, p. 44.

Figures, Rüpp. Vögel Nord-Ost-Afr. pl. xxx. Gray et Mitch. Gen. Birds, pl. lxxxvii. Reich. Singvögel, pl. xlv.

English. *Great White-headed Weaver. White-headed Dinemellia.*
French. *Tisserin de Dinnemell. Dinemellia teté blanche.*
German. *Weisskönfyer Webervogel. Weisskopfige Dinemellia.*
Native Names. "*Kinn, Tulich and Kiungamesi.*" Böhm.

Habitat. North-East and Eastern Africa. "Between about 12° n. lat. and 7° s. lat., from Shoa and Somali to Mamboio." *(Shelley).*

Localities. Shoa, Abyssinia *(Harris).* Addebarrak, North-Eastern Abyssinia and White Nile *(Lefebvre).* Bahr-el-Abiad, Olibo and Belinian *(Heugl.)* Sudan *(Knobleeker).* Malémboa in Ukamba *(Hildebrandt).* Mamboio *(Kirk).* Kokoma *(Böhm).* Jambara and Ambo-Karra *(Antin.)* Wapokomoland, Masai, Barawa and Pare *(Fischer).* Somali-Land *(Phillips).* Masai *(Thomsonn).* Lado *(Emin Bey).*

Male. Head, neck, under-parts, and speculum white; mantle, back, scapulars, wings and tail, dull chocolate brown; primary-coverts black; scapulars, secondaries, great-and lesser wing-coverts, broadly edged with buffish white; shoulders, lower rump, upper- and lower tail-coverts scarlet, varied in some with yellow; thighs black; margins and tips of tail feathers, pale buff; iris brown; lores and skin round eye bluish-black; bill blackish brown, paler at the tip; legs and feet blackish brown: length 7·4, wing 4·3, tail 2·9, tars. 1·1, culm. 0·9.

Female. Similar, but not so large as the male.

I have described below a very small pale coloured bird, probably a female, or an extreme variety.

Observ. The sexes appear to differ but little, according to authors, and I have not had an opportunity of examining a female, or a young bird, the dimensions of those I have seen, do not assist in the determination of the sex.

One specimen (No. 6.), in Capt. Shelley's collection from Somali, is a very striking instance of the extreme variation in a species; in this one, the white of the head and lower parts are strongly tinged with pale salmon; the back, wings and tail are pale earthy-brown, with the edges of the feathers nearly white; the white speculum is merged into the pale brown of the primaries, and all the quills white; the red on the shoulders, rump, upper-and lower tail-coverts, less brilliant; bill, legs and feet blackish.

The colour of the upper parts in many of the other specimens are varied with new feathers, which are always darker than the old and worn ones, some of these very old feathers, have completely lost the fine broad whitish edges, and the new primaries are quite as black as those in *T. Boehmi.*

Several of them are tinged on the breast with a dirty reddish brown substance, which can be removed, this must be obtained while the bird is in search of food, either in Ant hills, or on the ground.

The present species was first made known to science by Major Harris, who obtained it at Shoa in Abyssinia, and the figure appeared in the first part of Gray and Mitchell's 'Genera of Birds,' published in 1844, without a description, but in the following year Rüppell gave a good description and figure of it, in his 'Systematische Uebersicht der Vögel Nordost-Afrika's,' 1845. Since then it has been brought home by many travellers from Abyssinia and East Africa.

Respecting its habits, nidification and distribution, we are indebted to several German travellers, who have of late years greatly increased the knowledge we possess of the *Avi Fauna* of the country inhabited by this bird.

Herr Th. von Heuglin says, " In the stomach we found insects, berries and Durah *(African Millet)*. We received it in winter and spring from the Upper White Nile, viz., from the territories of the Kidj-negroes, from Olibo and the Bolinian. Living sociably like *Textor alecto* on cattle pastures with isolated trees and thickets, in the neighbourhood of rain beds, and is no less lively and talkative than its relations of the same tribe."

Dr. R. Böhm tells us "This prettily coloured weaver is common in the neighbourhood of Kokoma and is found in little flocks, usually in places where groups of trees standing together on expanses of grass form a sort of park-land. I here mention that it constantly lives together with *Urolestes*. (It may be reckoned as highly probable that the name *Kiungamesi* belonging to it, has been falsely mentioned to me for the latter species also). Here from bushes, but preferably from the summit of Acacia-trees he utters that loud, shrill, trumpet-like call which gives rise to his name of *Kiungamesi*. On the wing he utters a disconnected *Kick Kick* like a woodpecker, and a low *piep piep* may be the expression of his content. The Dinemelli weavers are clumsy and awkward in their movements, their flight also is heavy and fluttering. Left to themselves which is seldom the case as we have already seen, they maintain their usual character.

"The nests of this weaver, of which several are usually built together, are generally placed at the summit of thorny Acacias. They consist of large, rather untidy tufts of fine grass, mixed with single feathers and large leaves and are entered by an opening in the lower side. They are carefully fortified with twigs and sharply pointed little branches, which surround not only the nest but are massed deep down and high up on all the branches leading to it. On March 8th, I found a little pair building on a wide spreading Acacia-tree in the Masika Lake, near Itimbua in Wagalla, and on April 28th, I received a nest (without twigs) measuring 24 centimetres in diameter, containing a naked fledgling, which was distinguished by very swollen, yellow corners of its mouth. Two eggs also which I received on May 14th, one addled, the other containing a large embryo, are said to belong to the *Tulich*. They have a grey greenish-white ground, covered with brownish-black spots and marks."

"Plains near Pare, July 31st. Iris brown; bill, bare skin round the eye and feet black.

"I encountered six of these weavers on the ground, among a number of *Notauges superbus*. Their behaviour reminded me of that of the Starling." (G. A. Fischer).

Capt. G. E. Shelley gives us in the 'Ibis,' 1885, Mr. E. Lort Phillips's observations on this species, while in Somali-land. "These birds are fairly common throughout the country, frequenting the Mimosa-trees. They are very noisy when on the wing, and breed in colonies. Their eggs are green, thickly speckled with dark brown, and 0·95 inch long. In one of these colonies a pair of the small Hawk, *Poliohierax semitorquatus*, had usurped a nest, but were regarded apparently as welcome visitors by these sociable Weavers."

Specimens examined.

No.	Sex.	Mus.	Country.	Length.	Wing.	Tail.	Tars.	Culm.
1.	♂	G. E. Shelley.	Lado (*Emin Bey*)	7·4	4·3	2·9	1·1	0·9
2.	(?)	,,	Sudan (*Knoblecker*).	7·3	4·4	3·2	1·2	0·9
3.	(?)	,,	Mamboio (*Dr. Kirk*).	7·9	5·0	3·5	1·3	0·9
4.	(?)	,,	Masai (*Thomsonn*).	7·9	4·5	3·2	1·1	0·9
5.	(?)	,,	Somali (*Phillips*).	8·2	4·8	3·5	1·2	1·1
6.	(?)	,,	Somali (*Phillips*).	7·0	4·3	3·1	1·2	0·9
7.	♂	H. B. Tristram.	Lado (*Emin Bey*).	9·2	4·6	3·7	1·25	0·85

The figure (Plate 1. fig. 1.), is taken from No. 7, lent to me by the Rev. Canon Tristram, ¾ size.

TEXTOR BOEHMI.
BÖHM'S WEAVER.
PLATE I., Fig. 2.

Alecto dinemelli, Sclater, Proc. Zool. Soc. 1864, p. 109.
Textor Böhmi, Reichenow, Journ. für Ornith. 1885, p. 372.
Textor (Limoncres) Böhmi, Reichw. Journ. für Ornith. 1887, p. 67.
Textor Boehmi, Shelley, Ibis, 1887, p. 44.

English. *Böhm's Weaver. Grey-headed Weaver.*
French. *Tisserin de Böhm.*
German. *Böhm's Webervogel.*

Habitat. Central East Africa.

Female. Head, neck, and all the under-parts ashy white, darkest on the ear-coverts; mantle, back, wings and tail brownish black; shoulders red; speculum white; tortials faintly margined with pale buff; rump, upper-and under tail-coverts scarlet, varied with yellow; thighs black: iris reddish brown; lores and orbits, naked, bluish-black; bill brown, lower mandible pale brown; feet brownish-black: length 8·4, wing 4·8, tail 3·7, tars. 1·3, culm. 0·9.

Observ. This bird being a female, and no doubt a young one, may account for its smoky grey plumage. I notice that the new feathers on the head and breast are pure white; the only substantial characters by which it can be separated from the female of *T. dinemelli*, is the darker back wings and tail, and it is a trifle larger.

It is with great reluctance that I separate this bird from the true *Textor dinemelli*, knowing the changes to which the whole group of Weavers are liable, even the localities, difference of climate, seasons and sexes cause variation.

The only specimen (a female) which I have examined, was kindly lent to me by Capt. G. E. Shelley; it is one of Dr. Böhm's birds obtained at Gonda, and is identical, Capt. Shelley tells me, with the type in the Berlin Museum.

This bird is described in the 'Journal für Ornithologie' 1885, by Dr. Reichenow, who says that the specimen brought home by Capt. Speke in 1864, from Unyamuezi, which is now in the Bremen Museum, belongs to this species, and has remained under the name of *Alecto dinemelli*, Sclater, until lately. He also tells us that "The district where *Textor Boehmi* is found, extends over the territory between Tanjanyika and Victoria N'yanza," and it has since been discovered by Dr. Fischer at "Loeru, Massai-country, and builds its nest in Umbrella-Acacias near Seriau."

Capt. Speke's bird was "shot at Tura, in Unyamuezi, where it goes about in small flocks."

No.	Sex.	Mus.	Country.	Length.	Wing.	Tail.	Tars.	Culm.
1.	♀	G. E. Shelley.	Gonda (*Böhm*).	8·4	4·8	3·7	1·3	0·9

The figure (Pl. I., fig. 2) is taken from the above female, ¾ size.

CHRYSOMITRIS ATRATA.
THE BLACK SISKIN.
PLATE I.

Carduelis atrata, Lafr. et D'Orb. Syn. Av. i. p. 83 (1837).
Carduelis atrata, D'Orb. Voy. L'Amer. Merid. p. 364, pl. xlviii. fig. 2 (1835-44).
Fringilla atrata, Gray et Mitch. Gen. Birds, ii. p. 371 (1849).
Chrysomitris atrata, Bonap. Consp. Gen. Av. p. 515 (1850).
Fringilla atratus, Eyton, Catalogue of Birds, p. 257 (1856).
Chrysomitris atrata, Sclater, Catalogue Amer. Birds, p. 125 (1862).
Melanomitris atrata, Cassin, Proc. Acad. Nat. Sc. Philad. 1865, p. 91.
Chrysomitris atrata, Sclater, Proc. Zool. Soc. 1867, pp. 322, 323.
Chrysomitris atrata, Scl. et Salv. Proc. Zool. Soc. 1869, p. 152.
Fringilla atrata, Gray, Hand-List Birds, ii. p. 81 (1870).
Chrysomitris atrata, Scl. et Salv. Nom. Av. Neotr. p. 34 (1873).
Chrysomitris atrata, Tacz. Proc. Zool. Soc. 1874, p. 523.
Chrysomitris atrata, Scl. et Salv. Proc. Zool. Soc. 1879, p. 607.

Figure, D'Orb. Voy. L'Am. Mer. pl. xlviii. fig. 2.

English. *Black Siskin.*
French. *Le Tarin Noir.*
German. *Der Schwarze Zeisig.*
Italian. *Il Lucarino Néro.*
Spanish. *Gilguero.*

Habitat. Bolivia and High Peru.

Male. Black; speculum, lower belly, under-wing and tail-coverts, and basal two-thirds of the tail bright lemon-yellow; the yellow of the belly extending up to the centre of the breast; outer margin of the first primary black; an oblong yellowish white spot on the tertials; secondaries tipped with white; under surface of wing yellow, with blackish points; iris brown; bill dark slaty-brown, lower mandible paler; legs blackish-brown: length 4·7, wing 3·0, tail 2·0, tars. 0·6, culm. 0·4.

2

Young Male. Like the adult, but paler, with a small elongated black shaft-spot on the two longest under tail-coverts.

Female. Similar to male; duller, the yellow on the centre of the belly and breast, more extended; the two black shaft-spots on the under tail-coverts, longer and broader than in the young male; bill and legs as in the male.

Obs. The extent of the yellow markings of both sexes, depend upon age.

Although this curiously coloured Siskin was described by La Fresnaye and D'Orbigny in 1837, from specimens obtained by the latter at La Paz in Bolivia, comparatively little has been said respecting its habits.

M. D'Orbigny in his 'Voyage Dans L'Amerique Meridionale,' adds the following particulars to this species—" This Goldfinch is proper only to the great ravines of La Paz in Bolivia at a height of 3,700 metres above the level of the sea, latitude 17° degrees south. It rests on the bushes, flies in small flocks, especially in the winter, it is very familiar and has the manners of our European goldfinch. Its habits are lively, its flight easy and short. The people rear them in cages for their very agreeable song; the Spaniards call it *Gilguero* and the Aymaras *Chaijña*."

It was also obtained by Mr. Bridges in Bolivia, Mr. H. Whitely secured specimens at Pitumarca in High Peru, at an elevation of 11,000 to 14,000 feet above the sea-level, examples in my collection, were collected by Mr. Weishaupt at Mendoza in the Plata Confederation, and M. Jelski has lately procured it, with the nests and eggs at Junin in Central Peru, at an elevation of about 11,000 feet.

It is clear when we consider the altitude of the localities, in which this bird has been found, that it is exclusively a mountainous resident, keeping to the upper great valleys of the Andes, and occupying an area, as far as I am able to judge from the above localities, of about 11° n. lat. and 35° s. whether it extends its migration into Patagonia, we must leave to future observation.

The only account published respecting the nidification of this bird, is that given by M. L. Taczanowski in the 'Proceedings of the Zoological Society' 1874, from the nests and eggs obtained by M. Jelski at Junin.

"The nests found on the 28th of April and the 8th of June, 1873, were composed of an irregular layer of moss, mixed with a little wool, sprigs of dry herbs, small roots and branches, on this layer is arranged the nest of wool and different kinds of hair; rarely have they any feathers. All this construction is heavy and solid; the interior is rather deep but carefully arranged. Height 4·5, breadth 13, diameter of the interior 4·5, depth 2·5 centim. M. Jelski found them under thatched roofs.

"The eggs are greenish white and present different varieties of marking, some have a large ring composed of very small reddish spots on the upper end, and darker ones scattered over the surface, while others are more spotted and streaked with blackish-brown.

"Dimensions 18·6—13·3, 19·2—13, 19·2—13·1, 19·6—13·6 millim."

The following specimens are in my collection.

No.	Sex.	Mus.	Locality.	Length.	Wing.	Tail.	Tars.	Culm.
a.	♂	E. B.	La Paz, Bolivia (*D'Orbigny*).	4·7	3·1	2·1	0·6	0·4
b.	♂	E. B.	Interior of Bolivia (*Bridges*).	4·7	3·0	2·0	0·6	0·4
c.	♂	E. B.	Mendoza, Plata Confed. (*Weishaupt*).	4·0	3·1	2·2	0·6	0·4
d.	♀	E. B.	Mendoza, Plata Confed. (*Weishaupt*).	4·8	3·1	2·1	0·5	0·4
e.	♀	E. B.	Mendoza, Plata Confed. (*Weishaupt*).	4·0	3·1	2·1	0·5	0·4
f.	♂	E. B.	Mendoza, Plata Confed. (*Weishaupt*).	4·8	3·1	2·0	0·7	0·4

The figures are taken from *b* and *e*.

PAROARIA CUCULLATA.
THE CRESTED DOMINICAN CARDINAL.
PLATE I.

Le Paroare, Buffon, Hist. Nat. Ois. iii. p. 500 (1775).
The Crested Cardinal, Brown's, Illustr. of Zool. p. 54. pl. xxiii. (1776).
Loxia coronata, Miller, Cimelia Physica, p. 4. pl. ii, A (1776).
Le Cardinal Dominiquain hupé de la Louisiane. Pl. Enl. 103 (1777).
Fringilla dominicana cristata, Bodd. Tab. des Pl. Enl. 103 (1783).
Crested Dominican Grosbeak, Lath. Gen. Syn. iii. p. 123. Var. A (1783).
Pope Grosbeak, Penn. Arctic Zoology, ii. p. 350 (1785).
Crested Dominican Grosbeak, Lath. Gen. Syn. Suppl. i. p. 151 (1787).
Loxia dominicana, Gmel. Syst. Nat. ii. p. 848. 8. β (1788).
Loxia cucullata, Lath. Ind. Orn. i. p. 378 (1790).
Loxia cucullata, Daud. Trait. d'Ornith. ii. p. 331 (1800).
Loxia cucullata, Shaw, Nat. Misc. xi. pl. 433 (1800).
Crestudo roxo, Azara, Apunt. i. p. 461, num. cxxviii. (1802).
Le Paroare Huppé, Vieill. Ois. Chant. p. 105. t. 70 (1805).
Le Huppé rouge, Azara, Voy. dans l'Amer. Mérid. iii. p. 283 (1809).
Loxia cucullata, Shaw, Gen. Zool. ix. p. 264. pl. 48 (1815).
Fringilla cucullata, Vieill. Nouv. Dict. xii. p. 231 (1817).
Crested Dominican Grosbeak, Lath. Gen. Hist. Birds, v. p. 279 (1822).
Fringilla cucullata, Vieill. Encycl. Méth. p. 953 (1823).
Fringilla cucullata, Licht. Verz. Doubl. Mus. p. 22 (1823).
Crested Dominican Grosbeak (Cuv.), Griff. Anim. Kingd. ii. p. 137 (1829).
Paroaria cucullata, Bonap. Sagg. Distr. Metod. p. 141 (1831).
Fringilla cucullata, D'Orb. Syn. Av. p. 82 (1837).
Spiza cucullata, Gray et Mitch. Gen. of Birds, ii. p. 375 (1844).
Calyptrophorus cucullata, Cab. Arch. für Natur. Ornith. Notiz. ii. p. 329 (1847).

Paroaria cucullata, Reichb. Avium Syst. taf. lxxvi. fig (1850).
Paroaria cucullata, Bonap. Consp. Gen. Av. i. p. 471 (1850).
Calyptrophorus cucullata, Cab. Mus. Hein. pt. i. p. 145 (1850-1).
Paroaria cucullata, Gray, Gen. et Subgen. Birds, p. 78 (1855).
Paroaria cucullata, Burm. Syst. Ueb. Bras. iii. p. 210 (1856).
Paroaria cucullata, Sclater, Proc. Zool. Soc. 1859, p. 434.
Paroaria cucullata, Sclater, Cat. Amer. Birds, p. 108 (1862).
Passerina cucullata, Gray, Hand-List Birds, ii. p. 97 (1870).
Calyptrophorus cucullata, Sundev. Avium Dispon. Tentam. p. 34 (1872).
Paroaria cucullata, Sclater et Salv. Nomen. Av. Neotr. p. 30 (1873).
Paroaria cucullata, Durnford, Ibis, 1877, p. 171.
Coccothraustes cucullatus, Russ, Stubenvögel, i. p. 541. taf. xiii (1879).
Paroaria cucullata, Schmidt, Proc. Zool. Soc. 1880, p. 313.
Paroaria cucullata, Gibson, Ibis, 1880, pp. 19, 27.
Paroaria cucullata, Durnford, Ibis, 1880, p. 418.
Paroaria cucullata, E. W. White, Proc. Zool. Soc. 1882, p. 593.
Paroaria cucullata, Sclater, Vert. Anim. Gard. Zool. Soc. p. 248 (1883).

Figures. Brown's, Ill. Zool. pl. xxiii.   Miller's, Cim. Phy. pl. ii, A.   Pl. Enl. 103.   Shaw, Nat. Misc. pl. 433. Gen. Zool. pl. 48.   Vieill. O. C. t. 70.

English. *Crested Cardinal, Crested Paroare, Crested Dominican Cardinal of Louisiana, Pope Grosbeak, Crested Dominican Grosbeak, Red-headed Cardinal and Red-crested Cardinal.*

French. *Le Paroare, Le Cardinal Dominiquain Hupé de la Louisiane, Le Cardinal Huppé, Le Paroare Huppé, Le Huppé Rouge.*

German. *Dominikaner Kardinal-Fink mit einem Kamme. Der gehäubte graue Kardinal.*

Italian. *Il cardinal uccello ciuffetto.*

Habitat. Argentine Republic, Bolivia and Brazil.

Male. Crest, head and throat ending in a narrow point on the middle of the breast, scarlet; hind margins of ears black; upper part of neck, back, rump, upper tail-coverts, scapulars, great-and lesser wing-coverts, sides and patch on sides of chest, slaty grey; primaries black, outer edges silvery grey, first black; secondaries broadly edged with pale grey; tail black, outer ones margined and tipped with pale grey; centre of feathers on hind neck, narrow band across back of head uniting with sides of neck, breast, abdomen, under wing-and tail-coverts and thighs dirty white; under surface of wing and tail pale grey: iris reddish brown; bill pale brown, darkest at base of culmen, lower mandible nearly white; legs dark brown: length 7·2, wing 4·1, tail 3·6, tars. 1·0, culm. 0·55.

Male. Nearly adult. Similar, but with a few black margins on the feathers of the chest, thighs pale grey.

Female. Similar, but the scarlet of the head not so brilliant.

Young Bird. Similar, with head and throat pale rufous-brown, intermixed with scarlet; above tinged with pale olive-brown; primaries and secondaries dark brown; sides and flanks tinged with pale brown: bill and feet as in the adult.

Observ. The adult male and female are almost identical in colour and markings, the young are easily distinguished by the pale rufous head and throat, brown primaries and secondaries. In confinement they become more or less black all over, especially when fed on hempseed.

In the early days of Buffon, Latham, Gmelin, the older ornithologists and authors, this very beautiful Cardinal, was considered to be the male, or a variety of the more abundant species the Dominican Cardinal, so well known in Brazil and the adjacent countries to the south and west, and easily distinguished from the present bird by the absence of a crest, they had *reason* to suppose it was the male, on account of the sexes of this peculiar group of birds being so alike, that it is only by dissection this can be determined.

The area occupied by this bird is very extensive, being found throughout the middle and southern portion of Brazil, throughout Paraguay, the northern portion of the Argentine Republic, La Plata and extending its range into the great ravines of Bolivia.

With regard to its habits Burmeister says that it " Inhabits singly or in pairs, the damp bushy plains on the borders of the large rivers in the interior of Brazil, namely the Rio St. Francisco below its confluence with the Rio das Velhas.

"The bird is found in an area which extends southwards as far as Montivideo, and makes its nest in dense thickets, builds a fairly large nest with dry stalks, at a moderate height, and lays 3 to 4 longish oval white eggs, closely sprinkled with greyish-green spots darkest at the larger end."

Mr. H. Durnford on the Birds of the Province of Buenos Ayres says—"I scarcely think this ought to be included in my list, as all the specimens I have seen here, have probably been birds escaped from cages. I found it in April very common up the Parana at Baradero, where it frequented thickets and trees."

Mr. Durnford also "found it about six miles from Tucuman."

Mr. E. Gibson "On the Ornithology of Cape San Antonio, Buenos Ayres, 'Ibis,' 1880, gives us a very full and most interesting account of this species, which I take the liberty of quoting. He says—"Curiously enough, this pretty bird and sweet songster is now common in our district, while twenty-five years ago it was not to be found nearer than Dolores, sixty miles to the north-west. It remains during the whole year, and breeds with us. Quite a wood-frequenting bird, one rarely sees it either in the plains or about the swamps. It is not at all shy, and, particularly in the winter months, may be seen every day in the *patio*, looking for its share of food from the kitchens, in company with various other birds. One of our men was very successful in trapping them there; and even adult birds soon became tame after being caged. In Buenos Ayres it is one of the most common and prized of caged birds. Those I have seen were fed principally on thistle-seeds, millet, soaked bread, fruit, &c., &c. The leisurely sweet whistle is well known, and, as I have found, is not very difficult of imitation. I have kept a bird responding to me for some time before it discovered the nature of its rival. The young accompany the parents till well on into the winter, but do not sing or acquire their full plumage till the ensuing spring, the head and crest remaining of a dull brick-red in the interval.

"Breeding-Notes.—It nests from the end of October to the middle of November, retiring for that purpose to the woods.

"The nest is generally placed at the end of a branch of a tala tree, about eight or ten feet from the ground. It is a large shallow construction, built of wild vine tendrils or twigs and wood, and lined with horse-hair. Sometimes the last material greatly predominates; and I have then seen the nest so frail that one could see through the bottom of it. The uneasy approaches of the birds frequently betray its situation, should an intruder appear in the vicinity. Three is the largest and most usual number of eggs laid. The clutches of eggs vary greatly in appearance, and still more so in size.

"The commonest type measures about $\frac{11}{12} \times \frac{33}{40}$, and in colour is of a brownish ground, thickly marked with brown spots. One clutch of three, in my possession, fitly illustrates the above noted variation. The eggs average $1\frac{1}{10} \times \frac{33}{40}$, while the ground-colour, of which there is a good deal seen, has a greenish tinge; the spots also incline to the blunt end; and in addition there is a dark ring there, more or less pronounced."

Among the notes which I have collected is one "On the Birds from the Argentine Republic" written by my lamented friend Mr. E. W. White, he says it is "A tolerably common bird in the upper Riverine provinces; and much kept as a cage bird in Buenos Ayres, as it has a very fine whistle, almost rivalling that of the English Blackbird in power, but not in variety."

Specimens examined.

No.	Sex.	Mus.	Locality.	Length.	Wing.	Tail.	Tars.	Culm.
a.	♂	E.B.	Buenos Ayres.	8·0	4·1	3·6	1·0	0·0
b.	♂	E.B.	Brazil.	7·2	4·1	3·6	1·0	0·55
c.	♀	E.B.	Brazil.	7·5	3·8	3·5	1·0	0·55
d.	jun.	E.B.	(?)	7·0	3·6	3·2	0·9	0·55
a.	(?)	M.M.	Brazil.	0·0	3·6	0·0	1·0	0·55

The figures (Plate I.) are taken from *b* and *d*, life size.

PYRRHULA NIPALENSIS.
THE NEPAULESE BULLFINCH.
PLATE I.

Pyrrhula nipalensis, Hodgs. Asiat. Res. 1836, xix. pt. i. p. 155.
Pyrrhula nipalensis, Gray et Mitch. Gen. Birds, ii. p. 387 (1844).
Pyrrhula nipalensis, Blyth, Jour. Asiat. Soc. Beng. 1844, xiii. p. 951.
Pyrrhula nipalensis, Gray, Zool. Misc. 1844, p. 85.
Pyrrhula nipalensis, Hodgs. Cat. Birds of Nepal in B. Mus. p. 111 (1846).
Pyrrhula nipalensis, Blyth, Cat. Birds in Mus. Asiat. Soc. Beng. p. 122 (1849).
Pyrrhula nipalensis, Bonap. Consp. Gen. Avium, p. 525 (1850).
Pyrrhula nipalensis, Gould, Birds of Asia, v. pl. v. (1853).
Pyrrhula nipalensis, Horsf. Cat. Birds in Mus. E. I. C. ii. p. 455 (1856-8).
Pyrrhula nipalensis, Blyth, Ibis, 1862, p. 389.
Pyrrhula nipalensis, Hodgs. Cat. Birds of Nepal in B. Mus. p. 60. 2nd ed., (1863).
Pyrrhula nipalensis, Blyth, Ibis, 1863, pp. 440-1-2.
Pyrrhula nipalensis, Jerdon, Birds of India, ii. pt. i. p. 390 (1863).
Pyrrhula nipalensis, Gray, Hand-List Birds, ii. p. 99 (1870).
Pyrrhula nipalensis, Tristram, Ibis, 1871, p. 233.

Figure. Gould's Birds of Asia, Vol. V. pl. v.

English. *Nepaulese Bullfinch, Brown Bullfinch.*
French. *Le Bouvreuil de Népaul.*
German. *Der Gimpel aus Nepal.*
Italian. *Il monachino da Nepaul.*

Habitat. Northern and Central Regions of Nepal. S. E. Himalaya, Darjeeling, Sikkim and Bootan.

Male. Head, back and lower parts ash-coloured, tinged with brown, darkest on mantle and scapulars; feathers on the crown, tipped with pale cinereous; a narrow band of dark brown round the base of the bill; band across rump, wings, outer margins of great wing-coverts, upper tail-coverts and tail purple black; margins and tips of same black; centre portion of tertials and the two centre tail feathers rosy-copper; outer margin of last tertials, bright red-brown, paler at its base; great wing-coverts broadly tipped with pale cinereous, darker at the base; spot under eye, on each side of breast, belly, under part of wing-and coverts, band across rump, and under tail-coverts white: eye brown; bill greenish horn, margin and tip black, lower mandible bluish black; foot fleshy brown: length 5·4, wing 3·3, tail 2·8, tars. 0·7, culm. 0·4.

Female. Similar, but rather more tinged with pale brown; the dark brown band at base of bill, less distinct; the elongated spot on the last tertial yellowish-white.

Young Male. Similar, rather more tinged with pale brown; without the dark brown band at base of bill; feathers on the crown, not margined with cinereous; the black band on rump very indistinct; the elongated spot on the last tertial, nearly as bright as in the adult: bill greenish brown, margin and tip darker, lower mandible yellowish brown, tip darker.

Nestling. Without the elongated spot on the last tertial.

"The young at first, want this distinctive sexual mark," (*Hodgson*).

This sombre coloured Bullfinch, which so much resembles the females of the other species known to science, was first described by Mr. B. H. Hodgson in the 'Asiatic Researches' in 1836, and mentioned by other ornithologists, including Mr. T. C. Jerdon, who gives an excellent description of it in his 'Birds of India,' 1863, at the same time, it is to be regretted that nothing is known respecting its habits, migration, or nidification.

The species was obtained by Mr. Hodgson in Nepal, it has since then been found in the S. E. Himalayas, Darjeeling, Sikkim, and Bootan.

Mr. W. E. Brooks procured it at Sikkim, a pair being in the collection of the Rev. Canon Tristram, who very kindly lent them to me. Mr. Jerdon says that in Sikkim "it is not very rare in winter, in summer seeking the higher elevations." Mr. E. Blyth says: "It does not appear that *P. Nipalensis* has been observed westward of Nepal."

Specimens examined.

No.	Sex.	Mus.	Country.	Length.	Wing.	Tail.	Tarsus.	Culm.
a.	♂	E. B.	N. India.	5·4	3·3	2·8	0·7	0·4
b.	♀	E. B.	Darjeeling (*Beavan*).	5·4	3·3	3·0	0·6	0·5
c.	♀	E. B.	Darjeeling.	5·2	3·3	2·8	0·6	0·4
d.	♂ jun.	E. B.	Darjeeling.	5·3	3·4	3·1	0·7	0·4
e.	♂	E. B.	India.	5·65	3·4	3·0	0·65	0·47
			Rev. H. B. Tristram's collection.					
a.	♂	H. B. T.	Sikkim (*Brooks*).	6·0	3·3	3·0	0·6	0·4
b.	♀	H. B. T.	Sikkim (*Brooks*).	5·9	3·6	3·2	0·6	0·4

The figures are taken from *a* and *c* in my collection.

MUNIA ORYZIVORA.
THE JAVA SPARROW.
PLATE I. and II.

The Padda, or Rice-Bird, Edw. Nat. Hist. Birds, i. p. 41. pls. 41-42 (1743).
Le Padda, Edw. et Catesby, Samml. Ausländ. Vög. i. t. 81-83 (1749).
Coccothraustes caerulescens, Klein, Av. Prodr. p. 96 (1750).
Loxia fusca, Linn. Mus. Adol. Frid. p. 18 (1754).
Loxia oryzivora, Linn. Amœn. Acad. iv. p. 243 (1759).
Coccothraustes sinensis cinerea, Briss. Orn. iii. p. 244. pl. xi. f. 4 (1760).
Coccothraustes sinensis cinerea, Briss. Syn. Méth. i. p. 377. No. 12 (1763).
Loxia oryzivora, Linn. Syst. Nat. i. p. 302 (1766).
Coccothraustes sinensis cinerea, Gerini, Stor. Nat. Ucc. iii. pl. 328. fig. 1 (1771).
Loxia oryzivora, Müll. Volls. Natursystem, 3. p. 550 (1773).
Le Padda, ou l'oiseau de Riz, Buff. Hist. Nat. Ois. iii. p. 463 (1775).
Gros-Bec de la Chine, Buff. Pl. Enl. 152. fig. 1 (1777).
Le Calfat, Buff. Hist. Nat. Ois. iv. p. 371 (1778).
Le Padda, ou l'oiseau de Riz, Bodd. Tabl. des Pl. Enl. 152. 1 (1783).
Java Grosbeak, Lath. Gen. Syn. iii. p. 129 1783).
Red-Eyed Bunting, Lath. Gen. Syn. iii. p. 210 (1783).
Java Grosbeak, Lath. Gen. Syn. Suppl. 1. p. 151 (1787).
Loxia oryzivora, Gmel. Syst. Nat. i. p. 850 (1788).
Emberiza calfat, Gmel. Syst. Nat. i. p. 887 (1788).
Loxia javensis, Sparrm. Mus. Carls. Fas. 4. tab. lxxxix. (1788).
Loxia oryzivora, Lath. Ind. Ornith. i. p. 380 (1790).
Emberiza calfat, Lath. Ind. Ornith. i. p. 418 (1790).
Loxia oryzivora, Licht. Cat. Rer. Nat. Rar. p. 43 (1793).
Loxia oryzivora, Daud. Trait. d'Ornith. ii. p. 393 (1800).
Sunda Grosbeak, Lath. Gen. Syn. Suppl. ii. p. 195 (1801).

Loxia javensis, Lath. Ind. Ornith. Suppl. ii. p. xlv. (1801).
Le Padda, Vieill. Ois. Chant. p. 94. pl. 61 (1805).
Loxia javensis, Shaw, Gen. Zool. ix. p. 300 (1815).
Loxia oryzivora, Shaw, Gen. Zool. ix. p. 316. pl. 51 (1815).
Emberiza calfat, Shaw, Gen. Zool. ix. p. 415 (1815).
Coccothraustes oryzivora, Vieill. Nouv. Dict. xiii. p. 545 (1817).
Fringilla oryzivora, Horsf. Trans. Linn. Soc. 1822, p. 161.
Fringilla oryzivora, Raffles, Trans. Linn. Soc. 1822, p. 314.
Java Grosbeak, Lath. Hist. Birds, v. p. 251 (1822).
Red-Eyed Bunting, Lath. Hist. Birds, v. p. 331 (1822).
Loxia oryzivora, Hahn und Küst. Vög. Asien, Lief. x. t. iii. (1822).
Fringilla oryzivora, Swains. Zool. Ill. iii. pl. 156 ♂ et ♀ (1822-3).
Fringilla oryzivora, Licht. Verz. Doubl. p. 89 (1823).
Emberiza calfat, Vieill. Encycl. Méth. p. 923 (1823).
Coccothraustes oryzivora, Vieill. Encycl. Méth. p. 1016 (1823).
Coccothraustes oryzivora, Shaw, Gen. Zool. xiv. p. 87 (1824).
Loxia javensis, Shaw, Gen. Zool. xiv. p. 88 (1824).
Loxia oryzivora, Cuv. Règn. An. p. 412 (1829).
Red-Eyed Bunting, (Cuv.), Griff. Aves, ii. p. 129 (1829).
Java Grosbeak, (Cuv.), Griff. Aves, ii. p. 153 (1829).
Loxia javensis, Gulliver, Proc. Zool. Soc. 1842, p. 111.
Amadina oryzivora, Strickl. Proc. Zool. Soc. 1842, p. 167.
Amadina oryzivora, Blyth, Journ. Asiat. Soc. 1846, xv. p. 285.
Amadina oryzivora, Gray et Mitch. Genera Birds, ii. p. 369. No. 4 (1849).
Amadina oryzivora, Blyth, Cat. Birds Mus. A. S. Beng. p. 118 (1849).
Munia oryzivora, Bonap. Consp. Gen. Av. p. 451 (1850).
Padda oryzivora, Reichb. Avium. Syst. Nat. pl. lxxvi. fig (1850).
Oryzornis oryzivora, Cab. et Hein. Mus. Hein. i. p. 174 (1851).
Oryzornis oryzivora, Gray, Gen. et Subgen. Birds, p. 76 (1855).
Oryzivora leucotis, Blyth, Indian Orn. MS (1855).
Oryzivora orizivora, Blyth, Ind. Ornith. MS (1855).
Coccothraustes oryzivora, Eyton, Cat. Birds, p. 247 (1856).
Padda orizivora, Horsf. et Moore, Cat. Birds Mus. East Ind. Comp. ii. p. 504 (1856-8).

Padda orizivora, Moore, Proc. Zool. Soc. 1859, p. 443.
Oryzornis oryzivora, Swinh. Ibis, 1860, p. 60.
Padda oryzivora, Reichb. Singvögel, p. 42. pl. xv. f. 135-139 (1861).
Padda verecunda, Reichb. Singvögel, pp. 41, iv. pl. xv. 133 (1861).
Munia oryzivora, Swinh. Ibis, 1861, p. 45.
Munia oryzivora, Newton, Ibis, 1861, p. 115.
Munia oryzivora, Bernst. Journ. f. Ornith. 1861, p. 179.
Munia oryzivora, Scl. Proc. Zool. Soc. 1863, p. 219.
Munia oryzivora, Swinh. Proc. Zool. Soc. 1863, p. 299.
Munia oryzivora, Wall. Proc. Zool. Soc. 1863, p. 486.
Munia oryzivora, Jerd. Birds of Ind. ii. p. 359 (1863).
Loxia oryzivora, Martins, Journ. für Ornith. 1866, p. 14.
Munia oryzivora, Schl. Proc. Zool. Soc. 1866, p. 424.
Munia oryzivora, Hartl. Proc. Zool. Soc. 1867, p. 826.
Munia oryzivora, Schl. et Poll. Madag. p. 154 (1868).
Oryzornis oryzivora, Cab. Decken's, Reis. O.-Afr. iii. p. 30 (1869).
Amadina oryzivora, Gray, Hand-List Birds, ii. p. 55 (1870).
Munia verecunda, Gray, Hand-List Birds, ii. p. 54. No. 6760 (1870).
Oryzornis oryzivora, Finsch et Hartl. Vögel Ost-Afr. iv. p. 433 (1870).
Padda verecunda, Finsch et Hartl. Vögel Ost-Afr. iv. p. 433 (1870).
Padda oryzivora, Swinh. Proc. Zool. Soc. 1871, p. 385.
Loxia oryzivora, Walden, Trans. Zool. Soc. 1872, viii. p. 72.
Fringilla orizivora, Bligh, Journ. As. Soc. (Cey. Br.), 1874, p. 67.
Padda oryzivora, Salvad. Cat. Ucc. Borneo, p. 263 (1874).
Padda orizivora, Hume, Nests and Eggs, ii. p. 454 (1875).
Loxia javensis, Gulliver, Proc. Zool. Soc. 1875, p. 490.
Padda oryzivora, Wald. Trans. Zool. Soc. 1875, ix. p. 207.
Padda oryzivora, Tweedd. Ibis, 1877, p. 317.
Munia oryzivora, Hartl. Vög. Madag. p. 404 (1877).
Oryzornis oryzivora, Fisch. et Reichn. Journ. für Orn. 1878, p. 266.
Padda oryzivora, Salvad. Cat. Uccelli. Sum. p. 263 (1879).
Padda oryzivora, Legge, Hist. Birds Ceylon, pp. 646-7 (1879).
Padda oryzivora, Sharpe, Proc. Zool. Soc. 1879, p. 344.

Spermestes oryzivora, Russ, Stubenvögel, i. p. 136. pl. viii. (1879).
Loxia oryzivora, Licht. Cat. Rer. Nat. Rar. p. 43 *(ed.* 1882).
Padda oryzivora, Scl. Vert. An. Gar. Zool. Soc. p. 240 (1883).
Oryzornis oryzivora, Böhm, Journ. für Ornith. 1883, p. 201.
Oryzornis oryzivora, Schal. Journ. für Ornith. 1883, p. 363.
Oryzornis oryzivora, Fisch. Journ. für Ornith. 1885, p. 136.
Padda oryzivora, Kütter, Journ. für Ornith. 1885, p. 352.
Munia orizivora, Shelley, Ibis, 1886, p. 312.

  Figures. Edwards, Birds, pl. 41-42. Edw. et. Catesb. pl. 81-83. Briss. pl. xi. f. 4. Gerini. pl. 328. f. i. Pl. Enl. 152. f. i. Sparrm. pl. lxxxix. Vieill. O. C. pl. 61. *Good.* Shaw, G. Z. pl. 51. Hahn et Küst. t. iii. Swains. Z. Ill. pl. 156. Reichb. Singvög. pl. xv.

 English. *Padda, or Rice Bird. Java Sparrow. Java Grosbeak. Red-Eyed Bunting. Sunda Grosbeak. Paddy bird. Verecund Padda.*
 French. *Le Gros-bec cendré de la Chine. Le Padda, ou l'oiseau de Riz. Le Gros-bec de la Chine. Le Galfat ou Calfat. Le Padda Modest.*
 German. *Reis-vogel. Reismäher. Reisfresser. Riesfink. Der Padda. Gatterer. Der Reis Kernbeisser. Der Vescheidene Reisvogel.*

 Native Names.
  Java. *Glate,* Horsfield.
  Sumatra. *Gelatik,* Raffles.
  Bengal. *Ram Gira,* Blyth.

 Habitat. Java and Malay Archipelago.
  Introduced into India, China, Mauritius, Réunion, S. and E. Africa and Australia.

Male. Crown of head, nape, outer margin of ear-coverts, chin, lower rump, upper tail-coverts and tail black; hind neck, back, all the wing-coverts, secondaries, throat and breast pale slaty grey; primaries pale ashy brown, edges of outer web pale slaty grey;

quills dark brown; large patch occupying cheeks and ear-coverts and under tail-coverts white; belly, sides, flanks, thighs and under wing-coverts dark vinous, tinged with pink; under side of wing grey: bill crimson, with white margins and tip; iris reddish brown; lids red; feet pinkish flesh colour: length 5·2, wing 2·8, tail 1·0, tars. 0·7, culm. 0·6. Plate I. fig. 1.

Female. Similar in every detail: length 4·75, wing 2·7, tail 1·9, tars. 1·7, culm. 0·6. Plate I. fig. 2.

WITH BLACK HEADS.

Male. Head entirely black with faint indication of the white patch on cheeks and ear-coverts; entire upper parts and breast dark slaty grey; in the centre of belly a blackish lunar patch; belly greyish white; under tail-coverts white. Pl. II. fig. 1. supposed ♀ of authors.

Female. Similar, with less black on the centre of belly, the vinous blended into the grey of breast and white of under tail-coverts.

Young Bird. Upper parts and chest pale slaty grey, tinged with buff, palest on the margins of the feathers, darkest on the crown; primaries and tail dark slaty brown; cheeks, chin, centre of belly, thighs and under tail-coverts white, tinged with buff; a few upper tail-coverts black: bill and legs pale fleshy-brown, reddish on the culmen. "iris brownish-red," (*Bernstein*).

Pl. II. fig. 2. This is *Loxia javensis*, Sparrm. and *Padda verecunda*, Rchb.

Young. Upper parts and chest dark slaty grey, strongly tinged with reddish brown, darkest on the crown; primaries and tail slaty brown; cheeks, chin and under tail-coverts whitish, tinged with pale rufous; belly and flanks pale rufous-brown, paler in the centre: bill and legs pale fleshy brown, tinged with pink on the culmen.

Pl. II. fig. 3.

Observ. Having carefully examined a large series of adult specimens, I am enabled to say that it is almost impossible to distinguish the male from the female when alive, even in dimensions, the males vary as much as the females, therefore it would be useless to take the size as a guide for the selection of either sex, and doubtless large numbers of people who purchase supposed pairs, in most instances get two males or two females.

The birds with black heads have been described and figured by many authors as a variety, and by others as the female, now I have carefully dissected a number of these and found both male and female are alike, at the same time I have searched for an account of the black headed birds in a state of nature, and failed, but they do change in confinement, as my father (Mr. A. D. Bartlett) tells me "they will moult into white cheeks again. I am unable to give any reason for their changing from white cheeks to black, and back again, but this they certainly do, as far as I can make out; this change does not depend upon age, sex or season."

It will be seen by reference to the synonymy that I have united four described species viz:—*Loxia oryzivora*, Linn. *Emberiza caljat*, Gmel. *Loxia javensis*, Sparrm. and *Padda verecunda*, Reichb.

There are but few general works on ornithology which do not contain an account or figure of this very lovely weaver-bird, and without hesitation, I may say that the Java Sparrow is one of the best known foreign cage-birds throughout the world; it is kept by vast numbers of persons, not for its song (for it has none), but for its very beautiful plumage, it is also a bird which is easily managed in confinement and requires little attention, the food being simple and dry, viz:—rice, canary-seed, millet, wheat, and similar seeds.

The true habitat of this species is Java; from that island it has been conveyed by man, from a very early period, to all parts of the world, and in many places it has been liberated, where it thrives and increases very rapidly; in its native island it is exceedingly abundant where it does much damage to the seed-crops. According to various authors it is plentiful throughout China and is used by the Chinese artists in their beautiful landscape paintings; it is found on most of the islands of the Malay Archipelago, Madras, East Indies, Ceylon, Mauritius, Réunion, Sumatra, Madagascar, Australia and South and East Africa.

From the mass of material which I have brought together respecting this bird, I hope the following extracts may fulfil the object of the present work.

Bechtein says:—"These birds are brought in great numbers by ships from Java, and the Cape of Good Hope; where, on account of the ravages they commit in the rice fields, they have as bad a reputation as the sparrows among ourselves. They are prized only for their beauty. Their cry is "*Tak! Tak!*" Their song is very monotonous, and consists of two notes, "*Dirr! Dirr! Dchi!*" The first note is given with a humming sound; the second is higher in the scale, and much more clearly uttered."

The most interesting notes on this bird in its native haunts, are given by Dr. H. A. Bernstein from his own observation, he says:—" Just like our European field-sparrows the rice-bird inhabits exclusively cultivated tracts of land, and here he is very commonly to be seen. During the time when the rice-fields (*Sawah's*) are placed under water, that is in the months November till March or April, when the sown rice is growing up and ripening for harvest, the rice-birds live in pairs or in small flocks in gardens, villages, woods and thickets, where for food they have the seeds of various plants, several small fruits and probably insects and worms, for I have frequently seen them on country roads etc., looking about on the ground where it was hardly likely they could find anything else. As soon however, as the rice-fields begin to turn yellow and are laid dry by drawing off the water, they resort thither, often in large flocks, and not uncommonly do a considerable amount of damage, so that every kind of trouble is taken to drive them away. In neighbourhoods which suffer specially from these feathered thieves, one, or if the field is large, several little watch-houses are erected in the middle of the field resting on four high bamboo stakes, whence numerous threads run in all directions to thin bamboo sticks set up at certain distances from one another through the whole field : to these threads are hung large dry leaves, gay rags, dolls, wooden clappers and such like things. Now when the person sitting in the little watch-house, like a spider in a web, pulls the threads, at the same moment all the dry leaves rustle, the dolls shake, the clappers sound and the unbidden guests fly away frightened. Also after the harvest the birds find their table well spread in the rice fields lying fallow to the commencement of the rainy season, that is till towards the beginning of November, as numerous acres not only lie fallow but also all kinds of weeds spring up among the stubble in an incredibly short space of time, whose seeds quickly ripening afford them a welcome nourishment. At this time they are fairly plump and well nourished and offer, especially the young ones, a favourite dish, on which account they are snared in large numbers.

"I have several times found the nest of *Munia oryzivora*: sometimes at the summit of various trees, sometimes among the numerous creepers which cover the stems of the Areng palms. They vary in size and form according to their position: whilst those attached to trees are for the most part larger and possess, on the average, a fairly regularly half ball shaped form, those placed among creepers on the stems of Areng palms are smaller and of a less decided, irregular form, only slightly hollowed out in the centre. All nests however are almost exclusively composed of the stalks of various grasses which are not very firmly twined together, so that the whole build is of no great solidity. The number of the shining white, somewhat long-shaped eggs varies between six and eight in the nests found by me. Their diameter lengthwise amounts to 21 mill., their greatest diameter through the middle 14 millim."

Mr. R. Swinhoe saw it on the "Amoy, in flocks, and occasionally met with it during winter and spring," and he says it is "wild at Hong Kong during the early spring, and found about Canton and Shanghai. A South China bird, extending to the Straits of Malacca and Java."

Mr. E. Newton procured it in the Mauritius, and Dr. Hartlaub in his 'Birds of Madagascar,' says:—"Introduced from India to Bourbon and the Mauritius, but has become rare on the former island, where it is called Calfat. Pollen saw this bird building in the niches of the façade of the town council-house at St. Denys, together with our house-sparrow."

In Mr. R. B. Sharpe's paper 'On the Birds of Labuan,' he tells us that "Governor Ussher observes":—"This bird was introduced to the island by Mr. Low; it has thriven, and is now in prodigious numbers."

Mr. James Mottly of Benjermassing, South-Eastern Borneo says they are "Rather common here, and exceedingly destructive to the rice-fields, feeding on them in vast flocks. These birds are taken in thousands by the natives, and are a favourite article of food, being exceedingly fat. In confinement they become very familiar, and breed readily. I have a great number of them; and many which have escaped do not leave the house, but are constantly on the outside of the cage which formerly held them."

It was also "observed by Dr. v. Martens in the Museum of the Military Library at Manilla, and, in all likelihood, an indigenous species." *(Arthur, Marquis of Tweeddale).*

Capt. W. V. Legge, in his admirable work on the 'Birds of Ceylon,' tells us "This well-known bird which is largely imported into Ceylon as a cage-pet, has been successfully acclimatized in Ceylon. It is now no uncommon occurrence to meet with a small flock on the compound surrounding the Colombo Lake."

Mr. Jerdon tells us that it is wild in Madras, Capt. W. V. Legge mentions specimens from Tenasserim, it was procured according to E. Blyth in the Merqui province, Mr. Buxton obtained specimens at Lampong in Sumatra, Mr. A. R. Wallace found it at Lombok, and "It has been introduced into St. Helena, and according to Mr. Melliss, is numerous there." It has been collected by Dr. Kirk, Dr. Böhm and others at Zanzibar, where it was introduced some years ago.

In the 'Birds of Ceylon,' above mentioned, Capt. W. V. Legge concludes his article on this species with the following passage— "Habits.—This bird appears to affect trees as much as the nearly allied Munias resort to the ground. It flies swiftly, and is restless and shy. In confinement it is as docile as all birds of its kind, and it is consequently a favourite cage-pet. It feeds on the ground, tripping quickly on the grass, and clings, with the agility of its family, to stalks of grain, to which it is no doubt very destructive during harvest-time."

Mr. Allan Hume, in his valuable and interesting volume of 'Nests and Eggs of Indian Birds,' gives the following particulars of the nidification.

"This species, the well-known Java Sparrow, a native of that island but now naturalized in Mauritius, Ceylon and other places, has naturalized itself also in the neighbourhood of Madras, whence I have had many specimens, killed wild, as well as the eggs sent to me by my friend the late Captain Mitchell. He "found a nest near Madras in August containing five eggs. It was placed like a Munia's in a thorny bush 7 or 8 feet from the ground. The nest was globular and very large, chiefly composed of fine grass but with a few broad-bladed leaves of millet intertwined. The entrance small, circular, and lateral."

"The eggs were very regular ovals, pure, glossless white, and varied from 0·7 to 0·75 in length, and were (all the three he sent me) 0·55 in breadth."

Specimens examined.

No.	Sex.	Mus.	Locality.	Length.	Wing.	Tail.	Tars.	Culm.
a.	(?)	E.B.	Java.	5·65	0·0	2·0	0·7	0·6
b.	(?)	E.B.	Java.	5·55	2·65	1·95	0·7	0·6
c.	(?)	E.B.	(?)	5·6	2·65	2·0	0·7	0·68
d.	♂	E.B.	Java (H. Blyth).	5·2	2·8	1·9	0·7	0·6
e.	♀	E.B.	India (A. Johnstone).	4·75	2·7	1·9	0·75	0·6
f.	♂	E.B.	(?)	5·7	2·7	2·0	0·75	0·65
g.	(?)	E.B.	(?)	5·5	2·7	1·95	0·75	0·65
h.	(?)	E.B.	(?)	5·1	2·65	2·0	0·7	0·65
i.	♂	E.B.	Malacca.	5·5	2·75	2·0	0·75	0·65
j.	♂	E.B.	Australia.	5·0	2·75	2·0	0·7	0·65
k.	(?)	E.B.	Lombok.	5·2	2·6	2·0	0·6	0·6
l.	(?)	E.B.	Java.	5·5	2·6	2·0	0·7	0·6
m.	♂	E.B.	(?)	5·2	2·6	2·0	0·7	0·6
n.	♂	E.B.	(?)	5·1	2·6	2·0	0·7	0·65
o.	(?)	E.B.	Java.	5·35	2·7	1·9	0·7	0·65
p.	♂	E.B.	(?)	5·5	2·75	2·0	0·75	0·65
q.	♀	E.B.	(?)	5·45	2·65	1·9	0·7	0·55
r.	♀	E.B.	(?)	5·0	2·65	1·9	0·75	0·6
s.	♀	E.B.	(?)	5·5	2·5	2·0	0·7	0·6
t.	jun.	E.B.	Saigon.	5·4	2·7	1·6	0·75	0·6
u.	jun.	E.B.	India.	4·55	2·55	1·6	0·67	0·55

Figures (Plate I.) are taken from d and e.

Figures (Plate II.) are taken from p, t and u.

CARDINALIS VIRGINIANUS.
THE VIRGINIAN NIGHTINGALE.
PLATE I.

Virginian Nightingale, Ray, Syn. Meth. Av. p. 85 (1713).
Red Bird, Catesby, N. H. Carol. i. pl. 38 (1731).
Red Grosbeak, or Virginia Nightingale, Albin, Birds, i. p. 55. pl. 57 ♂ (1738); iii. p. 57. pl. 61. ♀ (1740).
Loxia cardinalis, Linn. Amœn. Acad. iv. p. 242 (1749).
Coccothraustes indica cristata, Klein, Hist. Av. Prodr. p. 94 (1750).
Coccothraustes rubra, Cates. et Edw. Samml. Ausl. Vögel, i. Tab. LXXVI (1751).
Cardinal, Du Pratz, Gent. Mag. xxiii. p. 460 (1753).
Loxia cardinalis, Linn. Syst. Nat. i. p. 172 (1758).
Coccothraustes virginiana, Briss. Ornith. iii. p. 253 (1760).
Le Gros-bec de Virginie, ou le Cardinal Hupé, Briss. Ornith. Suppl. vi. p. 88 (1760).
Coccothraustes Virginiana, Briss. Syn. Meth. i. p. 379 (1763).
Loxia cardinalis, Linn. Syst. Nat. i. p. 300 (1766).
Loxia rubra, Scop. Ann. i. p. 139 (1769).
Crested Grosbeak, Forster, Cat. Anim. N. Am. p. 11 (1771).
Red Bird (Kalm.), Forster, Trav. into N. Amer. ii. p. 71 (1771).
Loxia cardinalis, Gerini, Stor. Nat. Ucc. iii. pl. 329 (1771).
Le Cardinal Hupé, Buff. Hist. Nat. iii. p. 458 pl. xxviii (1775).
Le Gros-bec de Virginie, Buff. Pl. Enl. 37 (1777).
Red Grosbeak, Albin, Song Birds, p. 84. pl. 84 (1779).
Cardinal Grosbeak, Lath. Gen. Syn. iii. p. 118 (1783).
Cardinal Grosbeak, Penn. Arct. Zool. ii. p. 349 (1785).
Cardinal Grosbeak, Lath. Gen. Syn. Suppl. i. p. 150 (1787).
Loxia cardinalis, Gmel. Syst. Nat. i. p. 847 (1788).

Cardinal, Browne, Nat. Hist. Jam. p. 647 (1789).
Loxia cardinalis, Lath. Ind. Orn. i. p. 375 (1790).
Loxia cardinalis, Shaw, Nat. Misc. iii. pl. 105 (1792).
Loxia cardinalis, Licht. Cat. Rer. Nat. Rar. p. 42 (1793).
Le Cardinal Huppé (Buff.), Sonn. Ois. xlvii. p. 23 pl. 103. f. 2 (1801).
Virginian Nightingale, Benn. Mag. Nat. Hist. 1828, p. 418.
Cardinal Grosbeak, Lath. Gen. Hist. Birds, v. p. 274 (1822); Bechst. Cage and Ch.-Birds, p. 196 (1856); Wood Nat. Hist. Birds, p. 458 (1869).
Le Cardinal, Moine, Nat. Canad. i. 1869, pp. 225, 231.
Loxia cardinalis, Daub. Trait. d'Ornith. ii. p. 375 (1800); Wils. Amer. Orn. ii. p. 38 pl. xi. fig. 1. 11 (1810); Shaw, Gen. Zool. ix. p. 248. pl. 46 (1815); (Cuv.), Griff. Aves. ii. p. 156 (1829); Stanl. P. Z. S. 1834, p. 81; Parker, P. Z. S. 1863, p. 516; Lamp. Zool. Gart. vi. 1865, pp. 228-9.
Coccothraustes cardinalis, Vieill. Nouv. Dict. xiii. p. 526. pl. B. 30. f. 2 (1817); Vieill. Encycl. Méth. iii. p. 1001 (1823); Shaw, Gen. Zool. xiv. p. 87 (1824).
Coccothraustes virginianus, Russ, Stubenvögel, p. 524. taf. xiii (1879).
Fringilla (Coccothraustes) cardinalis, Bonap. Obs. on Wils. Ornith. No. 79 (1825).
Fringilla cardinalis, Wils. et Bonap. Const. Misc. B. N. Amer. ii. p. 273 (1831); Nutt. Man. of Ornith. i. p. 519 (1832); Aud. Ornith. Biog. ii. p. 336; v. p. 514. pl. clix (1834); Sacc, Zool. Gart. viii. 1867, pp. 440-1.
Cardinalis virginianus, Bonap. Sagg. Dist. Met. Anim. Vert. p. 53 (1831); Bonap. P. Z. S. 1837, p. 111; Bonap. Comp. List. B. Eur. et Am. p. 35 (1838); De Gregory, Rev. Zool. 1843, p. 127; Gr. et Mitch. Gen. Birds, ii. p. 358. pl. 88. fig. 4 (1844); Maund. Treas. Nat. Hist. p. 283 (1849); Blyth, Cat. B. Mus. As. Soc. App. p. viii (1849); Reichb. Av. Syst. Nat. pl. LXXIX (1850); Bonap. Consp. Gen. Av. p. 501 (1850); Cab. Mus. Hein. i. p. 144 (1851); Gray, Gen. et Subgen. p. 72 (1855); Scl. P. Z. S. 1856, p. 302; Eyton, Cat. Birds, p. 266 (1856); Baird, B. N. Amer.

p. 509 (1858); Scl. P. Z. S. 1859, pp. 365, 378; Scl. Ibis, 1859,
p. 104; Scl. Cat. Amer. Birds, p. 100 (1862); Taylor, Ibis,
1862, p. 128; Dresser, Ibis, 1865, p. 491; Lawr. Ann. Lyc.
N. Y. ix. 1868, p. 201; Scl. P. Z. S. 1869, p. 627; Gray Hand-
List Birds, ii. p. 102 (1870); Jones, Am. Nat. v. 1871, p. 176;
Scl. et Salv. Nomen. Av. Neotr. p. 27 (1873); Baird, Brew. et
Ridgw. H. N. Amer. B. ii. p. 100. pl. 30. figs. 6, 7 (1874);
M'Cauley, Geol. Surv. U. S. iii. p. 666 (1877); Merr. P. U. S.
Nat. Mus. 1878, p. 129, 132; Senn. Geol. Serv. U. S. iv. 1878, p
21; Jones, Forest and Stream, x. 1878, p. 275; M'Ches. Gibbs
et Senn. Geol. Surv. U. S. v. pp. 78, 394, 487 (1879); Schmidt,
P. Z. S. 1880, p. 313; Salv. Cat. Coll. Birds Strickl. p. 218
(1882); Salv. P. Z. S. 1883, p. 421; Bouc. P. Z. S. 1883, p. 444;
Scl. List Vert. Z. S. Gard. p. 250 (1883); Salv. et Godm. Biol.
Cent. Amer. Aves, p. 340 (1884).
Cardinalis carneus, Less. Rev. Zool. 1842, p. 209; Gray et Mitch. Gen.
Birds, ii. p. 358 (1844); Bonap. Consp. Gen. Av. p. 501 (1850).
Cardinalis virginianus var. carneus, Lawr. Bull. Nat. Mus. iv. 1876, p. 20.
Cardinalis lessoni, Bonap. Consp. Gen. Av. p. 501 (1850).
Cardinalis cardinalis, Licht. Nomencl. Avium. Mus. Zool. Berol. p. 44
(1854); Coues and Ridgw. Check-List N. Amer. Birds, p. 286
(1886).
Cardinalis var. coccineus, Baird et Ridgw. Hist. N. Amer. Bird, ii. p.
299 (1874); Merr. Proc. U. S. Nat. Mus. 1878, pp. 129, 132.
Cardinalis saturatus, Ridgw. Proc. Biol. Soc. Wash. iii. 1884-5. p. 24;
Auk, ii. 1885, p. 295.
Pitylus cardinalis, Aud. Synopsis, p. 131 (1839); Aud. Birds Amer.
iii. p. 198. pl. 203 (1841); Mart. Journ. für Ornith. 1859, p. 214.
Guiraca cardinalis, Trist., Jard. Contr. Orn. 1850, p. 5.

Figures. Albin's Birds, pl. 57. et 61. Cates. et Edw. Vögel. pl. LXXVI.
Gerini, Ucc. pl. 329. Buff. Ois. pl. xxviii. et Pl. Enl. 37. Shaw,
Nat. Misc. pl. 105. Sonn. Ois. pl. 103. Wils. Ornith. pl. XI.

Shaw, Gen. Zool. pl. 46.   Vieill. N. D. pl. B. 30.   Aud. Biog. pl.
clix.   Aud. B. Am. pl. 203.   Russ. Stubenv. taf. xiii.

English. Virginian or Virginia Nightingale. Cardinal. Red Grosbeak. Crested Cardinal. Red-crested Grosbeak. Red Bird. Cardinal-bird. Cardinal Grosbeak. Cardinal Redbird. Crested Grosbeak. Virginia Grosbeak. Scarlet Grosbeak.

French. Le Cardinal. Le Gros-bec de Virginie. Le Cardinal Huppé. Le Cardinal rouge.

German. Cardinal. Kardinal. Der Rothvögel. Virginische Nachtigal. Kardinalsvögel Der Cardinal Kernbeisser. Der rothe Kardinal.

Habitat. North America. From North Dakota and borders of Canada, South to Nicaragua in Central America, ranging from Newfoundland in the East to Colorado, New Mexico and Sonoro on the West Coast, including the Bermudas and Cozumel.

Male Adult. Crown, crest, cheeks and underparts vermilion red; above brick red, with pale greyish margins to the feathers; outer webs of primaries and tail-feathers bright brick red, inner webs darker, tips of same pale brown; quills dark brown; underside of wing for more than half its length, and-coverts pale vermilion red, tips pale brown; a narrow frontal band, chin and throat black; basal portion of all the body feathers dark slaty-grey: iris reddish brown; bill red; feet dark greyish brown: length 7·8, wing 3·4, tail 3·7, tars. 0·95, culm. 0·75.

Female. Above pale olive brown, paler on the forehead: crest, outer webs of primaries, great wing-coverts, centre portion of secondaries, tail-feathers and thighs brick-red; secondaries and tail-feathers broadly edged with pale olive brown; underside of wing and-coverts rosy red; tips of primaries and tail very pale brown, quills dark brown; cheeks, breast and sides pale buffish brown, paling towards the abdomen and under tail-coverts; a narrow frontal band, chin and throat slaty-grey: iris reddish brown; bill red; feet pale brown: length 8·3, wing 3·6, tail 4·3, tars. 0·95, culm. 0·67.

Young. Similar to female, but paler; the tinges of brick-red on breast, wings and tail less defined.

Observations. From a series of twenty-six examples of both sexes, and different phases, from many localities, now before me, it is easy to recognise the gradation of forms, which have been described under the following names:—*Cardinalis virginianus*, C. var. *coccineus*, C. *carneus*, C. *lessoni*, C. var. *saturatus*, C. var. *igneus* and C. var. *superbus*.

Although these local forms are readily distinguished, it is my intention to unite the five former under the Eastern species C. *virginianus*, and the two latter under the North-western species C. *igneus*.

I am of opinion that a great deal more attention should be paid to the age, and especially the constitution of the wild bird, before an accurate estimate can be made of the extent to which it will vary.

To attempt to reproduce all that has been written on the vocal powers and habits of the Virginian Nightingale, would, I fear, lead to a vast amount of repetition, which it is my intention to avoid, by giving only the life history of this beautiful songster.

The Virginian Nightingale may be placed amongst the earliest cage-birds that ever left the shores of North America; its brilliant plumage and song combined, make it one of the most conspicuous objects throughout the swamp-and forest land of the Southern States. These two great qualities might have been the destruction of this much eulogized swamp-loving bird, had it not been for the vast territory which it occupies, for not only the natives but travellers to that country, do their utmost to procure it dead or alive. The skins were used ages ago by the natives like those of many other birds to adorn their head dresses and garments, for they, like the inhabitants of other parts of the world have great taste for showy colours, in this way the poor Virginian Nightingale has been a persecuted bird in its native haunts from the time of Columbus to the present day.

From a careful study of the localities in which this species has been obtained, and a calculation of the square miles, I find that the distribution from North to South and East to West covers about 3,698,000 or nearly 4,000,000 square miles, in this area, the bird becomes very variable in size and colour, the more southern forms being the smaller and richer coloured, while the northern are larger and paler.

Mr. Ridgway in a letter to me on the subject remarks, "you will observe that the difference between these two geographical races is most obvious in the females. Indeed this is the case with all the climatic or local forms into which the species is "split up," *Cardinalis cardinalis saturatus* from Cozumel, having the capistrum quite black, exactly the opposite extreme from *Cardinalis cardinalis igneus*." I may say the examples of *Card. var. coccineus*, from Yucatan and Southern Mexico most resemble the Cozumel bird, while those found in Bermuda are similar to the birds of the Alleghany Mountains.

The most north-western bird *Cardinalis igneus* (Baird), is undoubtedly the largest and most powerful billed bird of all the comparatively closely allied varieties; therefore, I shall retain it as distinct, placing Mr. Ridgway's very beautiful variety *Cardinalis* var. *superbus* with it, although the bill does not appear so robust as that of the former bird. I think the present bird in its wild state is an extraordinary illustration of the Darwinian principle, variability of a single race, gradually developing into no less than six or seven remarkably well defined races, this and the *Textors* of Africa are worthy of further study on this point.

The name Virginian Nightingale was according to Willughby (who wrote his Ornithology 1676 and translated by John Ray in 1678) given to this songster by the earliest settlers in Virginia, the appellation Red-bird appears to be of equal antiquity, although little used. Dr. Latham in his 'General Synopsis,' published in 1783, calls it the Cardinal Grosbeak and observes, "This species is met with in several parts of North America, and has attained the name of Nightingale deservedly, having a remarkably fine song not unlike that of the last named bird; in spring, and part of the summer, it sits on the tops of the highest trees singing early in the morning, so loud as almost to pierce the ears; is frequently kept in cages, in which it sometimes sings the year through, and the female is not greatly inferior to the male in respect of song." And in his 'General History of Birds,' 1822, he continues, "It generally comes into New York and the Jerseys the beginning of April; frequents the Magnolia Swamps during the summer, departing towards Carolina in autumn: although pretty numerous, it is not gregarious, rarely more than three or four being met with together: remains in Georgia and Pennsylvania the whole year."

Alexander Wilson observes, "from the clearness and variety of their notes, which both in a wild and domestic state, are very various and musical; many of them resemble the high notes of a fife, and are nearly as loud. They are in song from March to September, beginning at the first appearance of dawn, and repeating a favourite stanza, or passage, twenty or thirty times successively; sometimes, with little intermission for a whole morning together, which, like a good story too often repeated, becomes at length tiresome and insipid. But the sprightly figure, and gaudy plumage, of the Red-bird, his vivacity, strength of voice, and actual variety of note, and the little expense with which he is kept, will always make him a favourite. In Pennsylvania and the Northern States it is rather a scarce species; but through the whole lower parts of the Southern States, in the neighbourhood of settlements, I found them much more numerous; their clear and lively notes, in the months of January and February, being, at that time, almost the only music of the season. Along the roadsides and fences I found them hovering in half dozens together, associated with snow birds, and various kinds of sparrows.

"In the Northern States, they are migratory; but in the lower parts of Pennsylvania, they reside during the whole year, frequenting the borders of creeks and rivulets, in sheltered hollows covered with holly, laurel, and other evergreens. They love also to reside in the vicinity of fields of Indian corn, a grain that constitutes their chief and favourite food. The seeds of apples, cherries, and many other sorts of fruit, are also eaten by them; and they are accused of destroying bees.

"In the months of March and April, the males have many violent engagements for their favourite females. Early in May, in Pennsylvania, they begin to prepare their nest, which is very often fixed in a holly, cedar, or laurel bush.

"The few of our song birds that have visited Europe extort admiration from the best judges. "The notes of the cardinal grosbeak," says Latham, "are almost equal to those of the nightingale," yet these notes, clear and excellent as they are, are far inferior to those of the wood thrush; and even to those of the brown thrush or thrasher."

According to Messrs. Baird and Ridgway, in their 'History of North American Birds' 1874, "In New England and the more Northern States it is chiefly known by its reputation as a cage-bird, both its bright plumage and its sweet song giving it a high value. It is a very rare and only an accidental visitor of Massachusetts, though a pair was once known to spend the summer and to rear its brood in the Botanical Gardens of Harvard College in Cambridge. A single specimen of this bird was obtained near Dueñas, Guatemala, by Mr. Osbert Salvin.

"In its cage-life the cardinal soon becomes contented and tame, and will live many years in confinement.

"In Florida Mr. Audubon found these birds mated by the 8th of February. The nest is built in bushes, among briars, or in low trees, and in various situations, the middle of a field, near a fence, or in the interior of a thicket, and usually not far from running water. It has even been placed in the garden close to the planter's house. It is loosely built of dry leaves and twigs, with a large proportion of dry grasses and strips of the bark of grapevines. Within, it is finished and lined with finer stems of grasses wrought into a circular form. There are usually two, and in the more Southern States three, broods in a season.

"The eggs of this species are of an oblong-oval shape, with but little difference at either end. Their ground-color appears to be white, but is generally so thickly marked with spots of ashy-brown and faint lavender tints, as to permit but little of its ground to be seen. The eggs vary greatly in size, ranging from 1·10 inches to ·98 of an inch in length and from ·80 to ·78 in breadth."

Mr. H. E. Dresser says this species, is "Common throughout Texas during the summer and indeed almost all the year, excepting where *Pyrrhuloxia sinuata* is found. In such localities it is not so abundant as that bird. At Matamoras it is very common, and may be seen, caged, in almost every Mexican hut. I took quantities of the eggs of this species near San Antonio in April and May."

In 'Forest and Stream' for May 1878, is a note on the "Northernmost locality on record," of the "Cardinal Grosbeak in Nova Scotia in winter." Mr. J. Matthew Jones writes—"Observing in your Natural History column, headed "A cardinal Grosbeak in Central Park," stating that the writer had seen one of these birds in that locality on the 17th March, and expressing his surprise at the occurrence, I may mention that a pair of these birds were found in the spruce woods at Point Pleasant, near this city (Halifax, N.S.), on the last day of January, 1871."

I am indebted to the Rev. Herbert D. Astley for the following details respecting the Virginian Nightingale breeding at liberty in England:—
"Even to those uninterested in the ways and habits of birds, the following experiment must prove attractive. Experiment is hardly the word, for it was by an accident that a pair of Virginian Nightingales (*Cardinalis Virginianus*) made their escape from a large pheasantry, where they had been for two years, and had become inured to the many atmospheric changes of our climate; not that they are ever delicate birds, for they make little of a November fog or a January snowstorm. However, they escaped on the 15th of May (1885), and as they kept about I did not take much trouble to get them in again, but put out their tin of canary seed so that they might not starve, and also as an extra inducement for them not to wander far from home. The pheasantry in which they had been confined is situated amongst bushes, and close by a rookery, which is all paled in, and adjoins the front garden lawns and a fairly large shrubbery, the home of many a bird; rich in the growth of syringas, lilacs, box trees, and many other shrubs, amongst which spring up old elms, lime and firs. To this retreat, the Virginian Nightingales soon found their way, and the following morning after their escape, on going through the shrubbery, I saw the cock bird perched on the tip-top of a hawthorn. There he was, singing as loud and as fast as the notes would come, his beautiful scarlet breast looking more brilliant than usual in the full morning sun of a May day, whilst the intense green of the hawthorn showed up the bird in strong relief. I felt as I saw him, that it was a sight that few, if any, in England were enjoying at that moment, or indeed at any other time, for I have never before heard of these American cousins being allowed their

full liberty. Two days after this, in a very bare yew shrub, for it was nothing more, I observed a nest commenced. Although I never imagined that the nightingales had already set to work, yet the nest struck me as being built of an uncommon material, and its general appearance convinced me that no blackbird, thrush, bullfinch, goldfinch, &c., had been at work. The nest was, a very frail one, with no foundation; merely bits of dead grass and some old pieces of rush lightly interwoven, the whole structure being decidedly small for the size of the bird; in fact, a greenfinch would seem a more suitable occupant for it than its real owner.

"The shrub stands at a corner where four paths meet, and is therefore the most exposed position a bird could choose for such an object. The same day that I discovered the commencement of this nest, the gardener told me that he had actually seen the hen Virginian Nightingale on it, whilst the cock bird perched himself on the top of the shrub. Exactly a week after they had escaped, the first egg was laid; it was rather larger than a sparrow's in size, and dirty white in colour, with large blotches of reddish-brown, thicker at the round end than at the other. At present, all goes well; and the hen has laid five eggs in as many consecutive days, and is now sitting. To protect such an exposed position, I have tied some branches of yew all over the bush, thereby making it difficult for passers-by to see the bird on her nest. As soon as the young are hatched, I intend rearing them up when a week old, and I look forward to seeing the old birds go to nest again before the summer is over. In the meanwhile, the subject is so interesting, not to say exciting, that the future fate of the young nightingales shall be related at a date not far distant, so here I must cease from "counting my chickens before they are hatched."

"Since writing my last letter on this subject, four young birds have successfully hatched, the fifth egg being unfertile. They are now a week old, and are most carefully attended to by the parents; but I intend taking them, for by rearing them by hand they will become much tamer, whilst the old birds will soon build again, and I look forward to seeing another brood in about a month's time. The cock bird has almost entirely ceased singing since the young were hatched, and his state of alarm is great if anyone passes near the nest. The eggs took exactly a fortnight to hatch.

"*Addenda.*

The brood of young Virginians mentioned above soon came to grief, a bird or a beast of some kind, it is not known what, but jays were the suspected culprits, made off with a couple, the two remaining birds I tried to rear by hand, but they seemed unable to digest the food and to my grief, died. The old couple at once began hunting for another nesting place and fixed upon one quite close to the former site, but this time in a low box bush, the nest was quickly finished and four eggs deposited in it, strict injunctions being given to the gardeners not to disturb it in any way, and in order to try and guard against robbery from mice or squirrels, I tarred the stem of the bush as far as I could and also placed some more branches of box upon the thinner parts at the top, so as to hide the eggs from prying eyes of unfriendly feathered fowl. But no! after the hen bird had sat out more than half her time, the eggs disappeared, and—disappointment No. 2.

"The Virginian Nightingales themselves seemed to lose less heart than I did, for they actually commenced another nest the day after they had lost their second hope of a brood, and, *experientia docens*, they built their third nest in a holly tree of a somewhat weeping growth, placing it in the under side of an overhanging branch about 9ft. from the ground. Four eggs were again laid and hatched on the 5th of August of the same year (1885) in which they had escaped: but when the young birds which grew apace were about a week old, once more two disappeared, evidently taken by a jay or a squirrel, for the nest was rather demolished, so in despair the other two were carried into the shelter of the house. One was considerably larger than the other, and it was this one that succumbed in a day or two, either to injuries or indigestion; the other bird, an ugly uncouth little creature was fed upon sopped bread and plenty of fruit—strawberries, grapes, etc. :—

"He throve, and he turned out luckily to be a male bird. I have him now (1888) in his splendid scarlet plumage, insolently tame, and a delightful pet. He attained his red coat in the late autumn to a great degree, though perhaps owing to the vicissitudes of his early life, not nearly so bright in colour as he became in his second year. To any stranger approaching his cage with friendliness, he will put up his crest and sing himself hoarse, and if allowed to come out, he will fly to one's shoulder and with grotesque movements shout into one's ear, whereby he evidently thinks one is troubled with a loss in the sense of hearing. I must add, that the parent birds after having been decoyed back again into the pheasantry, were once more released in the following spring, much to their delight. They built again, but the hen bird, after laying two eggs, was found dead."

The number of instances of its breeding in aviaries are but few. Lord Stanley had a pair which reared three young ones in his menagerie at Knowsley in 1834. Dr. Sclater records it as having bred in the Zoological Society's Gardens, and in various private aviaries they often build and lay eggs, which generally come to grief.

In confinement I recommend millet, canary, buckwheat, rape, turnip-seed, wheat and Indian corn to be given; and when obtainable in a green or soft condition, at intervals, also hawthorn berries; hempseed should be very sparingly used.

Much valuable information can be gathered from Dr. Karl Russ's 'Stubenvögel,' and Dr. A. E. Brehm's 'Thierleben,' on this bird in captivity.

Specimens examined.

No.	Sex.	Mus.	Country.	Length.	Wing.	Tail.	Tars.	Culm.
a.	♂	E. B.	Miami, N. America.	7·8	3·4	3·7	0·95	0·75
b.	♀	E. B.	N. America.	8·3	3·6	4·3	0·95	0·67
c.	♂	E. B.	Wilson Co. N. America.	8·45	3·7	4·0	0·95	0·7
d.	♂	E. B.	Virginia, N. America (*D. W. Scott*).	7·95	3·65	3·9	0·95	0·67
e.	♂	E. B.	Alabama, N. America (*Kumlien* and *Bean*).	7·1	3·55	3·85	0·9	0·7
f.	♂	E. B.	Tamaulipas, Mexico	8·0	3·50	3·9	0·9	0·62

No.	Sex.	Mus.	Country.	Length.	Wing.	Tail.	Tars.	Culm.
g.	♂	E. B.	Mexico	8·7	3·55	4·15	0·97	0·73
h.	♂ jun.	E. B.	Mexico	8·4	3·65	4·15	0·95	0·65
i.	♀	E. B.	N. America.	7·5	3·35	3·75	0·95	0·65
j.	♂	E. B.	Yucatan, Mexico.	7·55	3·3	3·85	0·95	0·7
k.	♂	E. B.	Yucatan, Mexico.	8·2	3·3	3·95	0·9	0·7
l.	♂ jun.	E. B.	Yucatan, Mexico.	7·65	3·15	3·65	085	0·7
m.	♀	E. B.	Merida, Yucatan.	7·6	3·25	3·75	0·95	0·7
MAIDSTONE MUSEUM.								
1.	♂	M. M.	Bermuda	8·0	3·6	4·0	0·95	0·7
2.	♂	M. M.	Bermuda	8·0	3·45	4·0	0·95	0·7
3.	♂	M. M.	Bermuda	7·8	3·45	3·9	0·95	0·7

In heraldry the Cardinal Grosbeak forms the crest to the arms of the family of Huger (South Carolina; granted 1771).

"Arms. Ar. a human heart emitting flames, betw. two laurel branches fructed, saltireways, in chief, and an anchor erect, in base, all ppr. betw. two flaunches az. each charged with a fleur-de-lis or. *Crest*—a sprig, thereon a Virginia Nightingale, all ppr. *Motto* —Ubi libertas ibi patria."

CHRYSOMITRIS UROPYGIALIS.
THE YELLOW-RUMPED SISKIN.
PLATE II.

Chrysomitris atratus, Cassin, Gilliss's Expedition, ii. p. 181 (1855).
Chrysomitris xanthomelæna, Reichb. ? Journ. für orn. 1855, p. 55.
Fringilla sp. ? Eyton, Cat. Birds, p. 256. No. 3211 (1856).
Chrysomitris uropygialis, Scl. Cat. Amer. Birds, p. 125 (1862).
Chrysomitris uropygialis, Cassin, Proc. Acad. Philad. 1865, p. 91.
Chrysomitris uropygialis, Scl. Proc. Zool. Soc. 1867, pp. 322, 338.
Chrysomitris uropygialis, Phil. Anal. Univers. Chile, xxxi. 1868, pp. 263, 295, 303, 316, 325, 329.
Chrysomitris xanthomelæna, Phil. ? Anal. Univers. Chile, xxxi. 1868, p. 325.
Fringilla xanthomelæna, Gray, ? Hand-List Birds, ii. p. 81 (1870).
Fringilla uropygialis, Gray, Hand-List Birds, ii. p. 81 (1870).
Chrysomitris uropygialis, Scl. et Salv. Nom. Av. Neotr. p. 34 (1873).
Fringilla uropygialis, Russ. Stubenvögel, p. 395 (1879).
Chrysomitris uropygialis, Tacz. Orn. Pérou, iii. p. 54 (1886.)

English. *Yellow-rumped Siskin. Cordillerean Goldfinch. Chilian Siskin.*
French. *Le Tarin des Cordillères.*
German. *Goldbürzelzeisig. Kordilleren-Zeisig.*
Castelláno. *Jilgeuro de la Cordillera.*

Habitat. Chili, and Peruvian Andes.

Male. Head, chin, throat and back dull black; feathers of nape, mantle, scapulars and great wing-coverts edged with yellowish-green; wings blackish-brown, speculum lemon-yellow, first primary black; tertials broadly edged with yellowish-white; secondaries tipped with same; rump, breast, belly, under-wing and tail-coverts and basal two thirds of tail bright lemon-yellow; under side of wing pale yellow; upper tail-coverts and rest of tail blackish-brown: iris dark brown; bill dark slaty-brown, lower mandible paler; legs blackish-brown: length 5·2, wing 3·2, tail 2·15, tars. 0·6, culm. 0·4.

Young Male. Similar, not so black, the yellowish-green edges of the feathers of the back broader and extending to the crown of head; lower parts pale lemon-yellow; a small elongated shaft-spot on the two longest under tail-coverts.

Female. Above dull blackish-brown; darker on the chin and throat, the feathers of back more or less broadly edged with yellowish-green; margins of tertials, speculum and centre of abdomen very pale yellow, inclining to white; rest of under-parts and rump pale lemon-yellow; two blackish elongated shaft-spots on the under tail-coverts: bill and legs as in the male.

Observ. The very young birds are almost green above, the forehead and chin blackish; the broad yellow margins of the tertials and secondaries in many specimens of various ages are completely frayed away.

THIS very interesting species, which is so closely allied to *Chrysomitris atrata*, was first made known to science by Dr. P. L. Sclater in his 'Catalogue of American Birds' published in 1862, although well known to ornithologists prior to this date, it was not recognized as different from the young birds or females of *Ch. atrata*.

I have a specimen from Mr. Eyton's collection which must have been procured long before 1856, this example (an adult male) was still undetermined when it passed into my collection, and without doubt is one of Mr. T. Bridge's specimens obtained in Chili, as I have one of his skins of *Chrysomitris atrata* which is prepared in the same manner.

Mr. J. Cassin also places this species (which was collected during 'Gilliss's Expedition') under *Ch. atrata*, he says—"This little bird is stated to appear occasionally in flocks, though it probably visits Chili only in the season of migration:" but in the 'Proc. Acad. Philad.' 1865, he remarks that the "specimens from 'Gilliss's Exped. to Chili,' now in the National Museum, were mistaken by me for the preceding *(C. atratus,)* having at that time only the young specimen from D'Orbigny's collection, to which I above alluded, and relying on it for my determination of the species."

Dr. R. A. Philippi tells us that it "is known in the province of Santiago by the name of *Jilguero de la Cordillera*, and lives in the central Mountainous provinces extending its range into Peru."

The series of specimens from which the principle part of the details are taken, is now in my own collection and were procured by Mr. Weishaupt in the mountains of Chili at an elevation of about 3,000 to 5,000 feet above the sea-level, where they are found in small flocks, keeping always to the great ravines, and feeding on the various wild grass and other seeds. At present I am unable to give any further details respecting its habits.

To reduce the number of species, I have placed *Chrysomitris xanthomelœua*, Rchb. among the synonyms of this bird for the present.

The plant is *Porliera hygrometrica*.

Specimens examined.

No.	Sex.	Mus.	Country.			Length.	Wing.	Tail.	Tars.	Culm.
a.	♂	E. B.	Chili.	(*Weishaupt*).		5·2	3·2	2·15	0·6	0·4
b.	♂	,,	,,	,,		4·65	3·2	2·0	0·6	0·45
c.	♀	,,	,,	,,		4·0	3·25	2·0	0·6	0·4
d.	♀	,,	,,	,,		4·0	3·2	2·0	0·6	0·4
e.	♂	,,	,,	,,		4·95	3·25	2·2	0·6	0·4
f.	♀	,,	,,	,,		4·95	3·15	2·0	0·6	0·4
g.	♀	,,	,,	,,		5·3	3·25	2·2	0·6	0·4
h.	♂	,,	,,	,,		4·85	3·25	2·0	0·6	0·35
i.	♀ jun.	,,	,,	,,		4·95	3·2	2·1	0·6	0·4
j.	♂	,,	,,	(?)		4·9	3·2	2·0	0·6	0·4
k.	♂	,,	,,	(*Weishaupt*).		4·75	3·1	2·0	0·6	0·4
l.	♀	,,	,,	,,		4·5	3·15	2·0	0·6	0·35

The figures (Plate II) are taken from *e* and *l*.

PASSER DOMESTICUS.
THE HOUSE SPARROW.
PLATE I.

Passer domesticus, Ray, Syn. Meth. Avium, p. 86 (1713).
Passera domestica, Zinan. Uova, Nidi Uccelli, t. 11. f. 70 (1737).
House Sparrow, Albin, Birds, i. p. 59. pl. 62 (1738).
Fringilla domestica, Linn. Faun. Suec. p. 242 (1746).
Passer domesticus, Linn. Syst. Nat. p. 30 (1748).
Passer domesticus, Klein, Stem. Avium, p. 17. t. 18. f. 1. a, b (1759).
Passer domesticus, Briss. Ornith. iii. p. 72 (1760).
Passer flavus, Briss. Ornith. iii. p. 78 (1760).
Fringilla domestica, Linn. Faun. Suec. 1. n. 212 (1761).
Passer domesticus, Briss. Orn. Meth. i. p. 327 (1763).
Fringilla domestica, Linn. Syst. Nat. i. p. 323 (1766).
Passer domesticus, Klein, Ova Avium, p. 29. t. 9. f. 7 (1766).
House Sparrow, Penn. Brit. Zool. fol. 107 (1766).
Sparrow, Penn. Brit. Zool. i. t. 51 (1768).
Fringilla domestica, Scop. Ann. i. p. 220 (1769).
Passer domesticus, Gerini, Stor. Nat. Ucc. iii. p. 340 (1771).
Rauch-sperling, Günth. Nest. und Eyern, t. 57 (1772-77).
Fringilla domestica, Müll. Vollständ. Natursystem, iii. p. 592 (1773).
Passera domestica, Cett. Ucc. Sard. p. 204 (1774-77).
Le Moineau, Buff. Hist. Nat. iii. p. 474. t. 29. f. 1 (1775).
Sparrow, Penn. Brit. Zool. i. p. 338 (1776).
Moineau franc de France, Buff. Pl. Enl. 6. 1. et 55. 1 (1777).
Moineau, Bodd. Tab. des Pl. Enl. 6. 1. 55. 1 (1783).
House Sparrow, Lath. Gen. Syn. iii. p. 248 (1783).
Sparrow, Penn. Arct. Zool. ii. p. 383 (1785).
Passer candidus, Sparrm. Mus. Carls. i. pl. 20 (1786).

House Sparrow, Lath. Gen. Syn. Suppl. i. p. 163 (1787).
Fringilla domestica, Gmel. Syst. Nat. i. p. 925 (1788).
House Sparrow, White, Nat. Hist. Selb. (1789).
House Sparrow, Walcot, Syn. Brit. B. ii. pl. 215 (1789).
Haus-sperling, Bechst. Naturg. Dent. iii. p. 107 (1789-95).
Fringilla domestica, Lath. Ind. Orn. i. p, 432 (1790).
Fringilla inda, et domestica, Licht. Cat. Rer. Nat. Rar. pp. 46, 47 (1793).
House Sparrow, Russell, Nat. Hist. Alep. p. 70 (1794).
House Sparrow, Lewin, Brit. B. ii. t. 77, et Br. B. Eggs, i. pl. 12. f. 1 (1795).
House Sparrow, Bew. Brit. Birds, i. p, 154, fig (1797).
Le Moineau, Daud. Trait. d'Orn. i. p. 91. pl. 3 (1800).
Le Moineau, Buff, par Sonn. Hist. Nat. xlvii. p. 115. pl. 104. f. 1 (1801).
Passer domesticus, Pall. Zoogr. Rosso-Asiat. ii. p. 29 (1811); Koch, Baier. Zool. i. p. 219 (1816); Leach, Cat. Mamm. et Birds in B. M. p. 13 (1816); Shaw, Gen. Zool. xiv. p. 40 (1824); Hewit. B. Ool. pl. 41. f. 1. 2 (1831-44); Sykes, P. Z. S. 1832, p. 95; Selby, Brit. Ornith. i. p. 298. pl. 54. fig. 4. 5 (1833); Cox, P. Z. S. 1835, p. 106; Macgill. H. B. Birds, i. p. 340 (1837); Dunn, Ornith. Isl. Ork. p. 80 (1837); Keys and Bl. Wirbelth. Eur. p. xl (1840); Blyth, J. A. S. Beng. xiii. 1844, p. 946; Schl. Rev. Crit. Ois d'Eur. p. lxiv (1844); Mühle, Beitr. Orn. Griech. p. 44 (1844); Rüpp, Syst. Ueb. p. 78 (1845); Yarr. Brit. B. p. 521. 2nd ed. (1845); Tick. J. A. S. B. xvii. 1848, p. 303; Thomps. B. Irel. i. p. 251 (1849); Gray et Mitch. Gen. B. ii. p. 372 (1849); Blyth, Cat. B. A. S. B. p. 119 (1849); Cab. Mus. Hein. i. p. 155 (1850-51); Robert, Voy. Isl. et Groënl. pl. 3 (1851); Midd. Reis. Sibir. Zool. p. 149 (1851); Gray, Cat. Eggs B. Birds, p. 62 (1852); Schl. Vog. Nederl. pl. 161 (1854); Hewits. Eggs B. B. i. p. 155. pl. 42. fig. 3. 4 (1856); Yarr. Brit. B. p. 546. 3rd ed. (1856); Eyton, Cat. B. p. 259

(1856); Adams, P. Z. S. 1859, p. 177; Jaub. et Barth. Lapomm.
Rich. Orn. p. 127 (1859); Powys, Ibis, 1860, p. 137; Lind.
Vög. Griech. p. 57 (1860); M.-Tand. Ibis, 1860, p. 188; Marc.
S. Emul. Abbev. 1861, p. 271; Gould, B. G. Brit. iii. pl. xxxii.
(1862); Maill. Not. l'ile de Reun. i. p. 174 (1863); Gray, Cat.
B. B. p. 100 (1863); Lowne, N. H. Gt. Yarm. p. 57 (1863);
Rad. Reis. Sib. Vög. p. 179 (1863); Bartlett, P. Z. S. 1863, p.
160; Trist. P. Z. S. 1864, p. 446; More, Ibis, 1865, p. 127;
Schl. P. Z. S. 1866, p. 424; Degl. et Gerbe, Ornith. Eur. i. p.
241 (1867); Trist. Ibis, 1867, p. 369; Pollen et Schl. Madag.
p. 154 (1868); Pollen, Relat. de Vog. i. p. 68 (1868-77); Wright,
Ibis, 1869, p. 250; Fritsch, Vög. Eur. tab. 20 fig. 16 (1870);
Gray, Hand-List B. ii. p. 85 (1870); Swinh. P. Z. S. 1870, p.
438; Heugl. Orn. N.-O.-Afr. i. p. 628 et Append. p. cxl. (1871);
Elwes et Buckl. Ibis, 1870, p. 192; Gray, B. W. Scotl. p. 141
(1871); Shelley, Ibis, 1871, p. 141; Gurn. Ibis, 1871, p. 293; Tacz.
Zoologist, 1871, p. 2589; Shelley, Birds Egypt, p. 148 (1872);
Harting, B. Birds, p. 28 (1872); Sundev. Av. Disp. Tentam. p. 32
(1872); Cord. B. Humb. p. 52 (1872); Irby, Birds Gibr. p. 119
(1875); Seeb. Ibis, 1876, p. 114; Sharpe et Dress. B. Eur. iii. p.
587. pl. 176. fig. 1 (1876); Newt. Yarr. B. B. ii. p. 89 (1876); Hartl.
Vög. Madag. pp. 399, 401 (1877); Hume, Stray Feath. 1878, ii.
p. 64; Boucard, P. Z. S. 1878, p. 57; Legge, H. B. Ceyl. pp.
600-4 (1878-80); Shelley, P. Z. S. 1879, p. 678; Brehm, Thierl.
ii. p. 314 (1879); Salv. Cat. Strickl. Coll. p. 209 (1882); Hart.
Sketch. B. Life, p. 165 (1883); B. O. U. List B. Birds, p. 51
(1883); Seeb. Brit. B. Eggs, ii. p. 83 (1884); Tristram, Faun.
Palest. p. 67 (1884); Fergus, Zeitsch. Gesam. Orn. 1884, p. 48;
Radde, J. f. O. 1885, p. 80; Leverk. J. f. O. 1887, p. 83.

Passer domesticus, Bonap. Consp. Gen. Av. p. 509 (1850); Schiff, J. f.
O. 1854, p. 266; Gray; Gen. et Subgen. Birds, p. 78 (1855);
Rodd, Zoologist, 1870, p. 2234.

Passer indicus, Jard. et Selb. Illustr. Orn. t. 118 (184-?); Blyth, J.
A. S. B. xi. 1842, p. 108; J. A. S. B. xv. 1846, p. 37; xvi. p.

470; Cat. B. A. S. Boug. p. 119 (1849); Bonap. Consp. Gen.
Av. p. 509 (1850); Kelaart, B. Ceylon, p. 126 (1852); Kel. et
Lay. Cat. B. Ceyl. p. 59 (1853); Layard, Ann. Nat. xiii. 1854,
p. 258: Hors. et Moore, Cat. B. M. E.-I.-Comp. ii. p. 499
(1856-8); Adams, P. Z. S. 1858, p. 481; Irby, Ibis, 1861, p. 231;
Jerdon, B. Ind. ii. p. 362 (1863); Gray, Hodgs. Cat. B. Nep.
p. 57. (1863); Beavan, P. Z. S. 1864, p. 376; P. Z. S. 1865,
p. 693; Bulger, P. Z. S. 1866, p. 571; Gray, Hand-List B. ii. p.
86 (1870); Holds. P. Z. S. 1872, p. 464; Hume, Stray Feath.
1873, p. 209; Lloyd, Ibis, 1873, p. 413; Hume, Nest and Eggs,
ii. p. 457 (1874); Oates, Stray Feath. 1875, p. 156; Butl. et Hume,
Stray Feath. 1875, p. 499; Tweedd. et Blyth, Birds Burm. p. 93
(1875); Hume et Davis, Stray Feath. 1878, p. 406; Salv. Cat.
Strickl. Coll. p. 209 (1882); Oates, B. Brit. Burm. i. p. 346
(1883); Murr. Faun. Sind. p. 183 (1884).

Passer arboreus, Licht. Mus. Berol.; Bonap. Consp. Gen. A. p. 510
(1850); Heugl. Syst. Übers. Vög. N.-O.-Afr. p. 42 (1856); Antin.
Cat. Uccell. p. 74 (1864); Gray, Hand-List B. ii. p. 86 (1870).

Passer domesticus, var. indicus, Blyth, J. A. S. B. xiv. 1845, p. 553.

Passer indica, Moore, P. Z. S. 1857, p. 96.

Passer pyrrhopterus, Blyth, J. A. S. B. xiii. 1844, p. 947; Gray, Gen.
B. ii. p. 373 (1849); Bonap. Consp. Gen. Av. p. 508 (1850);
Gray, Hand-List B. ii. p. 86 (1870).

Passer rufidorsalis, Brehm, Naum. 1856, p. 376.

Passer rufidorsalis megarhynchus, Brehm, Naum. 1856, p. 376.

Passer rufidorsalis microrhynchus, Brehm, Naum. 1856, p. 376.

Passer tingitanus, Bonap. Cat. Parznd. p. 18 (1856).

Fringilla domestica, Retz. Linn. Faun. Souc. p. 249. (1800); Gérard.
Tab. élém. i. p. 171 (1806); Ill. Prodr. Syst. Mam. et Av. p. 222
(1811); Shaw, Gen. Zool. ix. p. 429. pl. 64. f. 1 (1815); Tem.
Man. d'Orn. p. 218 (1815); Meisn. und Schinz, Vög. der
Schweiz. p. 74 (1815); Meyer, Vög. Liv. und Esthl. p. 84
(1815); Forst. Cat. B. Birds, p. ii. (1817); Nilss. Orn. Suec. i.

p. 140 (1817); Temm. Man. d'Orn. i. p. 350 (1820); ? Licht. Doubl. Mus. Berl. p. 89 (1823); Naum. Vög. Deutsch. iv. p. 453. taf. 115. fig. 1. 2 (1824); Werner, Atlas, Gran. pl. 39 (1827); Stark, Nat. Hist. Vert. i. p. 244 (1828); Griff. Cuv., Aves, ii. pp. 135, 234 (1829); Staul. Mag. Nat. Hist. iii. 1830, p. 172; Schinz, Nest. und Eier der Vög. t. 36. fig. 1 (1830); Cook, P. Z. S. 1831, p. 96 ; Jeuyns, Man. Brit. Vert. Anim. p. 134 (1835); Nordm. Voy. Russ. Mérid. iii. p. 180 (1840); Gull. P. Z. S. 1842, pp. 71, 98, 99; Yarr. Brit. B. i. p. 474 fig. (1843); Thien. Fortpfl. Vög. Eur. t. 10. f. 4 (1845-56); Hare. P. Z. S. 1851, p. 145 ; Kjærb. Ornith. Dan. pl. xxvi. fig. 4 (1852); Radde, J. f. O. 1854, p. 61 ; Brehm, J. f. O. 1854, pp. xxxviii, xlvi ; Sundev. Svensk. Fogl. pl. 6. fig. 1, 2 (1856) ; Schl. Nederl. Vögels. pl. 16. fig. 11. 12 (1861); Hintz, J. f. O. 1867, p. 165.

Fringilla pyrrhoptera, Less. in Bélang. Voy. Ind. p. 274 (1834).
Fringilla passer, Crisp, P. Z. S. 1860, p. 179.
Pyrgita domestica, Cuv. Rêg. Anim. i. p. 385 (1817); Boie, Isis, 1822, p. 554; Flem. B. Anim. p. 83 (1828); Latr. Cuv., Rêg. Anim. i. p. 439 2nd ed. (1829); Brehm, Vög. Deutschl. p. 264 (1831); Gould, B. Eur. pl. 184. fig. 1 (1832-37); Gould, P. Z. S. 1834, p. 51 ; Rüpp. Neue Wirbelth. p. 100 (1835-40); Eyton, Cat. B. B. p. 19 (1836); Strichl. P. Z. S. 1836, p. 99; Bonap. Comp. List Birds, p. 31 (1838); Fraser, P. Z. S. 1839, p. 121 ; Jerd. B. Penins. Ind. M. J. xi. 1840, p. 28 ; Ewer, P. Z. S. 1842, p. 92; Blyth, P. Z. S. 1842, p. 93 ; Fraser, P. Z. S. 1843, p. 52 ; Hodgs. Gray's Z. Misc. 1844, p. 84 ; Gray, Hodgs. Cat. B. Nep. p. 107 (1846); Maund. Treas. Nat. Hist. p. 629 (1849); Reichb. Avium Syst. Nat. pl. lxxv (1850); Licht. Nomencl. Av. Mus. Berol. p. 47 (1854); Sch. J. f. O. 1854, p. 246 ; Gull. P. Z. S. 1875. p. 490.
Pyrgita pagorum, Brehm, Vög. Deutsch. p. 265 (1831).
Pyrgita rustica, Brehm, Vög. Deutsch. p. 266. t. 17. f. 2 (1831).
Pyrgita indica, Hutton, J. A. S. Beng. xvii. 1848, p. 693.
Pyrgita valida, Brehm, Vogelfang, p. 98 (1855).
Pyrgita minor, Brehm, Vogelfang, p. 98 (1855).

Pyrgita intercedens, Brehm, Vogelfang, p. 98 (1855).
Pyrgita brachyrhynchos, Brehm, Vogelfang, p. 98 (1855).
Pyrgita pectoralis, Heugl. J. f. O. 1867, p. 299.
Pyrgita cahirina, Heugl. J. f. O. 1867, p. 299.
Pyrgita castaneus, Heugl. Orn. N.-O.-Afr. i. p. 628 (1871).
Pyrgita castanotus, Heugl. Orn. N.-O.-Afr. i. p. 628 (1871).
Pyrgita melanorhynchus, Heugl. Orn. N.-O.-Afr. i. p. 628 (1871).
Domestic, or House Sparrow, Gmel. Syst. Nat. Hist. vii. p. 207. Eng. Ed. (1801).
Sparrow Finch, Penn. Brit. Zool. i. p. 456, pl. 58 (1812).
Black-breasted Finch, Lath. Gen. Hist. B. vi. p. 50 (1823).
House Sparrow, Mont. Ornith. Dict. ii. (1802); Buff. N. H. B. iv. p. 27. pl. 85. fig. 1. Eng. Ed. (1812); Pult. Cat. B. Dorset, p. 12 (1813); Low's, Faun. Orcad. p. 59 (1813); Bew. Brit. B. i. p. 174 (1816); Bew. Brit. B. i. p. 158 (1821); Hunt, Brit. B. iii. (1822); Lath. Gen. Hist. Birds, vi. p. 46 (1823); White's, Nat. Hist. Selb. p. 100. Ed. (1832); Gurney, Russell et Coues, The *House Sparrow*, 1885.
The Sparrow, Hone's, Every-Day Book, i. p. 495 (1826); id. i. p. 364 (1838); Wood, N. H. Birds, p. 475 (1869); Tristram, Nat. H. Bible, p. 201. 7th ed. (1883*)*.

> *Figures.* Albin, Birds, i. pl. 62. Pl. Enl. 6. 1, et 55. 1. Gould, B. Eur. pl. 184. fig. 1; et Birds Great Brit. iii. pl. 32. Sharpe et Dresser. Birds Eur. iii. pl. 176. fig. 1.
> Jard. et Selby, Ill. Orn. pl. 118.

Danish *Grasspurv*. Dutch, *De Huismusch, De Musch.* English *Sparrow, Philip Sparrow, House Sparrow, Sparrow Finch, Domestic Sparrow, Indian Sparrow, Indian House Sparrow, Common Sparrow.* French, *Le Moineau, Moineau domestique, Le Moineau franc, Grosbec Moineau.* Finnish, *Kolivarpunen.* Gaelic, *Gealbhan, Gealbhag.* German, *Der Sperling, Der Haus-sperling, Der Rauch-sperling.* Italian, *Passera.* Norwegian, *Grasspurv.* Portuguese, *Pardal.* Russian,

Vorobey. Spanish, *Gorrion*. Swedish, *Hussparf*. Swiss, *Tatting*, *Sparf*.
Bengalese, *Charia* or *Chatu* (Jerdon and Blyth). Hindoo, *Churi and Khas Churii* (Jerdon). *Gowrya* (Blyth). Tamils in Ceylon, *Gewàl-Kurulla* (Legge). Tam. *Adiki lam Kuravi* (Jerdon). Sinhalese, *Geh Kurulla* (Layard). Teluga, *Uri-pickike* (Jerdon).

Habitat. Europe, from Siberia in the North to Egypt and Nubia in the South, and from England in the West to Ceylon, the East Indies, and Siam, in the East.

Introduced into Australia, New Zealand, Mauritius, Reunion, Madagascar, Comoro Islands, United States of America, Canada, and many other places.

Male Adult Summer, India. Crown and nape pale grey; a chestnut band behind the eye widening and uniting on the hind neck; a small white spot above hind corner of eye; mantle, scapulars, greater and lesser wing-coverts chestnut-brown, the inner half of each feather nearly black, excepting the latter; primaries, secondaries and tail dull brown, edged with brownish-buff, broader on the secondaries, quills blackish; median coverts tipped with white, black at the base; rump, upper tail-coverts, sides of chest, sides and flanks dirty ashy grey; bastard-wing and primary-coverts blackish, edged with pale brown; cheeks and sides of neck white; a narrow frontal band, lores, chin and throat black; breast, underparts, undersides of wing-and coverts, and under tail-coverts dirty creamy white, paling towards the abdomen: iris hazel brown; bill black, legs light brown: length 5·3, wing 2·9, tail 2·3, tars. 0·65, culm. 0·4.

Female Adult Summer, Kingsbury. Above nearly uniform dirty brown; inner half of feathers of mantle, scapulars and wing-coverts blackish brown; margins of same tinged with rufous; primaries, secondaries and tail dark brown, more or less edged with rufous and buffish white, quills shining dark brown; median coverts creamy white, brown at base; band behind eye reaching to nape, and sides of lower neck, fawn-colour: bastard-wing and primary-coverts dark brown, faintly edged with buff; cheeks, breast, sides and flanks pale earthy brown, paling towards chin and abdomen; a slight indication of black on centre of throat, and faint centres to feathers of breast; underside of wing-and coverts dull white; under-tail coverts dirty white, darker in the centre, with brown shaft stripe: iris light hazel; bill brown, yellowish at base: length 6·0, wing 2·8, tail 2·2, tars. 0·7, culm. 0·45.

Young of first year. Similar to female but paler, especially the margins to the feathers; the young males assuming the breeding dress by the following spring.

Observations. The fully adult males shot in England in April, have assumed the dark chestnut back, and deep slaty grey of the crown; the black is more extended on the breast; the underparts conspicuously pale slaty grey; and the bill black.

In winter the black of the chin and throat in the male are slightly margined with white; crown brownish; margins to feathers of back broader and richer chestnut; underparts paler; bill brown, base yellowish.

In some young males, the margins of the median coverts, are rich rufous brown.

The female from the U. S. America exhibits more of the shaft stripes on the throat and breast, than in the English birds; the ear-coverts of the male are darker grey.

The type of Sir W. Jardines *P. indicus* in my collection is a young male, just assuming the breeding plumage of early spring.

The Indian form is readily distinguished by its pure white cheeks and sides of neck, and paler underparts.

Of all the birds perhaps none has been so persecuted as the common House Sparrow, and no wonder; I well remember when a boy while living close to the Crystal Palace, Sydenham, (to which I had daily access), associating with the workmen, who had to attend to all the roof and rain-water pipes of that building, I was in my glory watching the continuous and everlasting labour of clearing out basketsful of straw, hay, rags, feathers, tow, cottons, leaves, twigs and other refuse, carried there for the nests of two indefatigable birds. Sparrows and Starlings' eggs in any number came from every nook and corner, this accumulation of rubbish gave great trouble, stopping up and causing an over-flow of water and decay of iron pipes, which had to be replaced and many strengthened to support the building. Well may the farmers and owners of property condemn and place a high price on the head of a sparrow, which he well deserves, not only for the quantity of food he consumes, but the destruction on all sides, by his too sociable habits.

When reading Mr. J. H. Gurney's continental notes of this bird in Metz,—"The cottagers" he says, " put up pots of earthenware against the walls of their houses for the sparrows to nest in, not by way of encouraging them (as the English encourage Martins), but to make them into a pie when the young ones got big enough,"—reminded me that when the old thatched buildings such as the Wapiti House, Elephant House, and similar places existed in the Zoological Gardens, they formed a perfect paradise for our home loving and very domesticated enemy, which were in greater numbers even than now, the keepers used the very same kind of German or Dutch earthenware pots, but the young were utilized for a very different purpose, they being given to the small mammals; hawks, owls, lizards, snakes, &c.

It was during those early days of mine, that the Australian and New Zealand governments persuaded my father to prepare a large number of all our British Birds alive for those colonies, and it fell to my lot to undertake the management of them until they were shipped, it was amongst this mixed congregation of the feathered tribe, that many pairs of sparrows formed a most troublesome addenda, for they would not be tamed or stop on their perches, but always persisted in crawling through the bars at the bottom of the cage and sulking there until turned out again.

It is with feelings of humiliation and regret, that I ever had a hand (I am speaking of nearly twenty-five years ago) in sending to those colonies one of their greatest pests, for such are the reports of this bird which continually reach us.

Some enthusiastic person, did a similar act for the United States, which has brought about legislation and a whole army of scientific and other men to wage war against this corn-eating, seed devouring "ruffian."

The back of this institution (Maidstone Museum) is beautifully covered with ivy, which the sparrow has taken possession of for years, builds its nest and rears its young in perfect safety, but by permitting this to go on, I have lost (without thinking about it) a beautiful pink May-tree, they have by degrees eaten off all the small buds during the winter, thus preventing the tree from throwing out a single leaf, and since the dead tree has been removed, they have taken to two others close by, which will I fear, share the same fate as the first, for they make them a perfect feeding ground during the winter.

To use the words of Bewick written in 1816 respecting the plumage of the sparrow might appear to some of far too early a date for quotation, but, it is one of those passages, which I am more impressed with than those of later authors, " This bird, as seen in large and smoky towns, is generally sooty and unpleasing in its appearance; but among barns and stackyards the cock bird exhibits a very great variety of his plumage, and is far from being the least beautiful of our British birds."

Whenever I exhibit the lovely skins of the common house sparrow to those who never had the bird in their hands before, the exclamations of admiration and surprise are curious to relate; is it a thrush, a redwing, a chaffinch, a brambling, and some have gone so far as to ask if it is a goldfinch, a clean country sparrow puzzles many, however familiar they are with the dirty groping street bird, who cocks his eye up sideways, draws your attention, and seizing the crumbs from your feet, flies off, returning with all the impertinence in the world for the next. They will even go so far as to have a tremendous family quarrel and flog their lady friends under one's nose, be it summer or in the depth of winter. I have witnessed this quarrel when the snow was three inches deep, and they (four in number) appeared more like young rats fighting for the last crust than birds, the snow flying in all directions.

It would be almost impossible to form an adequate estimate of the literature on the sparrow, both for and against its habits :—In Griffith's edition of Cuvier's Animal Kingdom, I find an excellent calculation regarding the quantity of corn consumed by this bird; it is as follows —"Rougier de la Bergerie, a French writer on rural economy, has made an approximative calculation of what the sparrows cost, annually, to France. If their number be reduced merely to ten millions, a reduction much below the reality, it follows, that each of them eating a bushel of grain, weighing twenty pounds, ten millions of bushels will thus be withdrawn from the consumption and commerce of men; and, only reckoning the price of a bushel to be twenty sous, no less a sum than ten millions of francs per annum, will be withdrawn from agricultural produce. This calculation of an able agriculturist is confirmed by observation. The quantity of grain eaten by these birds, may be easily ascertained by those who bring them up in cages; and M. Sonnini, from whom we borrow these observations, says, that he found two-and twenty grains of wheat in the stomach of a sparrow just killed."

From the very interesting and most important "little work on the sparrow controversy" entitled 'The House Sparrow,' full of detail and careful observation, written by Mr. J. H. Gurney, Jun., Col. C. Russell, and Dr. E. Coues, I (although no friend of the sparrow), think that the observations of Mr. J. H. Gurney (p. 8) are worthy of great consideration. He says—"If one-fourth of the young sparrows hatched in England are fed for ten days on 14 caterpillars apiece, it is easy to make a calculation of how many they would eat in a large agricultural county like Norfolk. Norfolk contains 800 parishes: say that 800 young sparrows are annually hatched in each parish; that gives us a total of 640,000 sparrows. If one-fourth of them are fed on caterpillars, we should have 22,400,000 of these destructive creatures eaten in this one county alone, every year, by sparrows. So that there is a very nice balance to adjust in a matter which the most expert observer might find difficult. On the one hand the young sparrows are fed on a great many caterpillars; on the other hand they are fed with grain, but this is mixed with weeds and other vegetable matter. Again, there is a sidelight in which to look at the question :—If the sparrows were dead, how many of these caterpillars would be eaten by other small birds? We may be quite sure that a considerable portion of them would *not* be eaten, unless chaffinches and greenfinches become more numerous than they are now; and if this was so, would not they speedily become much more addicted to corn? I think there is not a doubt about it."

Mr. H. Seebohm in his British Birds' Eggs (p. 63) tells us that "In the hot months of the year the house sparrow is excessively fond of dusting itself, like the domestic fowl; and sometimes as many as half a dozen may be seen enjoying this luxury in company. In Derbyshire, where the roads are mostly limestone, sparrows are not unfrequently seen to fly from them with their plumage almost as white as snow. The sparrow's flight is rapid, and when prolonged for any great distance is undulating, but when only flying a little way it is almost direct. Upon the ground it progresses in a series of hops." Mr. Dresser says, "the sparrow is eminently gregarious: even during the breeding-season one observes it in small groups searching after food; and in the autumn and winter they collect in flocks and frequent the hedges and stack-yards, and are often seen in very large flocks in the corn-fields."

The distribution of this species is perhaps greater than any other known bird; it occupies every city, town, village, castle, manor, solitary church, private residence, hamlet, the smallest isolated cottage, to the woodman's hut in the depth of the most lonely forests throughout the whole of Europe, and from Siberia in the North to Egypt, Nubia and Bengal; as Mr. H. E. Dresser truly remarks, "it follows the footsteps of man almost like a domestic animal, and where he fixes his habitation there the sparrow also takes up its abode."

In England it is found in every county, from the borders of Scotland to the Scilly Islands, to the West throughout Ireland, to the North in Scotland and its adjacent islands, passing still farther North to the Orkney and Shetland Islands, I procured it in Unst the most northern of the latter group. It does not appear to be found in Iceland or the Faroe Islands, but is plentiful in the warmer valleys of Scandinavia.

Its range according to travellers and collectors, extends from Southern Europe to Madeira, the Canary Islands; Morocco, Algeria, and Tangiers in N.-W. Africa; throughout Turkey in Europe, Asia Minor, Palestine into Egypt, and Nubia, the shores of the Red Sea to the borders of the Blue Nile as far as Khartoum. To the east the vast territories in which it has been observed, gives further proof of its extension, wherever the cultivation of corn is practicable, there they are found by thousands. It is abundant in Persia according to Mr. Blanford; from thence it advances to Turkestan, Baluchistan, Afghanistan, and extremely common in the valleys of the Himalayas and India, from Calcutta, Bengal, Madras, Nepal, Cashmere, Burmah and Siam, to Ceylon and the adjacent islands. At present I am unable to find any account of its appearance in China, or Japan.

The introduction of it into Australia, New Zealand, and the United States is of comparatively modern date, but those found in Mauritius and Reunion must have been taken there at a very early period.

Nidification.—It matters little to a sparrow, as to choice of a nesting place, whether it be a Palace, the House of Lords or Commons, Nelson's Column, the National Gallery, the British Museum, Guildhall, the Mansion House, or the Royal Exchange, let it be a stone building or a galvanized iron one, there is sure to be an unlucky corner left for him, which he is not slow to discover, quite regardless of the sensitive nerves of the occupants; his dignity is not even lowered when in possession of a hut, or a pig-sty, so long as he can find an aperture large enough to drag in hay and rags. The crown of a rain water-pipe is always a most favourite position for a nest, although the bird heedlessly places it there, losing many broods during heavy rains.

The sparrow will occasionally build a dome-shaped nest in a tree or a bush, these structures are large and loosely constructed, some that I have seen were of such dimensions as to make it appear as though two nests were united.

I have a nest taken from an ivy covered wall, composed of hay, straw, bents and the tail feathers of pigeons, the latter are stuck in an upright position, and amongst them a dyed blue duck's and a green ostrich feather, no doubt belonging to a young lady's bonnet, the tips of each feather meeting, thus forming a complete bower; the interior is lined with the downy feathers of the fowl.

The eggs five in number, are of the usual types; the ground-colour is dirty white variously spotted and streaked with pale grey, blackish-brown, purplish-brown, and yellowish-brown, and many of the small blotches overlaping each other, while one is completely striated all over, in another the brown is dispersed over the surface.

The dimensions of each egg are, viz.:—L. 0·85, b. 0·60. L. 0·82, b. 0·64. L. 0·77, b. 0·63. L. 0·80, b 0·63. L. 0·82, b. 0·64.

The eggs are extremely variable, from almost chocolate-brown to pure white, with a few blackish-brown blotches unevenly scattered on the surface. From four to seven eggs are the usual numbers found in the nests.

Some of the largest eggs in my collection measure:—L. 0·9, b. 0·64. L. 0·95, b. 0·68, while others are only L. 0·79, b. 0·63. L. 0·85, b. 0·60.

Those of the Indian bird in my collection obtained by Capt. Beavan at Beerachalee in India, when placed side by side with those taken in England, cannot be distinguished, the general colours being identical, and the measurements vary to the same extent.

From a series of over 84 skins from India, Mauritius, Nubia, Egypt, Comoro Islands, United States, Shetland, and various counties of England, I have selected the under-mentioned examples for the dimensions.

Specimens examined.

No.	Sex.	Mus.	Locality.	Date.	Length.	Wing.	Tail.	Tars.	Culm.
1.	♂	E. B.	Kingsbury, N. London.	W.	6·2	2·9	2·3	0·7	0·5
2.	♀	E. B.	Kingsbury, N. London.	S.	6·0	2·8	2·2	0·7	0·45
3.	♂	E. B.	Maidstone, Kent.	Oct.	5·9	2·95	2·2	0·75	0·45
4.	♀	E. B.	,, ,,	,,	5·9	2·85	2·3	0·7	0·45
5.	♂	E. B.	Unst, Shetland.	Nov.	6·0	2·95	2·35	0·7	0·45
6.	♀	E. B.	,, ,,	,,	5·8	2·2	2·25	0·7	0·5
7.	♂	E. B.	Maidstone, Kent.	May.	5·8	2·95	2·25	0·75	0·45
8.	♂	E. B.	,, ,,	Dec.	5·75	2·9	2·25	0·75	0·5
9.	♀	E. B.	,, ,,	,,	5·8	2·95	2·3	0·7	0·5
10.	♂	E. B.	,, ,,	April.	5·45	3·0	2·4	0·75	0·55
11.	♂	E. B.	U. S. America (*Garrett*).	May.	6·0	3·0	2·3	0·75	0·5
12.	♀	E. B.	,, ,, (*Ridgway*).	June.	5·45	2·9	2·3	0·7	0·55

Passer indicus.

No.	Sex.	Mus.	Locality.	Date.	Length.	Wing.	Tail.	Tars.	Culm.
1.	♂	E. B.	Kotekbaie (*Hume*).	Feb.	5·25	2·85	2·25	0·7	0·45
2.	♀	E. B.	Jural in Khunaitee (*Hume*).	Dec.	4·75	2·85	2·25	0·7	0·45
3.	♂	E. B.	India	?	5·3	2·9	2·3	0·65	0·4
4.	♀	E. B.	India	?	4·9	2·8	2·2	0·6	0·4
5.	♂	E. B.	India (*Jardine*, coll.).	?	5·55	2·8	2·3	0·65	0·45
6.	♂	E. B.	S. India (*Jerdon*).	W.	5·5	2·95	2·25	0·7	0·5
7.	♂	E. B.	Nubia (*Adams*).	Jan.	5·55	2·85	2·3	0·7	0·5
8.	♀	E. B.	Nubia (*Adams*).	,,	5·3	2·75	2·25	0·7	0·45
9.	♂	E. B.	Egypt (*Adams*).	Dec.	5·25	2·9	2·25	0·65	0·45
10.	♀	E. B.	Egypt (*Adams*).	,,	5·35	2·8	2·2	0·7	0·45

The figures (Plate 1) are taken from Nos. 8 and 9 male and female, procured at Maidstone in December.

The abbreviations are W. winter S. summer.

LINES TO A SPARROW.
"Who comes to my Window every morning for his Breakfast."

"Master Dicky, my dear,
You have nothing to fear,
Your proceedings I mean not to check, sir;
Whilst the weather benumbs,
We should pick up our crumbs,
So, I prithee, make free with a *peck*, sir.

I'm afraid it's too plain
You're a villain in *grain*,
But in that you resemble your neighbours,
For mankind have agreed
It is right to *suck seed*,
Then, like you, *hop the twig* with their labours.

Besides this, Master Dick,
You of trade have the trick,
In all *branches* you traffic at will, sir.
You have no need of shops
For your samples of *hops*,
And can ev'ry day take up your *bill*, sir.

Then in foreign affairs
You may give yourself *airs*,
For I've heard it reported at home, sir,
That you're on the best terms
With the *diet* of *Worms*,
And have often been tempted to *Rome*, sir.

Thus you feather your nest
In the way you like best,
And live high without fear of mishap, sir;
You are fond of your *grub*,
Have a taste for some *shrub*,
And for *gin*—there you understand *trap*, sir.

Tho' the rivers won't flow
In the frost and the snow,
And for fish other folks vainly try, sir;
Yet you'll have a treat,
For, in cold or in heat,
You can still take *perch* with a *fly*, sir.

In love, too, oh Dick,
(Tho' you oft when love-sick
On the course of good breeding may trample;
And though often henpeck'd,
Yet) you scorn to neglect
To set all mankind an *eggsample*.

Your *opinions* 'tis true
Are flighty a few,
But at this I, for one, will not grumble;
So—your breakfast you've got,
And you're off like a *shot*,
Dear Dicky, your humble *cum-tumble*."*

* Hone's Every-Day Book, vol. III. p. 364 (1838). Copied from the Examiner, Feb. 12, 1815.

TEXTOR PANICIVORA.

TEXTOR PANICIVORUS.
THE GREAT RED-BILLED WEAVER.
PLATES II. and III.

Loxia panicivora, Linn. Syst. Nat. i. p. 302 (1766).
Loxia panicivora, Müll. Vollst. Natur. iii. p. 550 (1773).
Loxia panicivora, Gmel. Syst. Nat. ii. p. 851 (1788).
Loxia panicivora, Lath. Ind. Orn. i. p. 388 (1790).
Bubalornis niger, Smith, Rep. Exp. Centr. Afr. p. 51 (1836).
Textor erythrorhynchus, Smith, Illustr. Zool. S. Afr. pl. LXIV (1841).
Textor erythrorhynchus, Gray et Mitch. Gen. Birds. ii. p. 350 (1849).
Alecto erythrorhynchus, Bonap. Consp. Gen. Av. p. 438 (1850).
Textor niger, Strickl. et Scl. Birds Damar. Contr. Orn. p. 150 (1852).
Textor erythrorhynchus, Licht. Nomencl. Av. Mus. Berol. p. 50 (1854).
Alecto erythrorhyncha, Müll. Journ. für Orn. 1855, p. 460.
Alecto panicivora, Müll. Journ. für Ornith. 1855, p. 460.
Textor erythrorhynchus, Anderss. Lake Ngami, p. 215 (1856).
Bubalornis niger, Eyton, Cat. of Birds, p. 245 (1856).
Textor erythrorhynchus, Livingst. Trav. S. Afr. p. 545 (1857).
Textor erythrorhynckus, Reichb. Singvögel, p. 88. pl. XLV. fig. 329 (1861).
Alectornis panicivora, Reichb. Singvögel, p. 89 (1861).
Textor erythrorhynchus, Hartl. Journ. für Orn. 1861, p. 176.
Textor erythrorhynchus, Layard, Cat. Birds S. Afr. p. 178 (1867).
Textor erythrorhynchus, Chap. Trav. S. Afr. Append. p. 400 (1868).
Textor alecto, Sharpe, Proc. Zool. Soc. 1869, p. 566.
Textor panicivorus, Gray, Hand-List Birds, ii. p. 40 (1870).
Textor erythrorhynchus, Gray, Hand-List Birds, ii. p. 40 (1870).
Textor erythrorhynchus, Sharpe, Cat. Afr. Birds, p. 58 (1871).
Textor erythrorhynchus, Gurney, Ibis, 1871, p. 255.
Bubalornis erythrorhynchus, Anderss. et Gurn. Birds Damara-Land. pp. 165, 199 (1872).

Textor panivivorus, Pelzeln, Ibis, 1873, p. 115.
Textor erythrorhynchus, Lay. et Sharpe, Birds S. Afr. p. 445 (1875-84).
Ploceus erythrorhynchus, Russ, Stubenvögel, i. p. 318. taf. x. fig. 52. (1879).
Bubalornis niger, Waterh. Proc. Zool. Soc. 1880, p. 491.
Textor niger, Salvin, Cat. Coll. Birds, Strickl. p. 240 (1882).
Textor panivivorus, Shelley, Ibis, 1887, p. 43.

THE INTERMEDIATE RED-BILLED WEAVER.

Textor intermedius, Cab. v. d. Decken's Reisen, iii. p. 32. taf. xi (1869).
Textor intermedius, Finsch et-Hartl. Decken's Reis. O.-Afr. p. 385 (1870).
Textor intermedius, Gray, Hand-List Birds, ii. p. 40 (1870).
Textor intermedius, Cab. Journ. für Orn. 1878, pp. 217, 233.
Ploceus intermedius, Russ, Stubenvögel. p. 318 (1879).
Textor intermedius, Fischer, Zeitschr. Gesam. Ornith. 1884, p. 333.
Textor scioanus, Salvad. Ann. Mus. Civ. Gen. 1884, p. 195.
Textor scioanus, Salvad. Ibis, 1885, p. 232.
Textor intermedius, Shelley, Ibis, 1885, p. 410.
Textor intermedius, Fischer, Journ. für Orn. 1885, p. 132.
Textor intermedius, Reichen. Journ. für Orn. 1887, p. 67.

Figures, Smith's, Illustr. Zool. S. Afr. pl. lxiv. Reichb. Singvögel pl. xlv. f. 329. Russ, Stubenvögel, taf. x. f. 52. Decken's Reis. taf. xi.

English. *White-winged Grosbeak. Red-billed black Weaver-Bird. Buffalo Weaver-Bird. Millet eating Alectornis. Black Bubalorne or Rose-beaked Weaver. Intermediate Weaver.*

French. *Alectornis mangeur de Millet. Bubalornis noir ou à bec rose.*

German. *Rosaschnabeliger Büffel-weber. Hirse-Alectovogel. Büffel-Webervogel. Büffel-vogel. Der Kornfresser. Viehweber, Vieh-Weberrogel.*

Native Name. *Tsaba Gushoa*, Andersson.

Habitat. Central South and portion of West Africa, "with the exception of Cape Colony and Namaqua-land." *(Shelley).*

Localities. Damara-land *(Andersson)*. Kurrichaine *(Smith)*. Trans-vaal and Crocodile River *(Ayres)*. Kalahari Desert *(Moffatt)*. Bamangwato *(Buckley)*. Tati, Makalaka Kraal *(Oates)*. Koaroomoorooi Pan *(Jameson)*. Zambesi *(Bradshaw)*. Humbe, Cunene River, Quillengues, Caconda, Kiulo and Gambos *(Anchieta)*. Kalomo River *(Livingstone)*. River Coanza, Angola *(Montiero)*. Galunga, Loanda *(Sala)*.

Localities of Textor intermedius and Scioanus. Central and East Africa, extending its range into Southern Abyssinia. Kisuani and Dalaoni River *(Decken)*. Ikanga in Ukamba *(Heilderbury)*. Pare, Ultinei, Uruscha, Kilbaia, Victoria N'yanza *(Fischer)*. Daimbi, Shoa *(Antinori)*. Taf, Somali-land *(Philipps)*.

Male. Black, with slight brownish tinge; basal portion of feathers white; patch on each side of chest and centres of side feathers white; outer edges of second to eighth primary white, quills black; bastard and outer web of first primary black; under wing-coverts black; under side of primaries white for more than half their length, tips black: iris dark brown; bill and feet red: length 9·0, wing 4·7, tail 4·1, tarsus 1·2, culm. 0·9.

Female. Similar, dark brownish black; base of feathers slaty grey; chin and throat whitish: iris brown; bill pale reddish brown, darker at the tip; legs reddish brown.

Young Bird. Dull chocolate brown, darkest on crown and mantle; base of feathers slaty grey; chin, throat and breast variegated with dirty white, a submarginal brown band on each feather; under tail-coverts slightly edged with dirty white: bill and legs reddish brown. Pl. III. fig. 1.

Young Male. Blackish brown, shewing feathers at all stages of growth, from dull brown to nearly black; basal portion of feathers slaty grey; a submarginal heart-shaped brown band on feathers of chest, tips whitish; margins of under tail-coverts whitish: "iris dark hazel; bill and legs reddish brown." *(T. E. Buckley.)*

Young Bird, Somali. Dark brownish black, with slaty grey tinge on crown, neck and breast; showing brownish feathers on the back of various stages of growth; base of feathers greyish white; heart-shaped submarginal blotches on feathers of breast; bill yellowish brown at base, tip blackish; feet dark brown. Pl. III. fig. 2.

THE two large black weavers which I now wish to distinguish have, I may say, been intermixed to such an extent, that they are almost beyond separation, and in attempting to divide them I find it advisable to follow up the original diagnosis of the two birds from the earlier authors, but this is rather perplexing, for neither Brisson or Linnæus give a locality beyond Africa for the species under consideration.

In the diagnosis given by Brisson in 1760, the bill and feet of his *Pyrrhula Africana nigra* are described as follows—"*Rostrum cinereo-album. Pedes, unguesque cinerei,*" which is unmistakably meant for *Textor albirostris*. Six years after the above was published Linnæus describes in his 'Systema Naturæ' 1766, another species which he calls *Loxia panicivora*, described thus, "*Loxia nigra, alula alba, rostro incarnato,*" which cannot be any other bird than (*Textor erythrorhynchus*, Smith), at the same time he quotes Brisson's work for the species, and in doing so led all subsequent Ornithologists to follow up the entanglement he commenced, for I find all intervening authors up to within a few years of the present day, have used the same synonymy for the two birds; under these circumstances I have placed all the references to the white or grey-billed bird from N. E., E., and West Africa, under *Textor albirostris*; and those of the red-billed bird of South, and part of West Central Africa, under *Textor panicivora*; but in doing this another difficulty arises as to which species Dr. Cabanis's *Textor intermedius* belongs, then again there is *Textor sciounus*, Salvad., both described as having red bills and inhabiting the same country, in juxtaposition with *T. albirostris*.

I do here most candidly admit that the two latter birds, are as much entitled to be placed with one as the other, and on careful examination of a series of seventeen specimens now before me, I have no hesitation in saying that they are hybrids between the South and North-east African forms, unless the black or more Northern form is the older, or origin of the Southern, which may account for the gradation from one into the other. *Textor intermedius* has less white on the under side of the wing and a stouter bill than *T. panicivora*, and *T. scioanus* still less white, but the bill is the same as *T. intermedius*, the legs of both, being dark brown or blackish, as in *T. albirostris*, but the legs of all the examples of various ages of the true *T. panicivora* are red or reddish brown; the young of the two distinct forms in the dull liver-brown plumage are only distinguished by the white underside of the wings and red legs.

I propose to unite the synonomy of the species as follows :—

Red-billed white winged forms—
1. *Textor panicivora.* The most Southern form, Damara-land.
   „   *intermedius.* } The North-eastern forms, Shoa, and
   „   *scioanus.*   }   Somali.

White, grey or black-billed form—
2. *Textor albirostris.* The North and N. E. form, Abyssinia extending West to Senegambia.

I subjoin the most interesting portions of the literature, which I have brought together respecting the habits of these well known birds, the earliest being Dr. Andrew Smith's, published in 1841 :—

"It was not till after we had passed to the northward of the 25th degree of south latitude that we discovered this bird; and if we are to believe the natives, it rarely extends its flight farther to the southward, which they attribute to the scarcity of Buffaloes south of that parallel. Wherever it was discovered it was always in attendance upon herds of the animals just mentioned, and either flying over the members of which the group was composed, or else perched upon the back of some individual animal. While perched, it appeared, generally, to be employed in collecting articles of food from the hide; and while so occupied it passed quickly from one part of the Buffaloe to another, without the latter appearing to bestow the slighest attention upon its movements. On opening the stomachs of the specimens we procured we found, what we had been led to expect, namely, that its food consisted in part at least of parasitical insects ; and that to obtain them it selected the company in which, as has already been remarked, we always found it. According to the evidence of the natives, it also frequently alights upon the ground, examines the excrement of the Buffaloes, and from it collects certain articles of food. Sometimes a number of individuals were observed associated with a herd of the quadrupeds in question, frequently only one or two, and on many occasions we encountered troops of Buffaloes without even one in attendance. This bird, besides being of service to its huge associates, by ridding them of many of the insects with which their skins are infested, also performs for them another valuable service. On observing any unusual appearance in the neighbourhood, its attention is immediately directed to it ; and if alarm is eventually excited the bird flies up, upon which all the Buffaloes instantly raise their heads, and endeavour to discover the cause which had led to the sudden departure of the sentinel. If they are successful in the attempt, and see reason to fear for their safety, they take to flight in a body, and are accompanied by the birds who fore-warned them of their danger. On the herd again halting to feed, the birds return to their avocation, and pursue a course similar to that we have just described, provided the like circumstances recur. We never found this bird attaching itself to any quadruped but the Buffaloe, nor did we ever find the latter with any other attendants."

In Dr. David Livingstone's 'Missionary Travels in South Africa,' (p. 545. 1857,) will be found the following interesting particulars respecting this bird, which I give at length :—He says, " Buffaloes abound (Kalomo river) and we see large herds of them feeding in all directions by day. When much disturbed by man, they retire into the densest parts of the forest, and feed by night only. We secured a fine large bull by crawling close to a herd : when shot, he fell down, and the rest, not seeing their enemy, gazed about wondering where the danger lay. The others came back to it, and when we showed ourselves, much to the amusement of my companions, they lifted him up with their horns, and, half supporting him in the crowd, bore him away. All these wild animals usually gore a wounded companion and expel him from the herd ; even zebras bite and kick an unfortunate or a diseased one. It is intended by this instinct, that none but the perfect and healthy ones should propagate the species. In this case they manifested their usual propensity to gore the wounded, but our appearance at that moment caused them to take flight, and this, with the goring being continued a little, gave my men the impression that they were helping away their wounded companion. He was shot between the fourth and fifth ribs; the ball passed through both lungs and a rib on the opposite side, and then lodged beneath the skin. But though it was two ounces in weight, yet he ran off some distance, and was secured only by the people driving him into a pool of water and killing him there with their spears. The herd ran away in the direction of our camp, and then came bounding past us again. We took refuge on a large ant-hill, and as they rushed by us at full gallop, I had a good opportunity of seeing that the leader of a herd of about sixty, was an old cow; all the others allowed her a full half-length in their front. On her withers sat about twenty Buffalo-birds (*Textor erythrorhynchus*, Smith), which act the part of guardian spirits to the animals. When the buffalo is quietly feeding, this bird may be seen hopping on the ground picking up food, or sitting on its back ridding it of the insects with which their skins are sometimes infested. The sight of the bird being much more acute than that of the buffalo, it is soon alarmed by the approach of any danger, and, flying up, the buffaloes instantly raise their heads to discover the cause, which has led to the sudden flight of their guardian. They sometimes accompany the buffaloes in their flight on the wing, at other times they sit as above described."

Among the 'Notes on the Birds of the territory of the Trans-vaal Republic' Mr. T. Ayres says:—

"This Finch inhabits the bush, and is not, so far as I know, ever found in the open country; we met with but few of them, and then always in company with the little blue Hoopoe (*Irrisor cyanomelas*) in twos and threes. The stomach of the bird sent contained insects; but berries, seeds and fruits, were not to be had at that season, our trip being in midwinter."

Mr. Charles John Andersson gives us the following valuable details respecting the habits of this interesting Weaver bird:—

"This large finch-like bird is rather common in Damara-land and also in the Lake-regions, where it is known to the natives by the name of '*Tsaba Gushou*.' It is a noisy species, gregarious in its habits, breeding in colonies, and constructing many nests in the same tree : it seems to prefer the giraffe-acacia for the purpose of nidification ; and it is curious that when these birds have used a tree for this purpose it usually withers in a short time after the building of the nest is completed; but whether the birds instinctively select such trees as have a tendency to decay, I am unable to say. The collective nests consist externally of an immense mass of dry twigs and sticks, in which are to be found from four to six separate nests or holes of an oval form, composed of grass only, but united to each other by intricate masses of sticks, defying the ingress of any intruder except a small snake. In each of these separate holes are laid three or four eggs, exactly resembling Sparrows' eggs, but much larger. I obtained no less than forty of these eggs (all much incubated), on January 29th, from two low trees standing close together, at Amatoni, in latitude 18° south; and on the following day the birds were busy in repairing one of the collective nests, which had been injured during the collection of eggs which it contained. I believe these nests are annually added to; for, so far as I have been able to see, the same nest is retained for several consecutive seasons."

Mr. E. Lort Philipps procured *Textor intermedius* in Somali-land where it is "very plentiful in flocks near Taf in the interior of the Plateau, which in the rainy season becomes a lake. In March they were busily building colonies of nests in the higher trees. In habits they much remind one of Starlings, especially when feeding in flocks on the ground.

"Iris brown; feet black; ♂ bill red; ♀ bill dark brown."

I am indebted to Capt. G. E. Shelley and the Rev. Canon Tristram for the loan of their specimens, from which the following measurements have been taken.

The plant is *Patterlickia pyracantha*, of South Africa.

Specimens examined.

No.	Sex.	Mus.	Locality.	Length.	Wing.	Tail.	Tars.	Culm.
1.	♂	E.B.	Otjimbinque, Damara-land (*Andersson*).	9·0	4·7	4·1	1·2	0·9
2.	jun.	E.B.	South Africa.	8·9	4·5	3.95	1·1	0·8
3.	♂	G. E. Shelley.	Otjimbinque, Damara-land (*Andersson*).	9·65	4·7	4·2	1·15	0·85
4.	(?)	G. E. Shelley.	Zambesi (*Bradshaw*).	9·2	4·85	4·45	1·2	0·85
5.	♂	G. E. Shelley.	Transvaal (*Buckley*).	8·65	4·9	4·25	1·2	0·85
6.	♂	G. E. Shelley.	Humbe, Angola (*Anchieta*).	9·55	4·8	4·3	1·2	0·9
7.	♀	G. E. Shelley.	Kiulo, Angola (*Anchieta*).	9·0	4·4	4·05	1·1	0·85
8.	♂ jun.	G. E. Shelley.	Bamangwato (*Buckley*).	8·1	4·5	3·9	1·2	0·0
9.	♂	H. B. Tristram.	Otjimbinque Damara-land (*Andersson*).	9·0	4·7	4·1	1·2	0·9
			TEXTOR INTERMEDIUS, CAB.					
10.	(?)	G. E. Shelley.	Somali (*E. Lort Phillips*).	8·75	4·8	4·1	1·2	0·95
11.	jun.	G. E. Shelley.	Somali (*E. Lort Phillips*).	8·0	4·5	3·75	1·0	0·85
			TEXTOR SCIOANUS, SALVAD.					
12.	♂	G. E. Shelley.	Daimbi, Shoa(*Antinori*).	8·7	4·7	4·1	1·1	0·85

The specimens figured in Plate II. are No. I. (fig. 1) Damara-land. No. 7. (fig. 2). Angola. ¾ size.

Those figured in Plate III. are No. 2. (fig. 1) S. Africa. No. II (fig. 2) Somali. ¾ size.

TEXTOR ALBIROSTRIS.
THE GREAT BLACK WEAVER.
PLATE IV.

Pyrrhula africana nigra, Briss. Orn. iii. p. 317 (1760).
Pyrrhula africana nigra, Briss. Syn. Meth. i. p. 397 (1763).
Le Grand Bouvreuil noir d'Afrique, Buff. Hist. Nat. Ois. iv. p. 385 (1778).
White-winged Grosbeak, Lath. Gen. Syn. iii. p. 144 (1783).
Loxia panicivora, Daud. Trait. d'Ornith. ii. p. 413 (1800).
Loxia panicivora, Shaw, Gen. Zool. ix. p. 283 (1815).
Coccothraustes albirostris, Vieill. Nouv. Dict. xiii. p. 535 (1817).
White-winged Grosbeak, Lath. Gen. Hist. Birds, v. p. 249 (1822).
Coccothraustes albirostris, Vieill. Encycl. Méth. iii. p. 1008 (1823).
Textor alecto, Temm. Pl. Col. pl. 446 (1828).
Le Tisserin Alecto, Cuv. Règn. Anim. p. 407 (1829).
Textor alecto (Cuv.), Griff. Aves, ii. p. 133. Suppl. p. 232. pl. 16. (1829).
Tisserin alecto, Less. Traité d'Ornith. p. 434 (1831).
Ploceus alecto, Rüpp. Neue Wirb. Faun. Abyss. p. 100 (1835-40).
Dertroides albirostris, Swains. Nat. Hist. Birds, ii. p. 278 (1836-37).
Textor alecto, Less. Compl. Œuv. de Buff. ii. p. 303 (1837).
Dertroides albirostris, Swains. Birds, W. Afr. i. p. 163 (1837).
Textor alecto, Rüpp. Syst. Uebers. Vög. N.-Ost.-Afr. p. 76 (1845).
Textor alecto, Lefebv. Voy. Abyss. vi. p. 111 (1845-50).
Textor alecto, Gray et Mitch. Gen. Birds, ii. p. 350. pl. 87. fig. 1 (1849).
Textor alecto, Reichb. Syst. Nat. pl. lxxvi (1850).
Alecto albirostris, Bonap. Consp. Gen. Av. p. 438 (1850).
Textor alecto, Cab. Mus. Hein. i. p. 183 (1850-1).
Textor alecto, Brehm, Journ. für Ornith. 1853, p. 98. 1854. p. 76.

Textor alecto, Licht. Nomencl. Av. Mus. Berol. p. 50 (1854).
Alecto panicivora, Hartl. Journ. für Ornith. 1854, p. 105.
Alecto albirostris, Hartl. Journ. für Ornith. 1854, p. 105.
Textor alecto, Gray, Gen. et Sub-gen. Birds, p. 70 (1855).
Alecto albirostris, Müll. Journ. für Ornith. 1855, p. 460.
Textor erythrorhynchus, Horsf. et M. Cat. Birds M. E.-Ind. Comp. ii. p. 521 (1856-8).
Textor alecto, Hengl. Syst. Vögel N.-O.-Afr. p. 37 (1856).
Textor alecto, Hartl. Orn. Westafr. p. 131 (1857).
Textor panicivorus, Hartl. Orn. Westafr. p. 131 (1857).
Alectornis albirostris, Reichb. Singvögel. p. 89. pl. xlv. fig. 330 (1861).
Textor alecto, Hartl. Journ. für Orn. 1861, p. 176.
Alecto albirostris, Hengl. Journ. für Orn. 1862, p. 25.
Textor alecto, Hengl. Journ. für Orn. 1862, p. 405.
Textor alecto, Brehm, Reis. Nord-Ost-Afr. iii. p. 134 (1862).
Textor alecto, Brehm, Reise Habesch, pp. 217, 337 (1863).
Alecto albirostris, Antin. Cat. di Uccelli, p. 62 (1864).
Textor alecto, Hengl. Journ. für Orn. 1867, p. 366.
Textor alecto, Hengl. Peterm. Geogr. Mith. p. 413 (1869).
Textor alecto, Finsch, Trans. Zool. Soc. 1870, p. 261
Textor alecto, Gray, Hand-List Birds, p. 40 (1870).
Textor alecto, Blan. Geol. et Zool. Abyss. p. 402 (1870).
Textor alecto, Sharpe, Cat. Afr. Birds, p. 58 (1871).
Textor alecto, Hengl. Ornith. N.-O.-Afr. p. 532. Appen. p. cxxviii. (1871).
Textor alecto, Antin, Viag. Bogos, p. 123 (1873).
Ploceus alecto, Russ, Stubenvögel, i. p. 315 (1879).
Textor alecto, Brehm, Theirl. iii. p. 364 (1879).
Textor alecto, Rocheb. Faun. Sénégamb. p. 235 (1884).
Textor albirostris, Shelley, Ibis, 1887, p. 43.

Figures. Temm. Pl. Col. pl. 446. Griff. (Cuv.,) Aves, ii. pl. 16. Reichb. Singvögel, pl. xlv. f. 330.

English. White-billed nut-cracker. African Ox-Bird. White-beaked Alectorne. Weaver Alecto. Ox-Weaver Bird. Great black Weaver. Black Weaver.

French. Le Grand Bouvreuil noir d'Afrique. Le Gros-bec noir à bec blanc. Alectornis à bec blanc. Bouvreuil Panicivore. Tisserin Alecto.

German. Alectoweber. Alectovogel. Weissschnabel-Alectovogel. Weissschnäbelige oder Alekto-Webervogel. Der Schwarze Weber.

Abyssinian. (Tigré) Wudscherck.

Habitat. North-Eastern and East Africa, extending its range into Senegambia on the West Coast.

Localities. Kordofan, Sennaar and Abyssinia (*Rüppell*) White Nile (*Arnaud*). Samhara, Khartoom (*Brehm*). Bissao, Galam, Sénégambia (*Hartlaub*). Abyssinia (*Harris*). Anseba, Sobat, Mareb, Fazoglo (*Heuglin*). Anseba, Waliko, Bogos (*Jesse*). Bogos (*Antonori*). Bathhurst, &c., Senegambia (*Rochebrune*). Anseba (*Esler*). N. E. Africa (*Kotschy*). Nubia and Casamanze (*Verreaux*). River Gambia (*Sharpe*).

Male. Black, slightly tinged with brown; base of feathers greyish white, purer white on the scapulars, sides of chest and sides; primaries slightly edged with white; under wing-coverts dull black; under webs of primaries blackish-brown: iris dark brown; bill greyish white, tinged with yellow, brown at tip; legs dark brown: length 9·7, wing 5·0, tail 4·3, tars. 1·25, culm. 1·0. Pl. IV. fig. 1.

Male, Nearly Adult. Similar, not so black; base of feathers whiter; white edges of primaries more extended: bill ashy-brown, tip nearly black; legs dark ashy-brown.

Female. Not so black, more tinged with slaty-grey and brown; very slight white edges to primaries: bill blackish brown, palest at base; legs dark brown. Pl. IV. fig. 2.

Young Bird. Dull chocolate brown; base of feathers greyish white; outer edges of primaries dirty white: bill and legs ashy-brown.

Obser. Easily distinguished from the preceding species by the under side of the wing and coverts being dull black, instead of white or greyish white.

While collecting the materials connected with the present bird, it became evident from the extremely few localities given (which is the only means of determining the distribution of a species) that it occupied a very limited area, in comparison to the preceding species, T. *panicivora*.

The latter bird, whatever its origin, inhabits a triangular portion of East and South Africa, from Somali-land across Victoria N'yanza to Benguela on the South West and the whole of the central territories to the East Coast, while this black or more Northern bird, inhabits a large tract of country from Nubia and Abyssinia on the North East to Senegambia in N. West and West Africa, keeping apparently between 10° S. to 17° N. latitude, Capt. Shelley says—" South from about 16° N. lat."

The intermediate race taking the central lake country Victoria N'yanza to Shoa in the N. E. and Somali.

The habits and economy of this weaver, are I may say, very similar to the preceding species, living in colonies of no fixed number of individuals, always selecting high trees in which to construct its rude nest and rear its young, they are said to be a very noisy and quarrelsome congregation, seeking their food on the ground like flocks of starlings.

From among the detailed observations on this peculiar bird, it affords me much pleasure to add a translation of Dr. A. E. Brehm's account:—
" During our journey I found colonies of the great black weaver (*Textor alecto*) on some high Mimosa-trees in the Samchara. This bird is unquestionably one of the most extraordinary phenomena of his whole species. He is a finch, and yet he resembles the thrush in more than one particular; he is a weaver-bird, and builds himself a nest which is much more like that of our magpies than the elegant edifices erected by his relations. He differs from these in cry and in disposition in a more remarkable way than in his appearance.

" One cannot exactly say that the black weaver is a particularly common bird: I have only found him South of the 16° of Northern latitude and there by no means often. He forms settlements wherever he appears; he is not seen alone. The settlements are not large. I counted three, six, thirteen and eighteen nests on the trees. The tree however must be a fairly large one to carry so many of these curious edifices. Each nest namely is a truly huge structure of three to four feet in diameter. It consists of brushwood and twigs, sometimes of those of the Mimosa, which are used notwithstanding their thorns. The bird weaves and twines these twigs between forked branches so untidily that one can almost see the interior of the nest. From the outside the nest looks like a bristly brush. On one side usually, according to my observations on the west side, an entrance leads into the interior. This is at first so wide that a fist can enter comfortably, but it becomes gradually narrower till it is a passage just large enough for the bird, thus resembling the entrance to the starling-nests in our cases. The interior of the nest is lined with little roots and grass.

"A tree of nests like this is at certain periods of the year inhabited by an exceedingly noisy company. Near Khartoom I observed that the black weaver breeds at the commencement of the rainy season; in the Samchara he builds in April; therefore my previous observations may also apply to him.

"I do not know whether our birds make as much noise during the remainder of the year as they do in the breeding season. The settlements I became acquainted with were noticeable at a long distance owing to the screaming of the birds. Their voices are very loud and many-toned. During a few minutes I spent under a tree I wrote down the following sounds. One of the male birds began : " *Ti, ti, terr, terr, terr, zerr, zaili,*" another answered : " *Gai, gai, zai,*" a third uttered the sounds " *Guik, guik, guk, guk, gai.*" Others screamed : " *Gu, gu, gu, gu, gai,*" and a few listened intently. They behaved like a swarm of bees. Some came, others went, and it seemed almost as if all the grown fledglings had also collected on the tree; for the large number of birds did not correspond with the few nests.

"The flight of the black weaver is very easy and hovering and is marked by slow flappings of the wings. The wings are carried very high. His run is quick and nimble and the bird is also an adept at climbing."

Herr T. von Heuglin says—" I hold the bright-billed *Textor* to be a bird of passage in North-East Africa, who arrives with the first summer rains, and when the breeding season is over wanders in large companies about the pasture-grounds and steppes, and then disappears in December. I have not seen him at any great height on the mountains. He is to be met with in the coast lands of Abyssinia, in the Anseba-territory, in Barka, on the Mareb as far up as Sorawi, in Sennaar and in Kordofan, also on the White Nile and on the Sobat. We found them breeding there (Samchara) in August and September, and in East Sennaar and Kordofan in July and September. Each colony has a nesting-place partitioned off, of which several are often seen on a large Adansonia, Sycamore, Soap-or Acacia-tree. The nest-places are used for several years; the structure itself consists of an irregular-shaped mass of coarse, dry bits of wood and twigs of trees, which are heaped up on forked and horizontal branches at a height of 15 to 30 feet, and form a pile of 5 to 8 feet in length and 3 to 5 feet in width. In such quarters an isolated company of 3 to 8 pairs build, and each pair forms therein its own dwelling, like the sparrow in the stork's nest, and fairly deep down in the interior. This nest is thickly and cleverly lined with fine grass, rushes, small roots and wool, and contains three to four eggs, coloured much like those of the house-sparrow, with rather thick rough shells, of a blunt egg shape 11·13 lines long and $8\frac{1}{2}$·9 in diameter. The young with their big heads and large hanging bellies have an ungainly appearance, are half-naked and very greedy. The old ones too, have much dirt among their feathers, are quarrelsome and noisy as sparrows, and often mix with thrushes, with whom they wander about the cattle pastures. Their food consists of fruits, grain, beetles, and the smaller kinds of chafers, grass-hoppers, etc., and also as it seems of parasitic insects, which they find on the cattle. I also often saw them hunting for chafers among the offal. In the morning whole colonies of them may often be heard chattering and screaming. A quantity of food is brought to the young ones. When shot they defend themselves bravely with their strong bills, and their bite draws blood."

Dr. O. Finsch, in his paper "On Birds from North-Eastern Abyssinia and the Bogos Country," published in the 'Proceedings of the Zoological

Society' for 1870, gives the following particulars respecting this species which was obtained by Mr. W. Jesse, during the late Abyssinian Expedition. "Iris brown; beak light horn-colour at the tip, base thickly covered with a white rough coating, apparently not horn, and rather soft; legs and feet dirty grey.

"I only procured and observed this bird on the Anseba; it was not very plentiful. Mr. W. T. Blanford shot one without the white rough covering at the base of the beak, possibly a young bird. Those seen were in company with a flock of *Lamprocolius chalybæus*. Perhaps the peculiarity about the base of both mandibles may be better described as excrescences."

I here add Mr. W. T. Blanford's notes—"I saw this bird only on the Anseba. It is quite Starling-like in its habits and flight, and belongs, I think, to this family rather than to the *Fringillidæ*. I frequently saw it associating with *Lamprotornis æneus*, *Lamprocolius chalybæus*, *L. chrysogaster*, hunting for insects on the ground, especially about cattle pens. The massive nests are not unlike those of *Sturnopastor contra*. All which I saw were in high Acacia-trees, but the breeding season was over long before July."

The plant in this plate is *Tinnea æthiopica* from Tropical Africa.

Specimens examined.

No.	Sex.	Mus.	Locality.	Length.	Wing.	Tail.	Tars.	Culm.
1	♂	E. B.	(?)	9·7	5·0	4·3	1·25	1·0
2	(?)	E. B.	Bogos, Abyssinia (*Jesse*).	9·55	5·0	4·35	1·2	0·95
3	♀	E. B.	Senegal	8·5	4·45	4·0	1·1	0·85
4	♀	G. E. Shelley.	N.E. Africa (*Kotschy*).	8·6	4·45	4·15	1·1	0·9
5	jun.	G. E. Shelley.	Anseba (*Esler*).	8·8	4·25	3·75	1·0	0·8

The figures (Plate IV. fig. 1. 11) are taken from Nos. 1 and 3, in my collection. ¾ size.

MUNIA FUSCATA.
THE BROWN PADDA.
PLATE III.

Loxia fuscata, Vieill. Ois. Chant. p. 95. pl. lxii. (1805).
Coccothraustes fuscata, Vieill. Nouv. Dict. xiii. p. 545 (1817).
Coccothraustes fuscata, Vieill. Encycl. Méth. p. 1015 (1823).
Loxia fuscata, Griff. Cuv. Anim. Kingd. Aves, ii. p. 153. pt. (1829).
Amadina fuscata, Gray et Mitch. Gen. Birds, ii. p. 369 (1849).
Munia fuscata, Bonap. Consp. Gen. Av. p. 451 (1850).
Oryzornis fuscata, Cab. et Hein. Mus. Hein. i. p. 174 (1851).
Padda fuscata, Reichb. Singvögel, p. 43. pl. xv. fig. 140 (1861).
Munia fuscata, Wall. Proc. Zool. Soc. 1863, p. 486.
Amadina fuscata, Gray, Hand-List Birds, ii. p. 55 (1870).
Padda fuscata, Salvad. Uccelli di Born. p. 264 (1874).
Spermestes fuscata, Russ, Stubenvögel, p. 142 (1879).
Padda fuscata, Legge, Birds Cey. p. 647 (1880).

Figures, Vieill. Ois. Chant. pl. lxii. Reichb. Singvögel, pl. xv. fig. 140

English. *The Brown Java Sparrow. Brown Padda. Brown Grosbeak.*
French. *Le Padda Brun. Le Gros-bec-Padda Brun.*
German. *Der braune Padda. Die braune Reisamadine.*

Habitat. Java ?, Borneo, Molucca, and Timor.

Adult. Forehead, crown, nape of neck, upper tail-coverts, tail, chin, and narrow band across the lower part of breast very dark chocolate-brown, inclining to black; primaries dull black, tinged with chocolate-brown; whole of back, greater wing-coverts, secondaries, and breast brighter chocolate-brown; cheeks and ear-coverts, belly, sides, and under tail-coverts nearly pure white, tinged with pale grey on the flanks; the feathers forming the blackish band across the breast, narrowly margined with white, and blending into the white belly; iris dark brown, eyelids fleshy pink; bill pinkish tinged with purple, cutting-edges whitish; legs brownish flesh-colour: length 5·15, wing 2·5, tail 1·6, tars. 0·75, culm. 0·55.

Obser. The male and female, as in *Munia oryzivora*, are nearly identical in colour and markings. The young vary, and are similar to those of the preceding species.

It is now eighty-three years since M. L. P. Vieillot described and figured the Brown Rice-Bird, or Padda, in his elaborate work entitled 'Oiseaux Chanteurs,' published in 1805, and although many travellers and collectors have visited the country in which this peculiar form is found, and large collections of other birds have reached Europe from the Malayan Archipelago, yet this bird remains one of the rarest of the Munias in museums and private collections.

It is much to be regretted that nothing is known respecting the habits, nidification, or distribution of this species.

Mr. A. R. Wallace procured this beautiful bird at Timor; but he does not mention anything respecting its economy, which undoubtedly resembles that of the common Java Sparrow.

The figures of the male and female in the accompanying plate are taken from specimens in the British Museum, and are the natural size.

MUNIA MALACCA.
THE WHITE-CHESTED MUNIA.
PLATE IV.

Passer chinensis, The Chinese Sparrow, Albin, Birds, ii. p. 49. pl. 53. upper figure (1738).
Coccothraustes javensis, Briss. Ornith. iii. p. 237. pl. xiii. fig. 1 (1760).
Coccothraustes javensis, Briss. Syn. Méth. i. p. 375 (1763).
White-breasted Indian Sparrow, Edw. Glean. Nat. Hist. iii. p. 301. pl. 355. fig. 2 (1764); Osb. Voy. China, ii. p. 329 (1771).
Loxia malacca, Linn. Syst. Nat. i. p. 302 (1766) : Müll. Vollst. Natursystem, iii. p. 551 (1773); Gmel. Syst. Nat. i. p. 851 (1788) : Lath. Ind. Orn. i. p. 385 (1790); Daud. Trait. d'Ornith. ii. p. 401 (1800); Gmel. Nat. Syst. vii. p. 133. Eng. edit. (1801); Shaw, Gen. Zool. ix. p. 332 (1815); Raffles, Trans. Linn. Soc. 1822, p. 313; Lath. Hist. Birds, v. p. 244 (1822); Griff. Cuv. Anim. Kingd. Aves, ii. p. 152 (1829).
Loxia jacobin, Müll. Vollst. Natursystem, Suppl. p. 151 (1776).
Le Jacobin, Buff. Hist. Nat. Ois. iii. p. 468 (1775); Daub. Pl. Enl. 139. 3 (1777); Bodd. Tables des Pl. Enl. 139 (1783); Sonn. Buff. Hist. Nat. xlvii. p. 47 (1801); Vieill. Ois. Chant. pl. 52 (1805).
Malacca Grosbeak, Lath. Gen. Syn. iii. p. 140 (1783).
The Jacobine, Buff. Nat. Hist. xiv. p. 19. Engl. edit. (1812).
Coccothraustes malacca, Vieill. Nouv. Dict. xiii. p. 532 (1817); Vieill. Encyl. Méth. iii. p. 1005 (1823); Steph. Shaw's Gen. Zool. xiv. p. 87 (1824).
Spermestes malacca, Jerdon, Madras Journ. xi. 1840, p. 27.
Spermestes braccata, Licht. Nomencl. Av. Mus. Berol. p. 49 (1854).
Spermestes malaccensis, Russ, Stubenvögel, p. 169. taf. vi. fig. 31 (1879).
Dermophrys malacca, Cab. Mus. Hein. i. p. 174 (1851).

Amadina malacca, Strickl. Proc. Zool. Soc. 1842, p. 167 ; Blyth, Journ. Asiat. Soc. Beng. xv. 1846, pp. 36, 285 ; Gray et Mitch. Gen. Birds, ii. p. 370 (1849) ; Kelaart, Prod. Birds Ceyl. p. 125 (1852) ; Layard. Ann. Mag. Nat. Hist. xiii. 1854, p. 258 ; Eyton, Cat. Birds, p. 254 (1856) ; Gray, Hand-List Birds, ii. p. 54 (1870).
Munia malacca, Blyth, Cat. Birds Mus. As. Soc. Beng. p. 116 (1849) ; Bonap. Consp. Gen. Av. i. p. 452 (1850) ; Horsf. et Moore, Cat. Birds Mus. E.-Ind. Comp. ii. p. 507 (1856-8) ; Reichb. Singvögel, p. 39. pl. xiv. figs. 121-122 (1861) ; Jerdon, Birds India, ii. p. 352 (1863) ; Scl. Proc. Zool. Soc. 1863, p. 219 ; Blyth, Ibis, 1867, p. 40 ; Beavan, Ibis, 1868, p. 173 ; Walden, Ibis, 1871, p. 177 ; Holdsw. Proc. Zool. Soc. 1872, p. 464 ; Legge, Ibis, 1874, p. 25 ; Salvad. Uccelli di Borneo, p. 266 (1874) ; Legge, Ibis, 1875, pp. 274, 398 ; Rey, Journ. für Ornith. 1875, p. 291 ; Hume, Nests and Eggs of Ind. Birds, p. 443 (1875) ; Legge, Hist. B. Ceyl. pp. 652, 655 (1878-80) ; Scl. Proc. Zool. Soc. 1879, p. 449 ; Schmidt, Proc. Zool. Soc. 1880, p. 312 ; Salv. Cat. Coll. Birds, Strickl. p. 252 (1882) ; Scl. Vert. Anim. Zool. Soc. Gard. p. 238 (1883).

    Figures, Albin's Birds, ii. pl. 53. upper fig. Briss. Orn. iii. pl. xiii. fig. 1. Edwards' Gleanings, iii. pl. 355. fig. 2. Daubenton Pl. Enl. 139, 3. Vieillot, Ois. Chant. pl. 52. Reichb. Singv. pl. xiv. figs. 121-22. Russ, Stubv. taf. vi. fig. 31.

Dutch. *Jakobijn.*
English. *Chinese Sparrow. White-breasted Indian Sparrow. The Jacobine. Malacca Grosbeak. Malacca Finch. Malacca Munia. Black-headed Finch, or Munia. Black-bellied Munia. White-chested Munia or Nun. Chestnut-backed Munia.*
French. *Le Gros-bec de Java. Le Jacobin. Le Jacobin à ventre blanc et noir.*
German. *Der Jacobin. Nonne. Malakka-Munia, schwarzköpfiger Elster-Weberfink mit weisser Brust und schwarzem Bauchfleck. Die dreifarbige Nonne-Amadine. Der Malackische Kernbeisser.*
Hindoo. *Nakl-nore,* or *Nakal-nor,* Jerdon.

Portuguese in Ceylon. *Pastro de Neli.*

Residents in Ceylon. *Paddy-bird or Ortolan.*

Sinhalese. *Wé-Kurulla.* Tamils. *Tinna Kuruvi,* Legge.

Telugu. *Nalla jinuvayi,* Jerdon.

Habitat. Peninsular India; Ceylon; Sumatra; Lower Bengal, and extending into Malabar and Borneo.

Male. Head, neck, breast, belly, thighs, and under tail-coverts black; mantle and wing-coverts, dark cinnamon-brown; primaries and secondaries, dark brown tinged with cinnamon-brown on the outer webs, quills nearly black; lower rump and upper tail-coverts glistening maroon; tail, dark brown, the central feathers edged with glistening sienna, outer rectrices like the primaries; chest, sides, flanks, axillaries, and under wing-coverts white; under side of wing silvery-grey; iris hazel-brown; bill translucent silvery-white, lead colour at the base; legs lead-blue: length 4·15, wing 2·15, tail 1·55, tars. 0·6, culm. 0·5.

Female. Similar to the male; the rump and upper tail-coverts not so richly coloured; the white chest and sides strongly tinged with creamy-buff; thighs tinged with brown; bill and legs as in the male.

Young Male. Similar to adult, but showing traces of the first plumage, which is dull-brown above; underparts buffish-brown, intermixed with black and white.

The young are pale rufous-brown above, palest on the head and neck, darker on the rump; underparts pale buff, whiter on the chin and throat.

Obser. The sexes are nearly alike, but the female, when adult, may be distinguished from the male by the creamy-buff tinge on the chest.

NEARLY all the earlier authors greatly confuse the nomenclature of this group of *Munias,* which is most pardonable, owing to the great resemblance of the species to each other; it is easy to believe that the *Munia sinensis* was supposed by them to be the female of *Munia malacca.* Again, those early ornithologists were not so diligent in the anatomical examination of the birds, possessing but few specimens for the determination of the sexes, and only considering the general plumage when describing them.

Brisson, in 1760, characterised two distinct species, *Coccothraustes sinensis* and *C. javensis,* which were founded on the figures given by Albin and Edwards; in 1764 Edwards refigured the present species under the name of 'The White-breasted Indian Sparrow.' In 1766 Linnæus united the two above birds under *Loxia malacca*, and from his description omitted the white chest, sides, and flanks, but he appends a note, "*Dorsum, alæ, cauda, ferrugineo-rufa. Pectus et hypochondria alba; reliqua nigra.*" It may be presumed that Linnæus's accidental omission of the words "*Pectus et hypochondria alba*" was the reason for adding the above note, after he had attached the habitat Malacca, that locality not having been used by earlier writers, who stated that it came from Java and China.

This species is one of the most beautiful of the Black-headed group, the colours in the adult are exceedingly pure and most strikingly defined, and although without a song its beauty will always make it a cage-pet amongst the lovers of live birds; it is extremely active, and, according to the observations of Dr. Max Schmidt, it will live from one to ten years in confinement. It is easily kept, and feeds on various small seeds similar to the Java Sparrow.

I propose to distinguish this bird by a more definite appellation, 'The White-chested Munia,' which separates it from all the other Black-headed Munias.

Mr. E. Blyth (J. A. S. B. vol. xv.) tells us :—" The *Amadina malacca*, or 'White-breasted Indian Sparrow' of Edwards, is common in Southern India, occurs rarely in Bengal, mingled in flocks of *A. sinensis*, or the 'Chinese Sparrow' of Edwards, from which, indeed, it only differs in having the lower parts pure white, with the same abdominal black patch; and it is curious that a third race inhabits the Malayan peninsula, similar to *A. sinensis* excepting in having no black patch on the abdomen : whence the *malacca* is ill-applied to the white-bellied bird of Peninsular India."

Mr. Jerdon, who was one of our best authorities on Indian birds, contributes, in his 'Birds of India,' vol. ii., the following particulars respecting this species :—" The Black-headed Munia is chiefly found in Southern India and Ceylon, a few stragglers occurring in Central India, and even in Bengal occasionally. It is very abundant in parts of Southern India, especially on the Malabar coast, frequenting long grass by the sides of rivers and tanks, occasionally dry grain fields, and very commonly sugar-cane fields. It often associates in very large flocks.

" The nest is usually placed among reeds, in tanks, or in the beds of rivers; occasionally in long grass in the bunds of paddy-fields. It is a rather large, nearly round or oval nest, neatly but loosely made of grass, with the hole at one side, this in general being very artfully concealed by the interlacing of the fibres of grass, so that I have been puzzled for a few moments to discover the entrance ; and the four to six eggs in number are pure white."

Respecting the breeding of this Munia we are indebted to Mr. Allan Hume, whose valuable notes I have much pleasure in quoting. He says :—
" Our Indian bird breeds in many localities in Southern India, but though the eggs have been sent to me by many correspondents, only one or two have favoured me with any notes on its nidification.

" Mr. A. G. R. Theobald writes :—' I found the nests near Pothanore, in the Coimbatore District, during the latter half of October. They were placed amongst reeds growing in a small pond ; they were round, with a round hole in one side for an entrance, and were composed of dry reeds and leaves of some flag-leaved grass very like those of the Cholum (*Sorghum vulgare*). The lining was composed of the hair-like filaments from the broom grass of this country. Seven is, I think, the full complement of eggs ; I never found more in any one nest.'

" Mr. F. R. Blewitt says :—' On the 19th July we were encamped in the open forest country in the immediate neighbourhood of the western side of the hill ranges (branches of the great Vindhyian group) lying in the extreme eastern section of the Bhundara District.

" ' In a sugar-cane field not far distant from our camp we found five unfinished, and one all but complete nest, containing a single egg, of the Black-headed Munia. The parent birds were shot while busily engaged in finishing off the entrance of the nest.

" ' This latter was nearly globular, a mass of coarse grass lined with somewhat finer grass, between six and seven inches in diameter. It was more loosely constructed than those of *Estrelda formosa*, several of which we had found in a similar locality, about a mile distant, two days previously. Both this nest and the other unfinished ones were placed amongst and attached to the cane leaves, precisely after the fashion of the Green Amaduvat.'

" The eggs of this species, which I owe to Messrs. Carter, Theobald, and others, are of the usual *Munia* type—dull, pure white, somewhat elongated, oval eggs ; there is nothing that I can see to distinguish them from those of *M. punctulata* and *M. malabarica*, except perhaps that elongated varieties are more common amongst them.

"In length the eggs vary from 0·6 to 0·72, and in breadth from 0·44 to 0·5 ; but the average is 0·64 by 0·17."

In Ceylon Capt. W. V. Legge tells us :—" This fine *Munia* is common in the south of the island, particularly in the district lying between the Bentota river, round the south-west coast to the Wallaway river. Between Galle and the Kukkul Korale forests it is found in wild paddy-fields and small cultivated tracts of land near the inland villages in that wooded region. I met with it close to the sea between Tangalla and Hambantota, but did not see it in the coast-district east of the latter place. It re-appears in the Park country, and is not uncommon between Batticaloa and Madulsima ; it ascends into the hills between Bibile and Badulla, and inhabits all the region and the Uva patna-basin in considerable numbers, luxuriating in the long grass and tangled vegetation which clothe the maze of hills between Udu Pusselawa and Haputale. In the western parts of the Kandy country it is far less common. It does not seem to be common in the Western Province, except in certain localities, such as the sylvan paddy-fields in the lower part of the Pasdun Korale ; there I found it plentiful not far from Agalewatta. It inhabits the east coast from Batticaloa northwards as far as Trincomalie and the neighbourhood ; but further north it appears to be rare.

"The 'Chestnut-backed Finch' affects paddy- and grass-fields, situated among the woods and forests, and is also foun l in marshy land about tanks and water-holes. In the hills it is partial to the Maana-grass patnas, and those covered with tangled bushes and rank vegetation. It is very destructive in the paddy-fields of the Kandyans, necessitating the constant presence of call-boys, and the erection of all manner of scarecrows, for the protection of their crops. Like the two following species (*Munia punctulata* and *M. striata*), it is very sociable, feeding in large flocks, which are quite sufficient to inflict heavy damage in the fields of the hard-working Cingalese cultivator. It is very fond of the seed of the Maana-grass, and that of various reeds and rushes which grow in swamps and marshy spots. Its note is like that of the common species *M. punctulata*, but stronger, and its flight is also similar."

Continuing Capt. Legge's very interesting notes on the habits and nesting of this bird, he says :—" This *Munia* breeds often gregariously. The season of its nesting lasts from May until August. In the former month I found many nests among the gigantic 'maana'-grass and tangled 'brackens' which cover the Uva patnas; and in the latter I found it nesting, *a number together*, among reeds near Hambantota, in company with the Baya (*Ploceus manyar*?). The nest is sometimes placed in a low bush; but it is more frequently built in grass and 'brackens.' It is a large, strongly made, globular structure, composed of the material nearest to hand, either blades of grass and roots, or strips of reeds, with a large unfinished-looking opening at the side. The interior is roomy, and in some cases very deep, and is lined with flowering grass-stalks or fine grass itself. The eggs vary from four to six in number, but most commonly do not exceed the former figure; they are pure white, rather stumpy ovals, and larger than those of its congeners. I have found them to vary from 0·73 to 0·63 inch in length, and 0·45 to 0·5 inch in breadth.

" In India it breeds from July till October."

Specimens examined.

No.	Sex.	Mus.	Locality.	Length.	Wing.	Tail.	Tars.	Culm.
a.	♂	E. B.	Ceylon.	4·15	2·15	1·55	0·6	0·5
b.	♂	E. B.	Ceylon.	4·2	2·2	1·65	0·65	0·5
c.	♀	E. B.	Ceylon.	3·85	2·1	1·4	0·6	0·45
d.	♂	E. B.	India.	4·1	2·2	1·4	0·65	0·5
e.	?	E. B.	Ceylon.	4·85	2·2	1·45	0·65	0·5
f.	?	E. B.	Ceylon.	4·7	2·1	1·4	0·6	0·5
g.	♂	E. B.	India.	4·25	2·25	1·45	0·6	0·5

The figures of the adult birds are taken from *a* and *c*; that of the young from life.

CARDINALIS IGNEUS.
BAIRD'S CARDINAL.

Cardinalis igneus, Baird, Proc. Acad. Philad. 1859, p. 305.
Cardinalis igneus, Sclater, Cat. Amer. Birds, p. 100 pt. (1862).
Cardinalis virginianus, var. (*igneus*) Scl. et Salv. Exot. Ornith. p. 63 (1868).
Cardinalis igneus, Coues, Proc. Acad. Philad. 1868, p. 84.
Cardinalis igneus, Elliot, Birds N. Amer. i. pl. xvi. (1869).
Cardinalis igneus, Cooper, Orn. Calif. i. p. 238 (1870).
Cardinalis igneus, Gray, Hand-List Birds, ii. p. 102 (1870).
Cardinalis virginianus, Finsch, Abh. Nat. Brem. 1870, p. 339.
Cardinalis virginianus, var. *igneus*, Baird, Brew. et Rigdw. Hist. N. Amer. Birds, ii. p. 103 (1874).
Cardinalis virginianus igneus, Ridgw. Proc. U. S. Nat. Mus. iii. 1881, pp. 181, 218, 232.
Cardinalis virginianus igneus, Rigdw. Proc. U. S. Nat. Mus. iv. 1882, p. 212.
Cardinalis virginianus igneus, Belding, Proc. U. S. Nat. Mus. v. 1883. p. 541.
Cardinalis virginianus igneus, Belding, Proc. U. S. Nat. Mus. vi. 1884, pp. 343, 345.
Cardinalis cardinalis igneus, Stejn. Auk, i. p. 171 (1884).
Cardinalis igneus, Salvin et Godm. Biol. Centr.-Amer. i. p. 341 (1884).
Cardinalis cardinalis superbus, Ridgw. Auk, ii. p. 344 (1885).
Cardinalis cardinalis igneus (Baird), B. O. U. Check-List, N. Amer. B. p. 286 (1886).
Cardinalis cardinalis superbus, Ridgw. Check-List of N. Amer. B. p. 286 (1886).

Figure, Elliot, Birds N. Amer. pl. xvi.

English. *Saint Lucas Cardinal. Cape Cardinal. Fiery Cardinal and Arizona Cardinal.*

Habitat. North-Western America. Lower California. Arizona, and Western Mexico.

Cardinalis igneus, Baird.

Male. Similar to *C. virginianus*, but not larger; the bill is more powerful, with culmen greatly curved; the black frontal band not so decided, and divided by the culmen; the black of the chin and throat less extended; general colour paler, with a greater tinge of pink: length 8·5, wing 3·85, tail 4·5, tars. 1·0, culm. 0·7.

Female. Similar to the female of *C. virginianus*, but with the underparts pale ashy-grey.

Young. Similar to the female, but duller; "bill deep black" (*Baird*).

Cardinalis superbus, Ridgw.

Male. Similar, the vermilion of the crest, cheeks and underparts much purer; the brick-red of the back paler: length 8·65, wing 3·7, tail 4·6, tars. 1·0, culm. 0·7.

Female. Similar to female of *C. igneus* with the back dark ashy-grey; and general colours brighter.

Obser. The species, or varieties, above described, may readily be separated, from the more southern forms, by their less brilliant colours, and more powerful bills, the black frontal band being divided by the culmen. This bird is so closely allied to *C. virginianus*, that I have considered a plate of it unnecessary.

WE are indebted to Mr. John Xanthus for our first acquaintance with this north-western Cardinal, which was characterised by Professor Spencer F. Baird in 1859, and which I now propose to distinguish from all the other races by the appellation of Baird's Cardinal, in honour of the describer; the name Fiery Cardinal being more appropriate for one of the southern varieties.

From the material connected with the habits of this bird, I find they closely resemble those of the Virginian Nightingale; however, I subjoin the most interesting details from Messrs. Baird, Brewer and Ridgway's 'History of the Birds of North America.' They say: "There appears to be nothing in the habits of this form of Cardinal, as far as known, to distinguish it from the Virginian bird; the nest and eggs, too, being almost identical. The latter average about 1 inch in length and 0·80 in breadth. Their ground-colour is white, with a bluish tint. Their markings are larger, and more of a rusty than an ashy-brown, and the purple spots are fewer and less marked than in *C. virginianus*.

"The memorandum of Mr. John Xanthus shows that in one instance a nest of this bird, containing two eggs, was found in a Mimosa bush four feet from the ground; another nest, with one egg, in a like situation; a third, containing three eggs, was about three feet from the ground; a fourth, with two eggs, was also found in a Mimosa, but only a few inches above the ground."

Mr. R. Ridgway published in 'The Auk' for 1885 a "Description of a new Cardinal Grosbeak from Arizona," and remarks: "The Cardinal Grosbeak from Arizona, hitherto supposed to be identical with *C. igneus* from Cape St. Lucas, proves, on comparison of numerous specimens, to be easily distinguishable. I therefore propose for it the name *Cardinalis cardinalis superbus*." Although Mr. Ridgway kindly lent me specimens of this, his new form, I have united it with *C. igneus*, to which it is most closely allied; the bill is not so robust, but the vermilion is much brighter than in the latter bird.

Specimens examined.

Var. *Cardinalis igneus*, Baird.

No.	Sex.	Mus.	Locality.	Length.	Wing.	Tail.	Tars.	Culm.
a.	♂	E. B.	La Paz, Lower California.	8·5	3·85	4·5	1·0	0·7
b	♂	E. B.	La Paz, Lower California.	8·4	3·6	4·4	0·95	0·65
1.	♂	Smithn. Inst.	San Jose, North America.	8·25	3·65	4·4	0·95	0·7
2.	♀	" "	San Jose, North America.	7·95	3·45	3·9	0·95	0·7

Var. *Cardinalis superbus*, Ridgway.

3.	♂	" "	Camp Grant, Arizona (*Dr. Palmer*).	8·65	3·7	4·6	1·0	0·7
4.	♀ ?	" "	Tucson, Arizona (*E. W. Nelson*).	7·7	3·8	4·5	0·9	0·7

The specimens Nos. 1 to 4 were kindly lent to me by Mr. R. Ridgway, of the Smithsonian Institution, for examination, Nos. 3 and 4 being his types of *Cardinalis superbus*.

PHRYGILUS FRUTICETI.
THE ORCHARD FINCH.
PLATE I.

Fringilla campestris, Bonap. MS.
Fringilla campestris, Griff. Cuv. An. Kingd. Aves, ii. p. 303. pl. dated 1828 (1829).
Fringilla campestris, Russ, Stubenvögel, p. 476 (1879).
Fringilla fruticeti, Kittl. Kupf. der Vög. p. 18. pl. xxiii. fig. 1 (1833); Gould, Darwin's Zool. Beagle, iii. p. 94 (1841); Fraser, Proc. Zool. Soc. 1843, p. 113; Russ, Stubenvögel, p. 476 (1879).
Euspiza fruticeti, Gray et Mitch. Gen. Birds, ii. p. 376 (1844).
Chlorospiza fruticeti, Gay, Fauna Chilena, Aves, p. 357 (1847); Philippi, Zool. Chilena, An. Univ. Chile, xxxi. pp. 264, 304 (1868).
Phrygilus fruticeti, Bonap. Consp. Gen. Av. p. 476 (1850); Cass. Gilliss's Exped. ii. p. 179 (1855); Burm. Syst. Uebers. iii. p. 232 (1856); Eyton, Cat. Birds, p. 251 (1856); Burm. Reise La Platastaaten, ii. p. 487 (1861); Scl. Cat. Amer. Birds, p. 111 (1862); et Proc. Zool. Soc. 1867. pp. 322, 337; Scl. et Salv. Proc. Zool. Soc. 1867, p. 985, et 1868. p. 569; Scl. et Salv. Ibis, 1868, p. 185; et Proc. Zool. Soc. 1869, p. 152; Gray, Hand-List Birds, ii. p. 89 (1870); Hudson et Scl. Proc. Zool. Soc. 1872, pp. 537, 548, 550; Scl. Proc. Zool. Soc. 1873, p. 780; Scl. et Salv. Nomencl. Av. Neotr. p. 31 (1873); Tacz. Proc. Zool. Soc. 1874, p. 521; Scl. et Salv. Proc. Zool. Soc. 1874, p. 677, et 1876, p. 16; Durnf. Ibis, 1878, p. 393; Scl. et Salv. Proc. Zool. Soc. 1879, p. 606; Sharpe. Proc. Zool. Soc. 1881, p. 7; Scl. Proc. Zool. Soc. 1881, p. 486; Döring, Exped. al Rio Negro, Zool. p. 39 (1881-2); Salv. Cat. Birds Strickl. Coll. p. 228 (1882); Scl. Vert. Anim. Gard. Zool. Soc. p. 249 (1883); Tacz. Ornith. Pérou, iii. p. 37 (1886); Scl. Proc. Zool. Soc. 1886. p. 397; Scl. et Hudson, Argen. Ornith. i. p. 54 (1888).

Rhopospina fruticeti, Cab. Mus. Hein. i. p. 135 (1851) ; Gray, Gen. et Subgen. Birds, p. 79 (1855).
Fringilla erythrorhyncha, Less, Journ. l'Inst. ii. p. 316 (1834) ; Scl. Proc. Zool. Soc. 1871, p. 497 ; Russ, Stubenvögel, p. 476 (1879).
Chlorospiza erythrorhynca, Gay, Fauna Chilena, p. 358 (1847).
Emberiza luctuosa, Eyd. et Gerv. Mag. Zool. 1836, p. 24. pl. lxxi. ; D'Orb. et Lafr. Syn. Av. i. p. 80 (1837) ; Bridge, Proc. Zool. Soc. 1841, p. 94 ; Russ, Stubenvögel, p. 476 (1879).
Diuca luctuosa, Licht. Nomencl. Av. Mus. Berol. p. 43 (1854).
Phrygilus alaudina (*F. campestris*, Bp.), Bonap. Consp. Gen. Av. i. p. 476. pt. (1850).
Phrygilus alaudina (*F. erythrorhynchus*, Less.), Bonap. Consp. Gen. Av. i. p. 476. pt. (1850).

Figures, Griff. Cuv. An. Kingd. Aves, ii. pl. Kittl. Kupf. der Vög. pl. xxiii. Eyd. et Gerv. Mag. Zool. pl. lxxi.

English. Field Finch. Orchard Finch. Red-billed Finch. Mourning Finch.

French. Le Pinson du verger. Le Pinson triste. Le Pinson de champ.

German. Strauch-Ammerfink. Busch-Ammerfink. Strauch-Ammersperling.

Castelláno. Rara negra.

Mountaineers of Chili. Jalé.

Habitat. Patagonia, Chili, and Bolivia, extending its range into High Peru.

Male. Head, cheeks, and whole of back bright slaty-grey, slightly tinged with yellowish-brown on the mantle and secondaries ; centre of each feather on the crown, hind neck, mantle, and scapulars, more or less broadly streaked with black ; rump unstreaked and paler grey ; upper tail-coverts pale silvery-grey, with shaft streak and tips black ; lesser wing-coverts black, edged with pale grey ; median coverts black, half the outer web white, forming a band ; greater wing-coverts black, narrowly margined with silvery-grey, tipped on the outer web with white, forming a narrow band ; primaries, secondaries, bastard wing, primary-coverts, and tail black, narrowly edged with pale ashy-grey, broader on the secondaries ; eyelids white ; lores, chin, throat, and breast black, gradually blending into the grey of the chest; sides of chest, axillaries, sides, flanks, and thighs slaty-grey, tinged with yellowish-brown; under wing-coverts blackish, edged with slaty-grey; under side of wing dull brown; belly white; under tail-coverts greyish-white, slightly tinged with buff, with narrow black shaft streaks; "iris dark hazel; bill, legs, and toes brownish flesh-colour" (*H. Whitely*); length 6·8, wing 3·65, tail 3·2, tars. 1·0, culm. 0·55.

Female. Crown of head, neck, and whole of back dull grey, washed with yellowish-brown, each feather streaked with brown, darkest on the crown and mantle; rump and upper tail-coverts pale greyish-brown; tail blackish-brown, the outer and two central feathers paler, the base of the outer web of first rectrices, and tips of the first, second, third, and fourth whitish; scapulars like the mantle, but edged with rufous; lesser wing-coverts grey; median blackish-brown, with half the outer web dull white; greater coverts brownish, edged with buffish-grey, and tipped on the outer web with dull white; primaries and secondaries dull brown, the former faintly, the latter broadly edged with ashy-brown; superciliary stripe, lores, cheeks, chin, and throat whitish, base of feathers blackish; ear-coverts rufous, like the margins of the scapulars; malar line, breast, sides, and flanks dull greyish-brown, faintly streaked with brown; flanks and under tail-coverts strongly tinged with buff; chest and belly nearly pure white; axillaries and under wing-coverts ashy; under surface of quills tinged with pale brown; iris brown; bill brown, lower mandible paler; legs and feet browner than in the male.

Young Male. Above similar to the adult male, but with broad brown margins to the feathers of the mantle, scapulars, and tertials; the spots on the median and greater wing-coverts white, tinged with buff; primaries and tail blackish-brown, the former narrowly edged with white; the black of the throat less extended, and edged with greyish-white; belly greyish-white; under tail-coverts dark ashy-grey, broadly edged with buffy-white.

Obser. The series of immature skins in my collection exhibit gradations of colour and markings from the first year's plumage to the adult; the very young males having rufous ear-coverts, the chin and cheeks nearly pure white; the black of the throat not extending on to the breast; under tail-coverts buff like those of the female; some have subterminal grey spots on the under side of the outer rectrices.

The under tail-coverts of several females have narrow brown shaft streaks, probably attributable to age.

THE figure and description of *Fringilla campestris* given in the second volume (p. 304) of Griffith's edition of 'Cuvier's Animal Kingdom' are conclusively those of the bird now under consideration, and I here append Griffith's short notice of it, which is as follows:—" The opposite is the figure of a Finch brought to this country in the curious collection of the

Rev. Mr. Hennah, from Mexico, which does not appear to have been hitherto described. The general colour of the bird is blue slate, but on the top of the head this colour becomes nearly black; on the back are several oval patches, and on the throat and breast are waved spots of the like colour; the wing-feathers, in general, are black or dusky, with yellow margins, and the tail is nearly black."

The plate opposite page 304 is dated 1828. Here, as in many other instances, the present bird was found in a "collection from Mexico," which does not necessarily prove that it is a Mexican species, as it is well known not to extend its range north of High Peru; therefore, the locality "Mexico" led all earlier ornithologists to overlook the name given to this species by Prince Bonaparte before 1828, who afterwards, in his 'Conspectus,' unites it with *Phrygilus alaudina*, another species of the same genus equally unlikely to be found in Mexico. Again, Griffith's and Gray's omission of all mention of the white band on the inner webs of the tail-feathers, decidedly characteristic marks in both sexes of the latter bird, determines my retaining the older specific appellation *campestris* in the synonymy.

This species appears to be exclusively a mountainous bird, keeping always to the higher ridges of the great Southern Cordillera, extending its range from High Peru, just below the perpetual snow, into La Paz in Bolivia, south to Chili and Patagonia, where it remains during the breeding season, descending only to lower ground during the winter months.

Mr. T. Bridges tells us it is "found in valleys of the Andes, inhabits hedges and bushy situations, and sings delightfully in summer. Iris dark brown." Mr. C. Darwin "obtained specimens of this bird from Northern Chili and Southern Patagonia," and says:—" I saw it also in the Cordillera of Central Chili, at an elevation of at least 8,000 feet, near the upper limit of vegetation. In Patagonia it is not common; it frequents bushy valleys in small flocks from six to ten in number. These birds sometimes move from thicket to thicket with a peculiar soaring flight; they occasionally utter very singular and pleasing notes."

It was procured during Gilliss's Expedition; and Mr. J. Cassin adds the following note:—" This little Finch frequents field and shrubbery, but is not a common species. It extends its range over the whole of western

South America; but, having been seldom seen by members of the expedition, may be regarded as rare in Chili."

Mr. H. Whitely collected "specimens of both sexes of this species at Chihauta, Arequipa, Paucartambo and Tinta"; at the latter locality he "shot them off cactus plants. Eye dark hazel; bill, legs, and toes brownish flesh colour." M. C. Jelski found it plentiful at Haunta and Junin (11,000 to 14,000 feet), in High Peru.

Among many of the valuable contributions to the 'Proceedings of the Zoological Society' we have from the pen of Mr. W. H. Hudson the most interesting notes on the habits of the 'Birds of Patagonia,' from which I have much pleasure in adding those respecting the present species:—
"This is a pretty and elegant bird, though possessing no bright colours; they go in pairs in the warm season, but in winter unite in flocks, often of two or three hundred individuals, and have a graceful, undulating flight. On being approached they utter a series of low ticking notes, and occasionally a long squealing cry. The male has also a very agreeable song, which continues all the year. In pleasant weather the song is heard at all hours; on cold and cloudy days, only at sunset. The bird usually soars from his perch and utters his song while gliding down with wings depressed and tail outspread. When I first heard it, I was startled with its wonderful resemblance to the song of the Correndera Pipit (*Anthus correndera*); it is, however, much shorter and more powerful.

"This species is quite common in the thickets along the Rio Negro, in the neighbourhood of Carmen; but, following up the river, appears to become much rarer."

We are also indebted to Mr. H. Durnford for his observations on the habits of this bird (published in the 'Proceedings of the Zoological Society'), which he says is:—"Common at Chupat throughout the spring and summer, and often seen during our journey in the valleys; it never wanders far from water. On the 20th September I took a nest on the hills near the colony; it was a very neat structure of wool, feathers, and the flowers of a grass, and placed in the centre of a thick bush, about a foot above the ground. It contained two eggs, of a pale green ground-colour, thickly marked with dull chocolate spots and streaks. Iris wood-brown; beak dark flesh-colour, tip of both mandibles and the whole of the upper mandible darkest; legs and feet reddish flesh-colour."

It has been procured at La Paz by M. d'Orbigny; also at Tilotilo in the Province of Yungas, in Bolivia, by Mr. C. Buckley; at Coquimbo, by Mr. C. Darwin, Dr. Coppinger, and others.

Professor W. Nation ('P. Z. S.' 1881, p. 486) writing from Lima, W. Peru, says:—" Examples of males and females of this Finch have been sent to me from this side of the Cordillera, at an altitude of 14,000 feet. Food, seeds of the *Lupinus tomentosus*, which I saw growing on the sides of the Andes in 1851."

Specimens examined.

No.	Sex.	Mus.	Locality.	Length.	Wing.	Tail.	Tars.	Culm.
a.	♂	E. B.	Paucartambo, High Peru (*H. Whitely*).	6·8	3·65	3·2	1·0	0·55
b.	♀	E. B.	Tinta, W. Peru (*H. Whitely*).	6·35	3·65	3·15	1·0	0·55
c.	♂	E. B.	Santiago (*Weisshaupt*).	7·5	3·8	3·15	0·95	0·55
d.	♂ Imm.	E. B.	Chili (*C. Reed*).	7·05	3·8	3·25	0·9	0·55
e.	♂ Imm.	E. B.	Chili (*C. Reed*).	7·15	3·9	3·2	0·95	0·5
f.	♂ Imm.	E. B.	Chili (*C. Reed*).	7·15	3·8	3·1	0·95	0·5
g.	♀	E. B.	Chili (*C. Reed*).	6·75	3·85	3·1	0·95	0·5
h.	♀	E. B.	Chili (*C. Reed*).	6·75	3·7	3·15	0·9	0·5
i.	♀	E. B.	Chili (*C. Reed*).	7·05	3·75	3·15	0·9	0·5
j.	♂ Imm.	E. B.	Chili (*C. Reed*).	6·8	3·65	3·15	0·9	0·5
k.	♂ Imm.	E. B.	Rio Negro (*W. H. Hudson*).	7·1	3·9	3·15	0·95	0·55
l.	♂ Imm.	E. B.	Chili.	7·1	3·85	3·1	0·95	0·55
m.	♂	E. B.	Chili (*Bridges*).	6·15	3·75	3·3	1·0	0·55
n.	♂	E. B.	Chili.	6·5	3·75	3·1	0·95	0·55
o.	♂	E. B.	Chili (*Murray*).	6·7	3·8	3·1	0·95	0·55
p.	♂	E. B.	Chili (*Bridges*).	6·9	3·85	3·3	0·95	0·55
q.	♀	E. B.	Chili (*Bridges*).	6·6	3·15	2·95	0·95	0·5

The figures are taken from *a* and *i*.

PYRRHULA ERITHACUS.
BEAVAN'S BULLFINCH.
PLATE II.

Pyrrhula erythaca, Blyth, Ibis, 1862, p. 389.
Pyrrhula erythaca, Blyth, Journ. A. S. Beng. xxxii. 1863, p. 459.
Pyrrhula erithaca, Blyth, Ibis, 1863, p. 441, pl. x.
Pyrrhula erythaca, Jerdon, Birds of India, ii. p. 389 (1863).
Pyrrhula erythaca, Blyth, Ibis, 1867, p. 43.
Pyrrhula erithacus, Beavan, Ibis, 1868, p. 177.
Pyrrhula erythaca, Gray, Hand-List B. ii. p. 99 (1870).
Pyrrhula erithacus, Tristram, Ibis, 1871, p. 232.
Pyrrhula erythrocephala, Swinh. Proc. Zool. Soc. 1871, p. 387.
Pyrrhula erythaca, David. N. Arch. Mus., Bull. vii. p. 10 (1871).
Pyrrhula erythaca, Hume, Stray-Feathers, 1874, p. 455.
Pyrrhula erythaca, Sharpe and Dresser, Birds Eur. pt. li. Note (1876).
Pyrrhula erithacus, Prjev. Rowley's Orn. Miscell. ii. p. 297 (1876).
Pyrrhula erythaca, David et Oust. Oiseaux Chine, p. 349 (1877).
Pyrrhula erithacus, Russ, Stubenvögel, p. 503 (1879).
Pyrrhula erythaca, Hume, Stray-Feathers, 1879, p. 108.
Pyrrhula erithacus, Gould, Birds Asia, v. pl. xxxii. (1880).
Pyrrhula erithacus, Sharpe, Cat. Birds in Brit. Mus. xii. p. 455 (1888).

Figures, Blyth, Ibis, 1863, pl. x. Gould, Birds Asia, pl. xxxii.

English. *Red-breasted Bullfinch. Beavan's Bullfinch.*

French. *Le Bouvreuil de Beavan.*

German. *Der Rothschwänzige Gimpel.*

Habitat. Himalayas, Sikkim, Darjeeling, and Kan-su, N. W. China.

Male. Head, and whole of back, dark slaty-grey; frontal band, and band across rump black; lower part of rump white; wing-coverts dark slaty-grey, basal half of the greater coverts black, like the primaries and outer tail-feathers; secondaries, upper tail-coverts, and centre tail-feathers glossy purplish black; the black frontal band encircled with buffish white, which blends into the grey of the head and throat; breast, belly, and sides orange red; under wing-coverts, middle of belly, and under tail-coverts white; flanks, and thighs pale slaty-grey; axillaries white tinged with orange at the tips; under surface of wings ashy; "iris dark brown; bill black; feet fleshy-brown" (Prjevalski) : length 5·9, wing 3·2, tail 2·95, tarsus 0·7, culmen 0·38.

Female. Head and hind neck ashy-grey, blending into the brown of the back; whole of back and scapulars chocolate-brown; the narrow white band of the face strongly tinged with yellowish buff on the cheeks and throat; breast, belly, and sides pale chocolate-brown; rest of plumage as in the male.

Young Male. Similar; the buffish-white band encircling the face more extended on the cheeks and throat; breast bright orange, very slightly tinged with red; under wing-coverts and axillaries greyish white.

Obser. Mr. R. B. Sharpe remarks (Cat. B. B. Mus. vol. xii. p. 455) that "Mr. Hume's series consists of seven specimens, all varying but slightly in the extent and depth of the scarlet breast, which in some is tinged with olive-yellow. One specimen has the breast ashy-grey, with only an appearance of scarlet, but is otherwise quite adult. The scarlet breast is therefore evidently gradually acquired."

OUR first knowledge of the existence of this beautiful Bullfinch is contained in a letter from Mr. Edward Blyth (late curator of the Calcutta Museum), which was published in the 'Ibis' for 1862, wherein the writer says: "Lieut. Beavan has just returned here from Darjeeling, where (though chiefly on Tonglo mountain, 10,000 feet, on the Nepal frontier of Sikkim, and some thirty miles from Darjeeling) he has collected many good things in a very short time. Of novelties, a fine new true Bullfinch (*Pyrrhula erythaca*), being the fourth which the Himalaya has yielded."

This is only a single instance of the many valuable acquisitions to our scientific knowledge of the *Avifauna* of the vast mountainous regions of the Himalayas visited by Lieut. Beavan, who says: "I came across a flock of this new species on my way up Mount Tonglo in April 1862. There were two males and several females picking about the bushes near the path. The females all escaped; but I secured both the males, though one was too much damaged to preserve; the other I sent to Mr. E. Blyth, who described it in the 'Ibis' for 1862 (p. 389), and in the following year furnished its portrait ('Ibis,' 1863, pl. x.). This was the only occasion on which I observed the species. The elevation was about 9,000 feet."

The following note is appended to *Pyrrhula major* by Mr. H. E. Dresser in his 'Birds of Europe':—"*Pyrrhula erythaca* (Blyth) is perhaps the rarest of the known species of Bullfinch; and I am fortunate in being able to examine a specimen belonging to Captain Elwes, a male obtained in Sikkim in April 1864. It inhabits Sikkim, at great altitudes."

In 'Stray Feathers' for 1874 we have the following additional notes on this bird from the pen of the great collector Mr. Allan Hume, who writes:—"A specimen of that rare Bullfinch *Pyrrhula erythaca* has recently been obtained for me by Mr. Gammie (to whom I have repeatedly owed rare birds and eggs) at Jor Bungala, close to Darjeeling, at an elevation of between five and six thousand feet. As far as I know, this is the first specimen obtained since the late Lieutenant Beavan shot the type on Mount Tonglo. Perhaps others have been met with; and, if so, I should be glad to learn the localities and dates on which they were procured.

"Since this was in type Mr. Mandelli has also kindly sent me a specimen of Beavan's Bullfinch, procured in April, also at Sikkim. It would appear that it is only an occasional migrant to Sikkim (just as *Syrrhaptes paradoxus* in England); for we have for years maintained the keenest watch for this species, and heretofore without success. Where can the home of this species be? Swinhoe has not met with it in China, nor any of the Russians in Siberia, nor our people in Yarkand. However, there is a vast country outside all these explorations, to which *P. erythaca* must belong."

Colonel N. M. Prjevalski in his remarks on the 'Birds of Mongolia,' published in the second volume of Rowley's 'Ornithological Miscellany,' 1876, has given all I can gather respecting the exact country in which this bird is supposed to breed. He observes: "We met with it only in Kan su, where it principally inhabits woods of the lower and middle mountain-ranges, and only seldom visits the alpine regions. It is most abundant in the thickets on the sides of mountain-brooks.

"The voice of the male, either when on the wing or sitting, resembles that of our common Bullfinch, but is somewhat weaker. In spring the males sing very prettily.

"The present species is a quick and lively bird, which very seldom sits quietly, but usually flies from one branch to another. About the middle of May the small flocks had not yet paired.

"The Kan-su mountains form the northern boundary of distribution for the present species."

The nest and eggs have not yet been discovered.

The details of the male, female, and young male, are taken from examples procured by Colonel Prjevalski, at Kan-su in N. W. China, and are now in the collection of Mr. H. Seebohm, who courteously sent these beautiful skins to me for examination.

Specimens examined.

No.	Sex.	Mus.	Locality.	Length.	Wing.	Tail.	Tars.	Culm.
a.	♂	H. Seebohm.	Kan-su, N. W. China (*Prjevalski*).	5·9	3·2	2·95	0·7	0·38
b.	♂ Imm.	H. Seebohm.	Kan-su, N. W. China (*Prjevalski*).	5·65	3·2	2·75	0·65	0·4
c.	♀	H. Seebohm.	Kan-su, N. W. China (*Prjevalski*).	5·75	3·2	2·95	0·65	0·35

The figures (Plate II.) are taken from *a* and *c*.

COCCOTHRAUSTES PERSONATUS.
THE JAPANESE HAWFINCH.
PLATE I.

Coccothraustes personatus, Temm. et Schl. Faun. Jap. p. 91, pl. lii. (1850).
Hesperiphona personatus, Bonap. Consp. Gen. Av. p. 506 (1850).
Eophona personata, Gould, Birds Asia, v. pl. 18 (1851).
Coccothraustes nippon, Licht. Nomencl. Av. Mus. Berol. p. 46 (1854).
Coccothraustes melanurus, Scl. P. Z. S. 1860, p. 243.
Eophona personata, Swinh. P. Z. S. 1863, pp. 299, 337.
Coccothraustes personatus, Whitely, Ibis, 1867, p. 201.
Eophona personata, Swinh. P. Z. S. 1870, p. 448.
Coccothraustes personata, Gray, Hand-List Birds, ii. p. 88 (1870).
Coccothraustes nippon, Gray, Hand-List Birds, ii. p. 88, pt. (1870).
Eophona personata, Swinh. P. Z. S. 1871, p. 386.
Coccothraustes personata, David, N. Arch. Mus. vii. Bull. p. 11 (1871).
Eophona personata, Elwes, Proc. Zool. Soc. 1873, p. 664.
Eophona personata, Swinh. Ibis, 1875, pp. 121, 146.
Eophona personata, Dyb. et Tacz. J. für O. 1875, pp. 242, 254, et 1876, p. 199.
Eophona personata, Tacz. Bull. Soc. Zool. Fr. i. 1876, p. 181.
Eophona personata, David et Oust. Ois. Chine, p. 346, pl. 91 (1877).
Eophona personata, Swinh. Ibis, 1877, p. 145.
Coccothraustes personatus, Blak. et Pryer, Ibis, 1878, p. 245.
Coccothraustes personatus, Russ, Stubenvögel, p. 514 (1879).
Coccothraustes personata, Blak. et Pryer, Birds Japan, p. 175 (1882).
Eophona personata, Jouy, Pr. U. S. Nat. Mus. vi. p. 295 (1884).
Coccothraustes personatus, Blakiston, Amend. List B. Japan, pp. 18, 63 (1884).
Eophona personata, Sharpe, Cat. B. in B. Mus. xii. pp. 30, 818 (1888).

Figures, Temm. et Schl. Faun. Jap. pl. lii. Gould, B. Asia, pl. 18. David et Oust. Ois. Chine, pl. 91.

Chinese. *Ou-toung*, and *La-tsung*.

English. *Japanese Hawfinch. Masked Hawfinch. Masked Grosbeak. Japanese Grosbeak.*

French. *Le Gros-bec du Japon. Le Gros-bec masqué.*

German. *Der Maskenkernbeisser. Japanesischer Kernbeisser. Schwarzköpfiger Kernbeisser.*

Japanese. "*Ikuru.*"

Habitat. Japan, extending into North, North-western, and Central China.

Male. Crown of head, lores, base of cheeks, and chin glossy purplish-black; nape of neck, back, scapulars and rump pale ashy-grey, tinged with pale rufous-brown on the rump; lesser, median, and greater wing-coverts glossy steel-blue, the innermost half of the latter like the scapulars; secondaries black, broadly edged on the outer webs with steel-blue; tertials like the back; bastard-wing, primaries and coverts black; first feathers black, with a small white spot on the edge of the inner web, an irregular white band across the remainder, diminishing on the outer webs only of the three innermost feathers; upper tail-coverts and central tail-feathers steel-blue, tipped with black, outer ones black; ear-coverts, throat, breast and sides like the back, paling towards the black frontal band of face; axillaries, under wing-coverts, abdomen, thighs and under tail-coverts nearly pure white; under surface of wings brownish-black; "iris light hazel"; "bill yellow," base purple tinged with green; feet reddish flesh colour: length 8·1, wing 4·35, tail 3·25, tars. 0·9, culm. 0·95.

Female. Similar to male, but without the black crown; and generally paler; bill entirely yellow, without the purple base.

Obser. According to Mr. Gould, the black crown of the male is absent in the female, but subsequent authors and collectors state that the two sexes are scarcely separable, the purple base to the mandibles being only seasonal. When a black-crowned specimen is marked ♀, it occurs to me that the sex has not been carefully determined. The specimen kindly lent to me by Professor A. Newton from the Cambridge Museum has the feathers of the whole of the back, chest and flanks beautifully marked with four or five faint wavy water-lines; these bars are entirely absent in the three wild birds in my own collection.

THE Japanese Hawfinch is one of the largest and most beautiful of the group to which it belongs, and is easily distinguished from the Black-tailed Hawfinch of Southern China, by the black tips to the primaries, which are white in the latter bird when adult.

This species was first described by Messrs. Temminck and Schlegel in their 'Fauna Japonica,' published in 1850; since that date, and during the last thirty-eight years, many travellers and collectors have visited the countries inhabited by this bird, without obtaining any authentic detailed history of its habits or nidification; it is undoubtedly a peculiar mountainous resident, and is supposed to breed on the highest snow-clad volcanoes of Japan and Central China, and must endure extreme cold, from the great altitude at which it has been procured.

In Mr. J. Gould's 'Birds of Asia' will be found excellent figures of both sexes of this species, and from the text I give the following notes:—
"The bird is well figured in Messrs. Temminck and Schlegel's 'Fauna Japonica,' but no account whatever is given of its habits, nor have they even mentioned the localities in which it was found. I believe that a seasonal change of colour takes place in the bill of this species, as well as in that of *Eophona melanura*, as the examples in the Earl of Derby's collection exhibit a deep purple colouring around the base and at the tip. A considerable difference occurs in the sexes; the black of the face and head, so conspicuous in the male, being entirely wanting in the female."

Mr. H. Whitely procured "one specimen only (a male), shot in a wood at Hakodadi. It is a rather powerful bird, as, although very badly wounded, it flew nearly 300 yards before it fell. Length 8·75 in., wing 5·25. Bill—upper mandible yellow, marked with dark-green streaks towards the crown of the head; lower mandible yellow, with a slight tinge of green; legs and feet greenish flesh-colour; eye light hazel."

It is found at Pekin according to Mr. R. Swinhoe, and in his 'Ornithological Notes made at Chefoo' he says the "name in the MS. Illustrations is *La-tsung* (M. D. 6854, 11209), or *Wax-bill*. This is applied to *Eophona melanura* in the south, where this larger bird does not occur."

Messrs. Blakiston and Pryer state that it is "found commonly on Fujisan in July, has a pleasing whistle, and is capable of being made very tame. Examples were also obtained in Yezo, Oyama, and Shikoku. Specimens were also observed in the Museum at Tokio and Hakodadi."

It was collected by M. P. L. Jouy, who says :—" This species probably breeds on Fuji-Yama, as they were taken in June and July, but it is apparently not very common. It was also found at Tate-Yama, Shinshiu, in winter. The male from Fuji-Yama dated June 30, 1882, had the bill chrome yellow, base slightly greenish ; feet pale flesh-colour. The female from Tate-Yama had the iris dark reddish brown ; bill pale yellow, base slightly greenish ; tarsi and toes pale flesh-colour."

Mr. F. Ringer's collection contained examples from Nagasaki.

I am indebted to Mr. H. Seebohm for the loan of two (f and g) very beautiful skins from Fujisan in Japan ; which are in my opinion both males.

Specimens examined.

No.	Sex.	Mus.	Locality.	Length.	Wing.	Tail.	Tars.	Culm.
a.	♂	E. B.	Japan.	8·6	0·0	3·25	0·85	0·0
b.	♂	E. B.	Japan.	8·1	4·35	3·25	0·9	0·95
c.	♂	E. B.	Japan.	8·0	4·2	3·25	0·85	0·9
d.	♀ ?	E. B.	Japan.	8·1	4·3	3·3	0·85	0·9
e.	?	Acad. Cantab.	Japan.	7·35	0·0	3·2	0·92	0·9
f.	♂ ?	H. Seebohm.	Fujisan, Japan.	8·65	4·2	3·25	0·9	0·95
g.	♂ ?	H. Seebohm.	Fujisan, Japan.	8·3	4·25	3·3	0·9	0·9

The figures are taken from a male, b, in my own collection, and that of the female from Mr. J. Gould's " Birds of Asia."

COCCOTHRAUSTES MELANURUS.
BLACK-TAILED HAWFINCH.
PLATE II.

Le Gros-bec de la Chine, Sonn. Voy. Ind. Orient. ii. p. 199 (1782).
Grey-necked Grosbeak, Lath. Gen. Syn. iii. p. 145 (1783).
Grey-necked Grosbeak, Gmel. Syst. Nat. Hist. vii. p. 140. Engl. edit. (1801).
Grey-necked Grosbeak, Lath. Gen. Hist. Birds. v. p. 250 (1822).
Loxia melanura, Gmel. Syst. Nat. i. p. 853 (1788); Lath. Ind. Orn. i. p. 389 (1790); Daud. Trait. d'Ornith. ii. p. 385 (1800); Shaw, Gen. Zool. ix. p. 312 (1815); Griff. Cuv. Anim. Kingd. Aves, ii. p. 156 (1829).
Coccothraustes melanura, Shaw, Gen. Zool. xiv. p. 87 (1824); Jard. et Selb. Ill. Orn. ii. pl. 63 (1837); Strickl. P. Z. S. 1842, p. 167: Gray et Mitch. Gen. Birds. ii. p. 358 (1844); Gray. Hand-List B. ii. p. 88 (1870); Gray. Fasc. Birds China, p. 5. pl. vi. (1871); Blakiston, Birds Japan. p. 175 (1882); Blakiston, Amended List B. Japan, p. 30 (1884).
Hesperiphona melanura, Bonap. Consp. Gen. Av. i. p. 506 (1850).
Eophona melanura, Gould. Birds of Asia, v. pl. 19 (1851); Gray, Gen. et Subgen. Birds, p. 71 (1855); Horsf. et Moore, Cat. B. Mus. E.-Ind. Comp. ii. p. 462 (1856-8); Swinh. Ibis, 1867, p. 390; Swinh. P. Z. S. 1870, p. 602, P. Z. S. 1871, p. 386; Swinh. Ibis, 1873, p. 372, 1875, p. 121; Dyb. Journ. für Ornith. 1876. p. 199; Tacz. Bull. Soc. Zool. France, i. 1876, p. 181; David et Oust. Ois. Chine, p. 347, pl. 92 (1877).
Coccothraustes melamurus, Swinh. Ibis, 1860, p. 61, 1861, p. 45; Swinh. P. Z. S. 1863, p. 299; David, N. Arch. Mus. vii. Bull. p. 10 (1871); Ibis, 1872, p. 430; Blakiston et Pryer, Ibis, 1878, p. 246; Russ, Stubenvögel, p. 515 (1879); Scl. Vert. Anim. Zool. Soc. Gard. p. 255. pt. (1883); Seebohm, Ibis, 1884, p. 266.

Figures, Jard. et Selb. Ill. Orn. pl. 63. Gould, B. Asia, pl. 19 Gray, Fasc. B. China, pl. vi. David et Oust. Ois. Chine, pl. 92.

Chinese. *Hou-eull*.

English. *Grey-necked Grosbeak. Black-tailed Grosbeak. Fork-tailed Hawfinch.*

French. *Le Gros-bec de la Chine. Le Gros-bec à queue noire.*

German. *Der Schwarzschwänzige Kernbeisser. Kernbeisser von China.*

Japanese. *Shima-ikaru.*

Habitat. China, migrating into North China and Siberia during the breeding season ; and Japan ? (*Blakiston*).

Male. Head glossy black, encircled by a greyish-white line, which is blended into the neck and throat ; back dull chocolate-brown, blending on to the rump, which is ashy-grey with a white termination ; wings and coverts black, glossy steel-blue on the coverts and secondaries ; tips of primary-coverts, secondaries, and ends of primaries white ; upper tail-coverts and tail black, glossed with steel-blue ; centre of breast ashy-grey like the rump ; sides of chest and sides chestnut brown ; abdomen and under tail-coverts pure white ; thighs like the rump ; axillaries, and under wing-coverts black, tips white ; under surface of wing blackish ; iris brown ; bill yellow, base, tip and cutting edge purple, tinged with green ; feet fleshy-white : length 7·1, wing 3·95, tail 3·1, tars. 0·85, culm. 0·75.

Female. Similar to the male, but paler and without the black head, which is dark grey on the crown ; cheeks, and chin grey like the breast ; wings nearly black, glossy steel-blue on the secondaries ; lesser wing-coverts and tertials like the hind neck ; outer webs of great coverts, and inner web of tertials glossy black ; tips of primary-coverts, outer webs at the ends and tips of primaries, and tips of secondaries white ; rump dull grey, tinged with pale brown ; upper tail-coverts and centre tail feathers slaty-grey, the outer ones brownish, edges and tips steel-blue ; underparts like the male but paler ; iris brown ; bill yellow with a very slight purple tip ; feet fleshy-white : length 6·7, wing 3·75, tail 2·8, tars. 0·75, culm. 0·75.

Obser. The chestnut on the sides of the male is much richer in some specimens than others.

" Two males procured at Foochow with the ends of the primary quills entirely white. I have observed this peculiarity in individuals of this species before." (*R. Swinhoe*).

The Chinese or Black-tailed Hawfinch appears to be an extremely abundant species throughout the southern portions of China, and, according to the researches of travellers and ornithologists, it is found to extend its migration into Central and Northern China ; it is plentiful during the winter on the Amoy and in Eastern Siberia ; and Messrs. Blakiston and Pryer have stated that " a specimen supposed to be this species was obtained from a bird-dealer at Tokio, Japan," and was in " the Educational Museum " of that place ; they say it is "about the size of *C. japonicus*. The bill is yellow, tipped with black. Head and neck black all round as far down as 12 millimètres behind the eye."

The above description is conclusively that of the Black-tailed Hawfinch, but in the 'Amended List of the Birds of Japan,' published in 1884 by the same authors, the species is marked " doubtful."

Although I am unable to find another instance of its occurrence in Japan, I am inclined to retain it as an " accidental visitor."

The following passage is from Mr. J. Gould's 'Birds of Asia' :—" In a collection of birds obligingly lent me by J. R. Reeves, Esq., there are fine examples of this species, which had been procured in the neighbourhood of Shanghai ; Sir William Jardine gives the neighbourhood of Canton as a locality from which he had received specimens ; and I have also others from the island of Chusan ; it is evident, therefore, that its range extends over all those parts of China best known to Europeans. On a label attached to one of Mr. Reeves' specimens, it is stated that the crop was filled with grain and a small mixture of gravel."

Mr. R. Swinhoe "found it on the Amoy in winter," and says it "leaves before summer. Breeds in Shanghai. Very abundant about Canton ; evidently breeds there in great numbers. I have not traced it further north ; also procured on the Woosung River near Shanghai ; at Foochow."

In Mr. Swinhoe's notes made at Chefoo, he says the " name in the MS. Illustrations of this species is *Tsao-hwa* (M. D. 10564, 4199), the Tsao-flower (a water-flag or lily)."

In 'The Birds of China,' published by MM. David and Oustalet, they state that "the Black-tailed Grosbeak is very common at all seasons in Southern and Central China, and advances in summer in little flocks as far as the Northern provinces : every year they catch some of these birds in the environs of Pekin, which the Chinese of the capital designate by the name of *Hou-eull*, and M. Dybowski has sent to the Warsaw Museum an individual of the same species taken in the environs of Abrek Bay in Eastern Siberia."

Specimens examined.

No.	Sex.	Mus.	Locality.	Length.	Wing.	Tail.	Tars.	Culm.
a.	♂	E. B.	Amoy (*R. Swinhoe*).	6·5	3·85	2·8	0·85	0·75
b.	♂	E. B.	Amoy (*R. Swinhoe*).	7·1	4·0	2·75	0·8	0·8
c.	♀	E. B.	Amoy (*R. Swinhoe*).	6·3	3·75	2·7	0·7	0·75
d.	♀	E. B.	Amoy (*R. Swinhoe*).	6·7	3·75	2·8	0·75	0·75
e.	♀	E. B.	Amoy (*R. Swinhoe*).	6·6	3·85	0·0	0·75	0·75
f.	♀	E. B.	Amoy (*R. Swinhoe*).	6·7	3·75	2·6	0·75	0·75
g.	♂	E. B.	China	7·1	3·95	3·1	0·85	0·75

The figures are taken from *d* and *g*, two specimens in my own collection.

The plant is *Talauma Candollei*.

EUPLECTES FLAMMICEPS.
THE CRIMSON-CROWNED WEAVER.
PLATE I.

Euplectes flammiceps, Swains. Birds W. Afr. i. p. 186. pl. xiii. (1837).
Euplectes flammiceps, Rüpp. Neue Wirbelth. p. 100 (1835–40) ; Rüpp.
Syst. Uebers. p. 76 (1845) ; Gordon, Jard. Contrib. Ornith. p. 9
(1849) ; Bonap. Consp. Gen. Av. p. 446 (1850) ; Hartl. J. für
O. 1854, p. 112 ; Eyton, Cat. Birds, p. 245 (1856) ; Hartl. Orn.
W.-Afr. p. 127 (1857) ; Hartl. Proc. Zool. Soc. 1860, p. 111 ;
Hartl. J. für O. 1860, p. 180 ; et 1861, p. 175 ; Reichb. Sing-
vögel, p. 57. pl. xxiii. fig. 203 (1861) ; Mont. Ibis, 1862, p. 338 :
Scl. Proc. Zool. Soc. 1864, p. 109 ; Hartl. Proc. Zool. Soc. 1867,
p. 826 ; Heugl. (Würt. Icon. 26), J. für O. 1867, p. 297 ; Heugl.
Syn. der Vög. N.-O.-Afr. J. für O. 1867, p. 373 ; Bocage, Aves
des Posses. Portug. d'Afr. J. S. M. Lisb. i. 1868, p. 139 ; Heugl.
Peterm. Geogr. Mitth. 1869, p. 415 ; Cabanis, Decken-Reisen, i.
p. 59 (1869) ; Sharpe, Ibis, 1869, p. 191 ; et Cat. Afr. Birds, p.
62 (1871) ; Heugl. Ornith. N.-O.-Afr. p. 567, Append. p. cxxxii.
(1871) ; Shelley and Buckley, Ibis, 1872, p. 289 ; Sharpe, Ibis,
1874, p. 69 ; et Proc. Zool. Soc. 1874, p. 306 ; Bocage, J. für O.
1876, p. 426 ; Cab. J. für O. 1878, p. 231 ; Fisch. et Reichn. J.
für O. 1878, p. 263 ; Fischer, J. für O. 1879, pp. 280, 282, 289,
303 ; Fisch. et Reichn. J. für Ornith. 1879, p. 351 ; Fischer, J.
für O. 1880, p. 187 ; Shelley, Proc. Zool. Soc. 1881, p. 585 :
Schalow, J. für O. 1883, p. 362 ; Scl. Vert. An. Gard. Z. S. p.
243 (1883) ; Rochb. Fauna Seneg. p. 241 (1884) ; Fischer,
Zeitschr. Gesam. Ornith. 1884, p. 327 ; Fischer, J. für O. 1885,
p. 134.
Ploceus flammiceps, Gray et Mitch. Gen. Birds, ii. p. 352 (1844), et ii.

p. 353 (1849) ; Gray, Hand-List Birds, ii. p. 46 (1870) ; Russ, Stubenvögel, p. 241 (1879).
Pyromelana flammiceps, Finsch et Hartl. Decken's Reis. O.-Afr. p. 414 (1870) ; Salv. Cat. Coll. II. E. Strickl. p. 244 (1882) ; Shelley, Ibis, 1883, p. 552 ; Böhm, J. für O. 1883, p. 199 ; et J. für O. 1885, p. 59 ; Shelley, Ibis, 1886, p. 352.
Euplectes oryx, Fraser, Proc. Zool. Soc. 1843, p. 52 ; Hartl. Jardine's Contrib. Ornith. p. 131 (1850).
Pyromelana oryx, Horsf. et Moore, Cat. Birds Mus. E.-Ind. Comp. p. 519 (1856-58).
Euplectes Petiti, Des Murs, Rev. Zool. ix. 1846, p. 242 ; Bonap. Consp. Gen. Av. p. 446 (1850) ; Hartl. Ornith. W.-Afr. p. 127 (1857) ; Reichb. Singvögel, p. 58 (1861) ; Heugl. J. für O. 1867, p. 375 ; Finsch et Hartl. Orn. O.-Afr. p. 415 note (1870) ; Heugl. Ornith. N.-O.-Afr. p. 570. Append. p. cxxxii. (1871).
Loxia (*Euplectes*) *Petiti*, Des Murs, in Lefebv. Voy. Abyss. vi. p. 112. pl. x. fig. 1 (1845-50).
Ploceus Petiti, Gray et Mitch. Gen. Birds, ii. p. 353 (1849) ; Gray, Hand-List Birds, ii. p. 46 (1870).
Ploceus craspedopterus, Schiff, Mus. Francf.
Euplectes craspedopterus, Bonap. Consp. Gen. Av. p. 446 (1850) ; Heugl. Syst. Uebers. p. 39 (1856) ; Reichb. Singvögel, p. 58 (1861).
Euplectes flaviceps (laps. typ.), Hartl. Proc. Zool. Soc. 1863, p. 106.
Euplectes pyrrhozona, Heugl. J. für Ornith. 1864, p. 247.

Figures, Swains. Birds W. Afr. i. pl. xiii. et Des Murs ; Lefebv. Voy. Abyss. t. 10. 1.

English. *Crimson-crowned Weaver. The Flammiceps Oryx. Petit's Fire-Finch. White-bordered Fire-Finch.*

French. *Le Cardinalin flammiceps. Le Cardinalin Petit. L'Ignicolor de Petit. Le Cardinalin craspedoptère.*

German. *Der Flammen-Webervogel. Swainson's Flammenköpfiger Feuerfink. Petit's Feuerfink. Der Feuerfink mit weissem Flügelsaum.*

Habitat. North-East and West Africa. Extending "from Abyssinia to Linda on the east coast, and from the Quanza River to Senegal on the west coast" (*Shelley*).

Male. Crown, hind neck, sides and lower part of throat, fiery orange-red, which passes up to an acute point, to the angle of the lower mandible; mantle and scapulars bright chestnut, tinged with orange; rump and upper tail-coverts like the crown and throat; narrow frontal band uniting on the culmen, narrow line over the eye, lores, cheeks, ear-coverts, chin, upper part of throat, chest, and belly velvety-black; wings, wing-coverts and tail black, narrowly edged with white and pale buff; flanks, thighs, abdomen and under tail-coverts pale fawn-colour, slightly tinged with orange; axillaries pale buff; under wing-coverts, and under surface of wing nearly black; iris brown; bill black; feet brownish flesh-colour: length 5·3, wing 2·95, tail 2·1, tars. 0·75, culm. 0·65.

Female. Above rufous-brown; crown of head and hind neck narrowly striated, mantle and scapulars broadly striated with dark brown; rump and upper tail-coverts faintly striated and uniform pale brown; wings and coverts, and tail dark brown, narrowly edged with pale rufous-brown; eyebrows yellowish buff; cheeks and ear-coverts like the hind neck; moustachial-line faint yellowish buff; chin, throat, abdomen and under tail-coverts nearly pure white; breast, sides, flanks, and thighs, brownish buff, slightly tinged with yellow, and very faintly striated; axillaries, under surface of wing and coverts dull brown; iris pale brown; bill pale fleshy-brown, darker on the culmen; feet pinkish flesh-colour: length 4·65, wing 2·45, tail 1·7, tars. 0·75, culm. 0·6.

Young. Similar to the female but paler.

Obser. The brilliant colours of the male are assumed by a gradual moult of the whole of the feathers, and after the breeding season they become like the females and young males.

In the adult males, the fine shafts of the feathers on the crown and nape terminate in long black hair-like points; and immature males have the wing-coverts, secondaries and tail broadly edged with rufous-brown; in some the longest under tail-coverts are white; the bill being silvery-white at the base.

The secondaries of the adult female are narrowly, and in the young females broadly, edged with pale rufous-brown.

The group of Fire-Finches (so called from the brilliancy of their plumage) to which the Crimson-crowned Weaver belongs is one of the most extensive and beautiful of the whole family of *Ploceidæ* found on the continent of Africa. The exquisite arrangement of colours, although opposed to each other, harmonizes, and lends beauty to the everlasting activity of these very amusing birds; their movements and most ludicrous song, or I might say chatterings, always create merriment among those who keep them in confinement and watch the grotesque attitudes into which these extraordinary birds put themselves.

The distribution of this weaver-bird appears to be very great, and from the number of localities in which it has been procured by many ornithologists shows that it occupies in its migrations the whole of the central portion of Africa.

The vast humid reed-covered swamps of the interior are the homes of this beautiful bird; in these situations they assemble in countless hundreds, and during the breeding season suspend their globular grass nests on the tall reeds.

This species was first separated from the more southern form (*Euplectes oryx*) by Mr. W. Swainson in 1837, who described it from a skin sent from Senegal, and although easily recognised by its black wings, it has been confused with the South and East African birds of the same genera, in which the wings are dull brown.

During the Niger Expedition in 1840, Mr. Louis Fraser found it "common about Cape Coast, West Africa, frequenting the Indian-corn plantations," and placed it under the name *Euplectes oryx*. In 1847 it was obtained by Dr. Gordon at Cape Coast Castle, where according to his observations "they are very familiar, and hop from branch to branch, within a few yards of the person who visits their retreats."

In Angola, according to Mr. J. J. Monteiro, it was "very common at Bembe, Cambambe, and about the river Quanza, but not seen on the coast; keeping always among the high grass"; and Dr. Welwitsch obtained it at Golungo also in the interior of Angola.

Major Harris brought home examples from Abyssinia; specimens were also collected by Dr. Petit in Abyssinia in 1840 while travelling with M. T. Lefebvre's expedition, which were described by M. O. des Murs under the name *Loxia* (*Euplectes*) *Petiti*.

Captain J. H. Speke also found it at Mininga, in Central East Africa, where he says it "flies about in large flocks, feeding in corn-fields, and roosting at night in the rushes in the swamps."

Herr von Heuglin says he found "this magnificent Fire-Finch breeding in almost solitary couples in August and September in the high grass and thickets in the territory of the Djur and the Kosanga rivers. The nests are built like those of *E. ignicolor*, and contain three verdigris-green eggs,

8⅓ mill. in length, which are usually sprinkled at the blunt end with extremely small violet-black spots. They disappear from the above-mentioned regions when the breeding season is over. This species seems to be found in Abyssinia also, only during the rainy season, in the neighbourhood of Adowa and in the lowlands of the Takazze."

M. Bojor observed it at Zanzibar, and Dr. Kirk sent home specimens from Melinda and Usambara in Eastern Africa. Dr. R. Böhm says it is "common on the coast of Zanzibar, and near Kakoma, not, however, in particularly large numbers. They prefer to live in patches of very tall grass on fallow ground or (not only at night) on marshes. Killed here in its transition plumage in the first half of February. I found and received nests of three to five eggs from the beginning of April (on April 11 featherless nestlings), until now, the second half of May. I saw several nests, some with young birds quite close together in very tall, thick grass.

"As long as the Fire-Finches wear their ordinary brown plumage, they fly about in such close company with *Ploceus sanguinirostris* that a shot sent into the closely-flying swarm regularly brings down a number of specimens of both kinds (Mdaburu in Ugogo). At eventide these flocks settle among the reeds of almost dried-up swamps to drink and sleep. From every direction, first singly, then in ever-increasing numbers, the flocks come with a particularly rapid and loudly whirring flight, wheeling around closely packed together, with precipitate movements like a flock of grey plover, to and fro, then sinking down noiselessly into neighbouring bushes, where they begin their confused noise, which ever increases then decreases. Hence they fling themselves among the reeds, then back into the bushes, and soon increase so much in force that their ascent resembles distant thunder in quite a deceptive way. The masses thus gradually advance to the border of open lakes, and then throw themselves on to the water from suitable spots where the clumps of reeds are bent downwards in the form of a terrace owing to their constantly being used for this purpose; here they fly up and down for a long period, forming an unbroken stream. If one hid oneself in one of the thick bushes into which the birds were accustomed to fly, one felt a considerable compression of the air when the flocks flew towards and into it like a living wall; and if one goes through the reeds when it is dark, black, noisy waves, formed by the birds disturbed from their sleep, seem to roll over the marsh. The rapid, restless, shy and fugitive behaviour of the Fire-Finches at this time contrasts wonderfully with their composed, self-complacent manner when they are accustomed to sun themselves and strut on the tops of stalks, twittering and shaking their wings with bristling plumage in their garb of the mating season."

Specimens examined.

No.	Sex.	Mus.	Locality.	Length.	Wing.	Tail.	Tars.	Culm.
a.	♂	E. B.	West Africa.	5·4	3·05	2·0	0·8	0·65
b.	♂	E. B.	West Africa.	4·7	2·8	1·8	0·8	0·65
c.	♂ winter	E. B.	West Africa.	4·95	2·75	1·75	0·8	0·65
d.	♂ imm.	E. B.	West Africa.	5·25	3·1	2·0	0·85	0·65
e.	♀	E. B.	West Africa.	4·4	2·5	1·65	0·75	0·6
f.	♀	E. B.	West Africa.	4·65	2·45	1·7	0·75	0·6
g.	♀	E. B.	West Africa.	0·0	2·55	0·0	0·75	0·6
h.	Adult	E. B.	Fantee, W. Africa (*Ussher*).	4·7	2·9	1·85	0·8	0·6
i.	Adult	E. B.	Ushambala Mt., Pangani R. (*Kirk*).	5·1	3·1	2·0	0·8	0·65
j.	Adult	E. B.	Melinda, E. Africa (*Kirk*).	5·3	2·95	2·1	0·75	0·65
k.	Adult	E. B.	Somali, E. Africa.	5·4	2·9	2·0	0·8	0·65

The figures are taken from *f* and *j*.

MALIMBUS MALIMBICUS.
THE LARGE RED-CROWNED WEAVER.
PLATE I.

Tanagra malimbica, Daud. Ann. du Mus. Paris, i. 1802, p. 151, ♀ pl. 10, fig. 2.
Tanagra malimbica, Shaw, Nat. Misc. xiv. ♀ (1802).
Malimbus cristatus, Vieill. Ois. Chant. p. 71, pl. xliii. ♀ (1805).
Le Républicain à capuchon écarlate, Temm. Cat. Cab. Ornith. pp. 102, 234 (1807).
Textor malimbus, Temm. Auct. ?
Ploceus cristatus, Vieill. Nouv. Dict. xxxiv. p. 129, ♀ (1819).
Le Malimbe, ? Temm. Man. d'Ornith. i. p. lxx. (1820).
Ploceus cristatus, Vieill. Tabl. Encycl. Méth. ii. p. 700, ♀ (1823).
Fringilla textrix, Licht. Verz. Doubl. Mus. Berl. p. 24 note (1823).
Ploceus rubricollis, Swains. Anim. in Menag. p. 306 (1838).
Euplectes ruforelatus, Fraser, Proc. Zool. Soc. 1842, p. 142; Allen et Thomp. Exped. R. Niger, ii. p. 500 (1848); Fraser, Zool. Typica, pl. 46 (1849); Verr. Rev. et Mag. 1851, p. 419.
Sycobius rubricollis, Gray et Mitch. Gen. Birds, ii. p. 351 (1844); Jard. Contrib. Orn. p. 3 (1849); Reichb. Singvögel, p. 80, pl. lxi. figs. 332-334 (1861); Bocage, Orn. d'Angola, p. 332, Append. p. 558 (1877).
Ploceus ruforelatus, Gray et Mitch. Gen. Birds, ii. p. 352 (1844).
Sycobius malimbus, Bonap. Consp. Gen. Av. i. p. 438 (1850); Hartl. Journ. für Ornith. 1854, p. 105; Müller, Journ. für Ornith. 1855.

p. 460; Hartl. Orn. Westafr. pp. 132, 274 (1857) ; Cassin, Proc. Acad. N. S. Philad. 1859, p. 135 ; Heine, Journ. für Ornith. 1860, p. 143; Hartl. Journ. für Ornith. 1861, p. 257 ; Reichn. Journ. für Ornith. 1875, p. 38.

Malimbus rubricollis, Strickl. Contr. Ornith. 1851, p. 133 ; Elliot, Ibis, 1876, pp. 457, 458, 461.

Textor ruficollatus (error), Eyton, Cat. Coll. Birds, p. 245 (1856).

Sycobius nuchalis, Elliot, Ibis, 1859, p. 393 ; Sharpe, Ibis, 1869, p. 191, 1870, p. 472.

Malimbus textrix, Gray, Hand-List Birds, ii. p. 43 (1870).

Malimbus occipitalis, Gray, Hand-List Birds, ii. p. 43, pt. (1870).

Malimbus ruforclatus, Sharpe, Cat. Afr. Birds, p. 60 (1871) ; Ussher, Ibis, 1874, p. 68.

Sycobius ruforclatus, Sharpe et Bouv. Bull. S. Z. France, iii. 1878, p. 75.

Ploceus malimbus, Russ, Stubenvögel, p. 322 (1879).

Malimbus malimbicus, Shelley, Ibis, 1887, p. 40.

Figures. Daud. Ann. du Mus. Paris, i. pl. 10. fig. 2. ♀. Vieill. Ois. Chant. pl. xliii. ♀. Fraser, Zool. Typ. pl. 46. Reichb. Singvögel, pl. lxi. figs. 332–334.

English. *The Red-necked Malimbus. Red-crowned Euplectes. The Large Red-crowned Weaver.*

French. *Le Tanagra de Malimbe femelle. Le Malimbe femelle. Le Malimbe cou-rouge.*

German. *Der rothhalsige Malimbus. Der Malimbus.—Prachtweber-vogel.*

Habitat. West Africa ; Tributaries of the River Congo, Gold Coast, and Angola. Fernando Po (*Fraser*). Gaboon, Cape Lopez, and River Camma (*Du Chaillu*). Fantee country and Denkera (*Ussher*). Condé (*Lucan* et *Petit*).

Male. Forehead, crown, and hind neck shining scarlet; whole of back, lores, cheeks, chin throat, and under-parts glossy black; basal half of the under sides of the inner webs of the primaries greyish-white; primary quills and those of the tail white on the under side; iris dark brown; bill and feet black; length 7·55, wing 4·2, tail 2·9, tars. 1·0 culm. 0·9.

Female. Similar to the male, but with a broad black frontal band which passes over and beyond the eye, and united to the black ear-coverts and cheeks; iris dark brown; bill and feet black; length 7·2, wing 4·0, tail 2·85, tars. 0·9, culm. 0·9.

Young male. Dull black; no black frontal band; crown and hind neck dull red, bases of the feathers slaty-grey; chin, throat, and upper part of breast slightly tinged with red.

Young female. Dull black, frontal band, lores, cheeks, and ear-coverts reddish-brown, crown and hind neck pale scarlet with whitish bases; chin, throat, and upper part of breast slightly tinged with red.

Observ. After a careful examination of sixteen specimens of males, females, and young, I have come to the conclusion that the birds from Fernando Po form a local race, and can be readily distinguished by the much paler scarlet or orange-red of the crown and hind neck, and by the greater extent of the white at the base of the feathers; otherwise they are identical with the birds from the mainland of West Africa.

Captain G. E. Shelley very kindly lent me two young females of this species, in which the frontal band, lores, cheeks, and ear-coverts are of a most peculiar reddish-brown; the tips of the feathers are tinged with faint scarlet. The base of the culmen and under margins of the lower mandible in the youngest bird are yellowish.

In 1802 Daudin described two birds of this genus under the name of *Tanagra malimbica*, male and female, one with a crest, and the other with a black frontal band without a crest; and in the same year Mr. George Shaw redescribed the female under Daudin's appellation; in 1805 Vieillot refigured the two birds in his elaborate work 'Oiseaux Chanteurs' (pl. xlii. and xliii.) under the name of Le Malimbe huppé (*Malimbus cristatus*), mâle et femelle, and in 1807 Temminck distinguished the female above mentioned as Le républicain à capuchon écarlate (*male*), but the female, which he characterises thus, *La femelle est entièrement d'un noir rembruni*, is, in my opinion, *Ploceus nigerrimus*, Vieill., owing to the absence of the scarlet crown and hind neck, which is so conspicuous in the male, female, and young of the species now under consideration.

Following up the synonymy of this bird, which is very extensive, varied, and, to say the least, rather complicated, I here transcribe Mr. D. G. Elliot's researches (Ibis, 1879, p. 461). He says: "Somewhere about this time (1807), as given by writers generally, Temminck calls the species *Textor malimbus*; but, so far as I am concerned, this name cannot stand, for two reasons. One is that I have been unable to find it published anywhere by Temminck, and suppose his name is merely a manuscript one in the Leyden Museum, and therefore not to be considered; and another is that his term is a repetition of the name of the genus to which the bird belongs, and therefore could not be used, even if I should find it, on account of its liability to create confusion. Swainson, in his 'Menagerie,' in 1838, regularly described this species and called it *Ploceus rubricollis*, and by this specific name the bird should hereafter be known. In 1842 Fraser, in the 'Proceedings of the Zoological Society,' gave to it the name of *Euplectes rufovelatus*; and in the 'Ibis,' 1859, I bestowed upon the unfortunate creature the term *Sycobius nuchalis*. It is well figured by Fraser in his 'Zoologia Typica,' and by Vieillot in the 'Oiseaux Chanteurs.'"

Mr. L. Fraser says: "During my residence at Fernando Po, in the early part of the year 1842, I procured two male specimens of this species, the one having the head entirely red, and the other having the black extending across the forehead.

"On reference to my note-book I find the following brief observation: These birds, although in deep moult (in June), appeared to be pairing One specimen was shot from the top of a very lofty tree, the others much nearer the ground. In an apparently young male the black extends across the forehead. A very good songster, and are most active about 5 P.M."

At present nothing has been published respecting the habits or nidification of this bird, although the species appears extremely abundant along the west coast of Africa from the Gold Coast to Angola, and is regularly received in every collection from there.

Specimens examined.

No.	Sex.	Mus.	Locality.	Length.	Wing.	Tail.	Tars.	Culm
a.	♂	E. B.	West Africa.	7·55	4·2	2·9	1·0	0·9
b.	♂	E. B.	West Africa.	7·2	4·2	2·85	1·0	0·9
c.	♀	E. B.	West Africa.	7·2	4·0	2·85	0·9	0·9
d.	♂	E. B.	Abouri, West Africa.	6·95	3·95	2·65	0·95	0·85
e.	♂	E. B.	Fernando Po, West Africa (*Fraser*).	7·25	3·85	2·6	0·95	0·9
f.	♀	E. B.	Fantee, West Africa (*Ussher*).	7·1	3·9	2·75	1·0	0·85

No.	Sex.	Mus.	Locality.	Length.	Wing.	Tail.	Tars.	Culm.
g.	♂	E. B.	Fernando Po, West Africa (*Burton*).	7·55	4·0	2·6	1·0	0·85
h.	♀	E. B.	Fernando Po, West Africa (*Burton*).	7·3	3·8	2·6	0·9	0·85
i.	♂	E. B.	Gold Coast	6·85	4·1	2·75	0·95	0·85
j.	♂ juv.	E. B.	Fantee, West Africa.	6·5	3·25	2·8	0·8	0·75
k.	♂	E. B.	Gold Coast (*Ussher*).	7·8	4·15	2·75	1·0	0·9
l.	♂	E. B.	Gold Coast (*Ussher*).	7·5	4·15	2·75	1·0	0·85
m.	♀	E. B.	Gold Coast (*Ussher*).	7·35	3·85	2·6	0·95	0·8
n.	♂	A. Boucard.	Fantee, West Africa.	6·8	4·05	2·85	1·0	0·8
o.	♀ juv.	G. E. Shelley.	Gold Coast (*Ussher*).	6·65	4·2	2·75	1·0	0·8
p.	♀ juv.	G. E. Shelley.	Aburi, West Africa (*G. E. Shelley*)	6·6	4·1	2·8	1·0	0·9

The figures (Plate I.), male and female, are taken from a and f in my own collection.

MALIMBUS CRISTATUS.
THE RED-CRESTED WEAVER.
PLATE II.

Le malimbe, Sonn. édit. de Buff. Hist. Nat. xlvii. p. 111 (1801).
Tanagra malimbica, Daud. Ann. Mus. Paris, i. 1802, p. 151, pl. 10, fig. 1. ♂.
Malimbic Tanager, Shaw, Naturalist's Misc. ♂ pl. 581 (1802).
Malimbus cristatus, Vieill. Ois. Chant. p. 71, pl. xlii. ♂ (1805); Gray, Gen. et Subgen. p. 70 (1855); Gray, Hand-List Birds, ii. p. 43 (1870); Sharpe, Cat. Afr. Birds, p. 60 (1871); Sharpe, Proc. Zool. Soc. 1871, pp. 612, 615; Shelley et Buckl. Ibis, 1872, p. 289; Ussher, Ibis, 1874, p. 68; Elliot, Ibis, 1876, pp. 457, 459; Shelley, Ibis, 1887, p. 40.
Malimbe huppé, Vieill. Analyse (1816), p. 33.
Ploceus cristatus, Vieill. Nouv. Dict. xxxiv. p. 129, ♂ (1819); Vieill. Encycl. ii. p. 700, ♂ (1823); Griff. Cuv. Anim. Kingd. Av. ii. pp. 131, 231 (1829); Swains. Anim. in Menag. p. 305 (1838); Russ, Stubenvögel, p. 320 (1879).
Ficophagus cristatus, Vieill. Auct. ? (1820.)
Le malimbe, Temm. Man. d'Ornith. i. p. lxx, pt. (1820).
Malimbic Tanager, Lath. Gen. Hist. Birds, vi. p. 39 (1823).
Ploceus malimbicus, Steph. Shaw's Gen. Zool. xiv. p. 34 (1824); Stark, Elem. Nat. Hist. i. p. 241 (1828).
Sycobius cristatus, Steph. Shaw's Gen. Zool. xiv. p. 37 (1824); Gray et Mitch. Gen. Birds, ii. p. 351 (1844); id. p. 352 (1849); Bonap. Consp. Gen. Av. p. 438 (1850); Reichb. Syst. Nat. pl. lxxvi. (1850); Hartl. Journ. für Ornith. 1854, p. 105; Hartl. Orn. W. Afr. pp. 132, 273 (1857); Cassin, Proc. Acad. Nat. Sc. 1857, p. 36,

et Proc. Acad. N. S. Philad. 1859, p. 135; Heine, Journ. für
Ornith. 1860, p. 143; Reichb. Singvögel, p. 90, pl. lxi. f. 331
(1861): Sharpe, Ibis, 1869, p. 191, Ibis, 1870, p. 472; Sundev.
Avium Despon. Tentam. p. 29 (1872); Reichn. Journ. für Ornith.
1875, p. 38; Bocage, Jorn. Acad. Sc. Lisboa, 1876, p. 264, et
Ornith. d'Angola, p. 331 (1877–81).

Sycobius malimbus, Licht. Nomencl. Av. Mus. Berol. p. 50 (1854).
Sycobius nigrifrons, Hartl. Journ. für Ornith. 1855, p. 356.
Sycobius sp. ? Bocage, Jorn. Lisb. 1867, p. 140.

Figures. Daud. Ann. Mus. Paris, i. pl. 10, fig. 1 ♂. Shaw,
Nat. Misc. pl. 581 ♂. Vieill. Ois. Chant. pl. 42 ♂.
Reichb. Singvögel, pl. lxi. fig. 331.

English. *The Malimbic Tanager male. Red-crested Malimbus. The Hoopoe Malimbus. Red-crested Black Weaver.*

French. *Le Malimbe mâle. Le Tanagra de Malimbe. Le Tisserin huppé, ou le Malimbe. Le Malimbe huppé. Cardinal noir et rouge huppé.*

German. *Der Hauben-Malimbus. Der Hauben-Prachtweberrogel.*

Habitat. West Africa. Tributaries of the River Congo, Gold Coast, south to Angola. River Boutry (*Pel.*). Aguapim (*Rus.*). Gaboon (*Lecomte*). Rivers Muni and Camma (*Du Chaillu*). River Quito, Cabinda (*Anchieta*). Fantee country and Denkera (*Ussher* and *Kirby*). Abouri (*Shelley* and *Buckley*). Loango (*Falkenstein*).

Male. Crown, crest, cheeks, throat, and upper part of breast shining scarlet; narrow frontal band, lores, space round the eye, chin and whole of back and under parts glossy black; axillaries and under surface of wings dull brown; iris dark brown; bill and feet black: length 5·75, wing 3·3, tail 2·5, tars. 0·8. culm. 0·65.

Female. Similar to the male, but not crested, the scarlet of the crown extending to the mantle; the black frontal band narrow, and not united on the culmen; general plumage less glossy; iris brown; bill and feet dark brown: length 6·35, wing 3·3, tail 2·65, tars. 0·8, culm. 0·7.

Young. Similar to the female, but dull black; with the chin and throat blackish.

Observ. In some of the young birds in my collection, the red feathers of the throat are intermixed with the black, showing a gradual moult. The bases of the scarlet feathers of the crown and throat in the adult of both sexes are white; slaty-grey in the young birds.

Mr. D. G. Elliot devoted much time in working out the synonymy of the species of the genus *Malimbus*, which he published in the 'Ibis' for 1876. I cannot do better than quote his remarks, which are as follows:—
"This species was first described by Daudin (Ann. du Mus. Paris, 1802), from specimens sent from the Congo by Perrein. The type is now in the Paris Museum at the Jardin des Plantes. He called it *Tanagra malimbica*, and described as the female the species named afterwards *Ploceus rubricollis* by Swainson. Uncoloured figures are given of both, and descriptions in Latin and French. Vieillot, three years afterwards, figured and described the same specimens in his 'Oiseaux Chanteurs' under the name of *Malimbus cristatus*, by which specific appellation the species has been generally known. He merely followed Daudin, and repeated his error in figuring Swainson's species as the female. In the 'Analyse,' 1816, where he changed the name of the genus to *Symbius*, he gives no Latin name to the species, but calls it the *Malimbe huppé*; and in the 'Nouveau Dictionnaire,' 1819, three years afterwards, he places it in the genus *Ploceus*.

"Prof. Barboza du Bocage (Jorn. Sc. Math. Lisboa, 1867) describes a specimen of this genus from Rio Quito, Cabinda, which is evidently, as he states, in immature plumage. Judging from his description, I am inclined to think it is one of the phases of plumage assumed at a certain age by the young of this species."

It might be supposed that a bird of this size, although smaller than the preceding species, with such attractive colours, and extremely abundant in its native haunts, would have a long history of its mode of life and nidification; but this, I regret to say, is wanting; all I can gather respecting its habits was written by M. Perrein about 1801, which I transcribe from Griffith's edition of Cuvier's 'Animal Kingdom':—

"These birds usually sojourn on trees bearing figs, which exactly resemble those of Europe, and place their nests on such of the branches as form a triangle. The nest is of a round form, with the aperture worked on the side; the exterior is composed of fine plants, arranged ingeniously, and the interior is furnished with cotton. The eggs are from three to five, of a greyish colour, and the male and female partake of the incubation. It is in the months of October and November that these birds are found in Malimba; they remain on the fig trees above mentioned only while they are loaded with fruit; and when that disappears, the birds disappear also, and do not return till the following year."

Specimens examined.

No.	Sex.	Mus.	Locality.	Length.	Wing.	Tail.	Tars.	Culm.
a.	♂	E. B.	Gaboon.	5·75	3·3	2·5	0·8	0·65
b.	♂	E. B.	West Africa.	5·95	3·05	2·45	0·8	0·65
c.	♂	E. B.	West Africa.	6·15	3·2	2·41	0·75	0·65
d.	♀	E. B.	West Africa.	6·35	3·3	2·65	0·8	0·7
e.	♀	E. B.	West Africa.	6·4	3·25	2·6	0·8	0·7
f.	♂	E. B.	Fantee (*Kirby*).	6·5	3·15	2·41	0·75	0·65
g.	♀	E. B.	Fantee (*Ussher*).	6·15	3·15	2·6	0·8	0·65
h.	♀	E. B.	Fantee (*Ussher*).	5·75	3·05	2·65	0·75	0·65
i.	♂	E. B.	Gold Coast (*Kirby*).	6·35	3·35	2·65	0·7	0·65
j.	♀ juv.	E. B.	Fantee.	5·0	2·9	2·35	0·7	0·6
k.	♂	A. Boucard.	Lundana, West Africa.	6·3	3·4	2·45	0·85	0·75
l.	♀	A. Boucard.	West Africa.	5·95	3·1	2·6	0·75	0·65
m.	♀	A. Boucard.	Fantee.	5·6	3·3	2·55	0·75	0·6
n.	♂ (σ.) ♂	H. B. Tristram.	Gold Coast.	—	—	—	—	—

The figures (Plate II.), male and female, are taken from *a* and *g* in my own collection.

MUNIA ATRICAPILLA.
THE BLACK-HEADED MUNIA.

PLATE V. (Figs. 1, 2).

Loxia atricapilla, Vieill. Ois. Chant. p. 84, pl. liii. (1805).
Coccothraustes atricapilla, Vieill. Nouv. Dict. xiii. p. 535 (1817).
Coccothraustes atricapilla, Vieill. Encycl. Méth. iii. p. 1007 (1823).
Loxia atricapilla, Griff. Cuv. Anim. Kingd. Aves, ii. p. 154 (1829).
Loxia atricapilla, Less. Traité d'Ornith. p. 415 (1831).
Munia rubroniger, Hodgs. Asiat. Res. xix. 1836, p. 153; Blyth, Journ. A. S. B. xxii. 1854, p. 412; Horsf. et Moore, Cat. Birds, E.-Ind. Mus. ii. p. 507 (1856-8); Gray, Cat. Birds of Nepal, p. 56, 2nd edit. (1863).
Lonchura melanocephala, M'Clell. Proc. Zool. Soc. 1839, p. 163.
Spermestes melanocephalus, Blyth. Ann. and Mag. Nat. Hist. xii. 1843, p. 166; Hodgs. Gray's Zool. Misc. p. 84 (1844).
Amadina malacca, Blyth, Journ. Asiat. Soc. Beng. xiii. 1844, p. 949.
Munia malacca, Gray, Cat. Hodgs. Coll. Brit. Mus. p. 106 (1846); Bonap. Consp. Gen. Av. p. 452, Adult, pt. (1850).
Amadina sinensis, Blyth, Journ. Asiat. Soc. Beng. xv. 1846, p. 36; Motl. et Dillw. Nat. Hist. Labuan, p. 25, pl. vi. (1855); Eyton, Cat. Birds, p. 254 (1856).
Munia rubronigra, Blyth, Cat. Birds Mus. A. S. B. p. 116 (1849); Hartl. Journ. für Ornith. 1859, p. 284; Reichb. Singvögel, p. 39 (1861); Jerd. Birds India, ii. p. 353 (1863); Blanf. Ibis, 1870, p. 469; Walden, Ibis, 1871, p. 177; Holdsw. Proc. Zool. Soc. 1872, p. 464; Layard, Proc. Zool. Soc. 1873, p. 205; Legge, Ibis, 1874, p. 25; Walden, Trans. Zool. Soc. ix. 1875, p. 208; Legge, Birds of Ceylon, p. 652 (1878-80); Salvad. Ornit. Papuasia, p. 438 (1881); Salv. Cat. Strickl. Coll. Birds, p. 252 (1882); Scl. Vert. Anim. Gard. Zool. Soc. p. 239 (1883).

Amadina rubronigra, Kelaart, Prod. Birds Ceylon, p. 126, Append.
C. (1852); Kelaart et Layard, Journ. Ceyl. A. Soc. 1853; Layard,
Ann. and Mag. Nat. Hist. xiii. 1854, p. 258; Scully, Stray Feathers,
1879, p. 332.
Spermestes atricapilla, Licht. Nomencl. Av. Mus. Berol. p. 49 (1854).
Munia sinensis, Reichb. Singvögel, p. 39. pl. xiv. figs. 123-124
(1861).
Donacola atricapilla, Blyth, Ibis, 1870, p. 171.
Amadina atricapilla, Gray, Hand-List Birds, ii. p. 54 (1870).
Munia atricapilla, Salvad. Uccelli di Borneo, p. 265 (1874); Hume,
Nests and Eggs, ii. p. 444 (1875); Sharpe, Ibis, 1876, p. 50; id.
Proc. Zool. Soc. 1879, p. 344, 1881, p. 798; Kutter, Journ. für
Ornith. 1885, p. 352.
Munia rubrinigra, Tweedd. Proc. Zool. Soc. 1877, p. 764.
Spermestes sinensis, Russ, Stubenvögel, p. 167, pl. vi. fig. 30 (1879).

   Figures. Vieill. Ois. Chant. pl. liii. Motl. and Dillw. Nat. Hist.
    Labuan, pl. vi. Reichb. Singvögel, pl. xiv. figs. 123-124.
    Russ, Stubenvögel, pl. vi. fig. 30.

English. *Red-black Weaver-finch. Chestnut-bellied Munia. Black and Red Munia. Black-headed Nun.*

French. *Le Jacobin roux-noir. Le Mungul. Le Gros-bec Mungul.*

German. *Rothschwarze Munia. Die schwarzköpfige Nonnen-Amadine.*

Pora Munia; *Nuk-roul* at Mussouri (Blyth).

Habitat. India; extending its range to the Himalayas, Nepal, Burmah, Ceylon, Labuan, and Borneo.

Male. Head, neck, upper part of breast, mesial band, flanks, thighs and under tail-coverts black; whole of back, scapulars, wing-coverts, and outer edges of wings cinnamon brown, palest on the mantle; primaries and secondaries pale brown; lower part of rump and upper tail-coverts glistening maroon, tips of the latter and outer edges of the rectrices glistening orange; tail-feathers dark brown; chest and sides of body dark cinnamon-brown; axillaries and under wing-coverts yellowish-buff, inner webs buff; iris brown; bill translucent silvery white, bluish at the base: length 4·3, wing 2·1, tail 1·5, tarsus 0·63, culmen 0·5.

Female. Similar, but rather paler; the mesial band not so black, and slightly tinged with brown.

Young. Head, whole of back and wings dull brown; slightly tinged with rufous-brown on the rump; chin and throat buffish-white; breast and sides of body like the back; abdomen and under tail-coverts buffish-white.

Observ. During the past eighteen years I have had many opportunities of seeing *Munia sinensis* and *Munia atricapilla* alive and in skin, which I consider constitute two well-defined species; the former from Sumatra, the latter from India. In one the black mesial band is most decided, while in the other it is absent, but in the intermediate phases the black mesial band of the Indian bird is occasionally tinged with chestnut-brown; the crown and hind neck being slightly tinged with the same, which becomes entirely black in the fully adult birds.

In 1805 Vieillot, in his 'Oiseaux Chanteurs,' figured and described a Black-headed Munia under the name of 'Mungul' (*Loxia atricapilla*), from "Les Grandes-Indes," and, in doing so, he distinctly mentions that "*les parties postérieures sont de la couleur de la tête*"; he confirms this in the figure of the bird, which has a black abdomen, and again repeats the above quotation in the 'Nouveau Dictionnaire d'Histoire Naturelle,' xiii. 1817; he is even more concise in the Latin diagnosis of the same species in the 'Tableau Encyclopédique et Méthodique,' iii. 1823—viz., "*ab domine crissoque nigris.*" In comparing this latter description of the under-parts with that given by Mr. B. H. Hodgson in the 'Asiatic Researches,' vol. ix. (1836), of his *Munia rubronigra*, which is as follows: "Head, neck, and breast glossy black; centre of the belly, vent, and under tail-coverts the same"—and by a careful comparison of specimens, I have come to the conclusion that M. Vieillot's *Loxia atricapilla* is the true Indian species, and should have priority.

Messrs. Motley and Dillwyn state: "In Labuan, which is comparatively but little cleared and cultivated, this pretty Finch is rare; on the mainland of Borneo, however, it is a very common species, and immense flocks of them assemble and often clear a paddy-field in a single day; when feeding they are never still for a moment, and it is very amusing to watch them hanging on the leaves and stalks of the grass in every possible direction. Their nests (one of which is figured) are built in long grass by the sides of streams."

Mr. T. C. Jerom, in his 'Birds of India,' tells us: "This very closely allied species, which differs from the last (*Munia malacca*) only in having the belly chestnut in place of white, replaces it in the north of India, being found throughout Lower Bengal, and all along the foot of the Himalayas as far as the Dehra Doon, and also in some of the more wooded adjacent districts ; but it would appear to be rare in the open country of the N.W. Provinces. I have seen specimens from the eastern coast north of Madras, and Mr. Layard procured it in Ceylon, but it is certainly rare in Southern India. It is much more common in the countries to the eastward, Assam, and Burmah as far as the Tenasserim provinces, southwards of which it is replaced by *M. sinensis*, which wants the black abdominal stripe altogether.

" According to Mr. Frith the nest is ordinarily placed in a baubal tree in Lower Bengal, solitarily, and is composed of a large ball of the tufts of *Saccharum spontaneum*. I have always found its nest fixed to reeds or long grass, and suspect that Mr. Frith must have been mistaken in the identity of the owner of the nest above noticed, the more so because that is exactly the character, both as to materials and site, of the nest of the next species (*Munia punctulata*) noticed."

In ' Nests and Eggs of Indian Birds,' Mr. Allen Hume writes : " According to Mr. Hodgson the Chestnut-bellied Munia breeds in the lower valleys and cultivated plains of Nepal in open jungle or brushwood, forming a large globular nest in the midst of bamboos, thick bushes, or grass, on or close to the ground, composed of dry grass or straw loosely twisted together, and lined with finer rice straw. It lays from June to August four to six small, oval, pure white eggs.

" I have recently had an opportunity of examining a large series of this species, including specimens from various parts of India, Burmah, the Malay Peninsula, Sumatra, Borneo, Celebes, and I must say that I see great difficulty in dividing them as distinct species. They appear to grade wonderfully one into the other, and I should myself be disposed to suppress *sinensis*, Blyth, *brunneiceps*, Walden, &c., and retain all under Vieillot's name."

Captain W. V. Legge, in his ' Birds of Ceylon,' says : " Doubts exist whether Vieillot's name *atricapilla* (Ois. Chant. 84, pl. 53) applies to this bird or not. I retain Hodgson's name, however, as the species only takes a doubtful place among the ornis of Ceylon.

"Layard remarks that he found this Munia about Gallé; but as it has never since been seen in Ceylon, and is a bird which does not strictly belong to the south of India, its presence in the Galle district must have been owing to a flock having been let loose from a ship calling at the port. By such means, or by pairs escaping from confinement, the little Amaduvad became uncommon during several years of my residence at Colombo. I am not sure that it bred there; but it would appear that the present species (*Munia rubronigra*), if rightly identified, did not propagate itself in the south of Ceylon, or else it would have been met with subsequently.

"I do not find any other record of its occurrence in the South, or, in fact, any lower down the peninsula than Sambalpur. Mr. Cripps says it is nowhere common in Furreedpore; in North-eastern India it is, according to Mr. Inglis, common during the rains, breeding there in June, July, and August; in Upper Pegu Mr. Oates records it as likewise common; but to Tenasserim it is only a summer visitant, Mr. Davidson having observed it there from March until August. If identical with Vieillot's bird, it is found at Singapore, and at Sarawak and Labuan.

"In its habits and voice, Mr. Davidson remarks, 'they resemble other Munias, going about in larger or smaller flocks, and feeding on the ground, chiefly on the grass seeds.' Mr. Oates says it affects elephant-grass and swampy places in preference to others.

"The breeding season of this handsome Munia in Bengal, Burmah, and Cachar is from June until September; but in Tenasserim, further south, Mr. Davidson speaks of their laying in April and May. In Pegu Mr. Oates says it breeds in elephant-grass, attaching its nest to two or three stems at a height of four or five feet from the ground. It is 'a loose mass of grass, spherical, cylindrical, or heart-shaped; the inside is lined with finer grass, the following ends being brought forward to the entrance, which is small and difficult to find.' In 1874 Mr. C. Parker found it nesting in long grass near the top, the nest being a very conspicuous object; but in the following year, owing to the grass having been cut down, they selected prickly date-palms and small pines to build in. The eggs vary from two to five in number, and are elongated glossless ovals, from 0·58 to 0·68 inches in length, by 0·4 to 0·47 inch in breadth."

Mr. J. Scully, in his 'Contributions to the Ornithology of Nepal,' published in 'Stray Feathers,' 1879, adds the following details to this species, of which he obtained—" Twelve specimens, Nepal valley. Length, 4·4 to 4·65; expanse, 7·1 to 7·5; wing, 2·1 to 2·2; tail, 1·5 to 1·6; bill, from gape, 0·4 to 0·45; bill, at front, 0·48 to 0·5; closed wings short of tail, 0·95 to 1·1.

"Bill leaden blue; irides dark brown; feet dark plumbeous.

"Young birds, obtained about the middle of September, are uniform earthy, with, in some specimens, a small spot or two of chestnut appearing on the breast. The adults of this species have the bills stronger and deeper than in *punctulata*. The young birds above mentioned have the bill about the same size as in *punctulata*, adult.

"This Munia is common in the central part of the Nepal valley from the end of May to October, frequenting rice-fields and gardens. A nest taken on the 13th July in the Residency grounds was placed in a thorny hedge; it was a large globular structure with a trumpet-shaped entrance at one side; it contained five white eggs, slightly set."

Mr. R. B. Sharpe states that "this species was introduced into Labuan by Mr. Low, who sent several specimens and their eggs, which are dull white, like those of *Munia fuscans*, from which they are not to be distinguished." I have a MS. note to the effect that Kelaart sent home specimens of *Amadina rubronigra*, Horsf. (Nos. 143, 144) from Nuwara Elliya, in Ceylon, between the years 1852–3; if these birds are still in existence, I shall be pleased to get more details respecting them.

I am indebted to Prof. A. Newton and M. A. Boucard for the loan of several specimens.

Specimens examined.

No.	Sex.	Mus.	Locality	Length	Wing.	Tail.	Tars.	Culm.
a.	♂	F. B.	Borneo.	4·3	2·1	1·5	0·63	0·5
b.	♂	E. B.	Borneo.	4·15	2·0	1·55	0·6	0·47
c.	?	E. B.	Nepal (*Hodgson*).	3·65	2·1	1·5	0·65	0·45
d.	♂	E. B.	India.	4·0	2·15	1·55	0·6	0·5
e.	?	E. B.	India.	4·9	2·2	1·7	0·62	0·5
f.	♂	E. B.	India.	4·0	2·1	1·45	0·65	0·45
g.	♀ jun.	E. B.	Madras.	4·0	2·1	1·45	0·6	0·42
h.	♂	E. B.	Borneo.	4·2	2·15	1·55	0·65	0·45
i.	♀	E. B.	India.	3·9	2·1	1·5	0·65	0·45
j.	?	E. B.	Borneo.	4·15	2·1	1·4	0·65	0·5

No.	Sex.	Mus.	Locality.	Length.	Wing.	Tail.	Tars.	Culm.
k.	?	E. B.	Doon.	4·35	2·15	1·55	0·65	0·5
l.	Adult	Acad. Cantab.	India (*Hamilton*).	3·9	2·25	1·35	0·65	0·45
m.	Imm.	Acad. Cantab.	India (*Strickland*).	3·85	2·15	1·45	0·6	0·4
n.	♂	A. Boucard.	India.	4·2	2·1	1·45	0·6	0·6

The figures (Plate V. figs. 1 and 2) are taken from *a* and *g* in my own collection.

MUNIA SUMATRENSIS.
THE SUMATRAN MUNIA.
PLATE V. (FIG. 3).

The Chinese Sparrow, Edwards, Nat. Hist. Birds, i. p. 43, pl. 43. ♂ (1743).
Passer fuscus, capite nigro, Klein, Hist. Av. Prodr. p. 90 (1750).
Der chinesische Sperling, Catesby et Edw. Samml. ausl. selt. Vögel. i. Tab. lxxv. (1751).
Coccothraustes sinensis, Briss. Ornith. iii. p. 235 (1760).
Coccothraustes sinensis, Briss. Syn. Meth. i. p. 374 (1763).
Loxia malacca, Linn. Syst. Nat. i. p. 302, var. β (1766); Gmel. Syst. Nat. ii. p. 851, var. β (1788); Lath. Ind. Orn. i. p. 386, var. β (1790); Shaw, Gen. Zool. ix. p. 332, var. β (1815).
Malacca Grosbeak, Lath. Gen. Syn. iii. p. 141, var. A (1783); Lath. Gen. Syn. Suppl. i. p. 152 (1787); Lath. Gen. Hist. Birds, v. p. 244, var. A (1822).
Munia sinensis, Blyth, Cat. Birds Mus. A. S. B. Append. p. 337 (1849); Horsf. et Moore, Cat. Birds Mus. E.-Ind. Comp. ii. p. 508 (1856–8); Moore, Proc. Zool. Soc. 1859, p. 444; Swinh. Proc. Zool. Soc. 1871, p. 304; David et Oust. Oiseaux Chine, p. 342 (1877).
Amadina sinensis, Gray et Mitch. Gen. Birds, ii. p. 370, pt. (1849).
Amadina sinensis, Gray, Hand-List Birds, ii. p. 54 (1870).
Munia malacca, Bonap. Consp. Gen. Av. p. 452, pt. (1850).
Munia malacca, Bernstein, Journ. für Ornith. 1861, p. 181.
Munia rubronigra, Swinh. Ibis, 1860, p. 61, 1861, p. 45.
Munia atricapilla, pt. Walden, Trans. Zool. Soc. 1875, p. 208.
Munia atricapilla, Salvad. Ornit. Papuasia, p. 438 (1881).

Figure. Edwards, Nat. Hist. Birds, i. pl. 43, male (1743).

Dutch. *Jacobijn.*

English. *Chinese Sparrow. Malacca Grosbeak*, variety. *Chinese, or Chestnut and black-headed Jacobin or Munia. Black-headed Finch Chestnut-bellied Finch, or Munia.*

French. *Le Gros-bec de la Chine. Capucin à tête noire. Le Gros-bec Mungul. Le Jacobin de la Chine.*

German. *Der chinesische Sperling. Die chinesische Munia. Der Mungul, Mongole oder Chinese.*

Habitat. Java and Sumatra. Pinang (*Canton*); Sumatra (*Raffles*); introduced into China (*Swinhoe*).

Male. Head, neck, and upper part of breast black, slightly glossed; rest of upper and under parts cinnamon-brown, paler on the mantle; lower part of rump glistening maroon; upper tail-coverts edged with glistening ferruginous; tail-feathers pale cinnamon, edged with ferruginous; wings like the back; lower part of abdomen and under tail-coverts very faintly tinged with darker cinnamon brown; iris dark brown; bill translucent silvery white, blue at the base; feet plumbeous: length 3·65, wing 1·95, tail 1·45, tars. 0·6, culm. 0·4.

Female. Similar, but without the tinge of darker cinnamon brown on the abdomen and under tail-coverts.

Young. Very pale rufous brown; chin, throat, and abdomen buffish-white.

Observ. In some specimens of this species the tinge of dark cinnamon-brown on the abdomen and under tail-coverts is rather more decided than in others; but the absence of the black mesial stripe will always determine the species. It is decidedly much smaller than *Munia atricapilla*. The young of the various species of this group are so alike, it is with great difficulty that they can be separated.

This Munia, which is well figured and described by Edwards in his 'Natural History of Birds,' published in 1743, under the name of 'Chinese Sparrow,' is without doubt the same species which Brisson characterized in his 'Ornithologie,' published in 1760, as *Coccothraustes sinensis*. The absence of the black mesial band and black under tail-coverts in the present species is a well-marked distinction, which separates it at once from the 'Mungul,' *Loxia atricapilla*, of India, figured and described by Vieillot in his 'Oiseaux Chanteurs,' published in 1805.

The true habitat of this pretty *Munia* appears to be the islands of Pinang, Sumatra, Java, and probably the smaller islands in close proximity, and the Malayan Peninsula. Mr. R. Swinhoe includes it in his birds of China, but remarks: "I almost doubt whether this is a Chinese bird, as I have never yet met with it in a wild state. It is occasionally to be seen in cages, but I think it comes from the Straits."

To distinguish this *Munia*, which is almost exclusively a Sumatran bird, and not an indigenous species of China, only having been introduced as a cage bird to that country, I propose to call it the Sumatran Munia, *Munia sumatrensis*, the appellation *Munia sinensis* being inappropriate.

We are indebted to Dr. H. A. Bernstein for his observations "On the Nests and Eggs of the Birds of Java," which appeared in the 'Journal für Ornithologie' for 1861, from which I transcribe the details respecting this bird: "*Burung Prit* of the Malays and Sundanese. This smaller species appears as numerously as the two preceding (*Munia ferruginea* and *M. oryzivora*) everywhere in western Java, in inhabited neighbourhoods, as well as in places overgrown with alang-mang, glagah, in short in bushy places. On the other hand, in high forests you will seek in vain for one bird, as also for the species related to it. It is a dear, harmless little bird, who lives, except during the breeding season, in small companies or families, whose members are friendly together, and who are seldom far apart from one another. It is so tame that it will allow a person to come quite close up to it, and one often, therefore, has an opportunity of observing its ways and mode of living from a near point of view. Its voice, which is often heard, especially when it first takes flight, sounds delicate and gentle, '*piet*,' or rather '*piuht*,' and has given rise to its Malayan name. Its food is composed of all kinds of small seeds and grain; grains of rice are too hard and large for it when they are ripe; it probably, therefore, visits the fallow-lying rice-fields only on account of the numerous plants which spring up very rapidly between the stubble and soon bear seed. When caged it is easily fed on rice boiled in water, or, even better, on small seeds and grains. It usually builds its nest at a slight elevation from the ground, in the twigs of a bush or low tree, often close to much-trodden roads and paths. In form the nest is more or less round, with an entrance at the side opening upwards transversely, and is composed of small roots and stalks of various plants, principally of grasses, which materials are generally very loosely woven on the outside of the nest, but which, on the contrary, on the inner side, are more closely and carefully twisted together. The number found in one nest of the shining white eggs, which are 14 to 15 millimetres in length, and whose greatest diameter measured obliquely is 10 to 11 millimetres, amounts usually to five, seven sometimes, and rarely only to four."

For the knowledge of the existence of this species as a permanent resident in the Malayan Peninsula, we are indebted to Lieut. H. B. Kelham, who gives a very complete contribution on 'Malayan Ornithology,' which appeared in the 'Ibis' for 1881. He remarks that "*Munia atricapilla* (Vieill.) is common, though not so much so as *M. maja*. Like that species, it congregates in large flocks. My note book says :—

"Saigong, Perak, 23rd May, 1877. To-day, on the low ground bordering Saigong Jhell, I shot several Munias out of a large flock which rose from the paddy. They are very like *M. maja*, except that they have the head black instead of white.

"One of these, a male, is $4\frac{5}{12}$ inches in length, irides red-brown, beak plumbeous, head, neck, and upper part of breast black, upper tail-coverts golden-chestnut, rest of plumage chestnut, becoming dusky on the tail; its stomach contained a great many minute particles of quartz.

"At first I thought this bird was *Munia rubronigra* (Hodgs.), which it much resembles; but that species has the middle of the belly, the vent, and the under tail-coverts *black* instead of chestnut."

Mr. H. O. Forbes also procured this bird in Sumatra.

Specimens examined.

No.	Sex.	Mus.	Locality.	Length.	Wing.	Tail.	Tars.	Culm.
a.	♂	E. B.	Java.	3·65	1·95	1·15	0·6	0·4
b.	?	E. B.	Java.	3·7	2·0	1·45	0·6	0·45
c.	♂	E. B.	Sumatra (H. O. Forbes).	3·7	2·0	1·4	0·6	0·45
d.	juv.	E. B.	?.	3·95	2·2	1·3	0·6	0·4
e.	♂	A. Boucard.	Cochinchina, *Introduced*.	4·4	2·0	1.3	0·6	0·4

The figure (Plate V. fig. 3) is taken from the male *a* in my own collection.

PYRRHULA ERYTHROCEPHALA.
THE RED-HEADED BULLFINCH.
PLATE III.

Pyrrhula erythrocephala, Vigors, Proc. Zool. Soc. 1831, p. 174.
Pyrrhula erythrocephala, Gould, Cent. Birds Himal. Mount. pl. xxxii. (1832).
Pyrrhula erythrocephalus, Blyth, Journ. A. S. Beng. xiii. 1844, p. 951.
Pyrrhula erythrocephala, Hodgs. Gray's Zool. Misc. p. 85 (1844).
Pyrrhula erythrocephala, Gray et Mitch. Genera Birds, ii. p. 387 (1844).
Pyrrhula erythrocephala, Gray, Cat. Hodgs. Coll. Brit. Mus. p. 111 (1846).
Pyrrhula erythrocephalus, Blyth, Cat. Birds Mus. A. S. Beng. p. 123 (1849).
Pyrrhula erythrocephala, Bonap. Consp. Gen. Av. i. p. 525 (1850); Gould, Birds of Asia, v. pl. 36 (1853); Eyton, Cat. Birds, p. 262 (1856); Horsf. et Moore, Cat. Birds Mus. E.-Ind. Comp. ii. p. 454 (1856-8); Adams, Proc. Zool. Soc. 1858, p. 483, 1859, p. 177; Gray, Cat. Hodgs. Coll. Brit. Mus. p. 60 (1863); Jerdon, Birds of India, ii. p. 389 (1863); Blyth, Ibis, 1863, p. 442; Beavan, Ibis, 1867, p. 142, 1868, p. 176; Pelz. Ibis, 1868, p. 318; Gray, Hand-List Birds, ii. p. 99 (1870); Tristr. Ibis, 1871, p. 232; Brooks, Stray-Feathers, 1875, p. 255; Hume, Stray-Feathers, 1879, p. 108; Brooks, Stray-Feathers, 1879, p. 488; Russ, Stubenvögel, p. 502 (1879); Salv. Cat. Birds Strickl. Coll. p. 203 (1882); Marsh. Ibis, 1884, p. 420; Stewart, Zoologist, 1886, p. 321; Sharpe, Cat. Birds Brit. Mus. xii. p. 457 (1888).
Pyrrhula erythrocephala, Hodgs. Icon. Brit. Mus. pl. 308, fig. 1-4.

Figures. Gould, Cent. Birds Himal. Mts. pl. xxxii.; id. Birds of Asia, v. pl. 36.

English. *Red-headed Bullfinch.*

French. *Le Bouvreuil à tête rouge.*

German. *Rothkopfgimpel. Der rothköpfige Gimpel.*

Habitat. W. Himalayas, Nepal; rare in Sikkim and Bootan.

Male. Crown of head, nape, and sides of neck rich orange-brown; frontal band black, edged with ashy-grey; mantle, scapulars, and back ashy-grey, edged with a narrow blackish band across the lower back; rump white; lesser and median wing-coverts ashy-grey, tinged with orange-brown; greater coverts pale ashy-grey, with a purplish basal square patch on the outer webs; primaries and coverts black, slightly edged with purple; secondaries, upper tail-coverts, and outer edges of tail-feathers glossy steel blue, transversely barred with black, inner webs and outer rectrices black; cheeks, throat, breast, sides, and axillaries dull orange-brown; under wing-coverts, belly, and under tail-coverts white; under surface of wings, and tail, dull blackish-brown; "bill black; legs pale fleshy-brown; iris light brown" (*Jerdon*): length 5·5, wing 3·0, tail 2·6, tars. 0·65, culm. 0·4.

Female. Crown, nape, and sides of head yellowish-olive-green; frontal band dull black, edged with pale grey, which blends into the crown of the head; hind neck, mantle, scapulars, and back slaty-brown, faintly tinged with olive; rump white; wings, coverts, and tail as in the male, but duller; chin brownish-black, faintly edged with buff; cheeks, sides of neck, throat, and under parts pale slaty-brown, faintly tinged with orange-brown; thighs and under tail-coverts white; axillaries, under surface of wings and coverts whitish; iris, bill, and feet as in the male.

Young Male. Similar, but much paler, especially the under parts, which are grey, tinged with orange-brown on the sides of the neck and body.

THE Red-headed Bullfinch was first made known to science by Mr. N. A. Vigors, who characterized it in the 'Proceedings of the Zoological Society' for 1831, and figured for the first time in Mr. John Gould's 'Century of Birds from the Himalayan Mountains,' which was published in 1832, and refigured with the female in his 'Birds of Asia' in 1853.

From all I can gather respecting this very beautiful Bullfinch, it appears to inhabit the higher ranges of the mountainous regions of the Himalayas, Nepal, and Bootan; and although the species does not associate in vast numbers, it is tolerably plentiful in those regions, being scattered over the country in small flocks of from six to twelve in number. It is remarkable for a bird like the present, so conspicuous for its beautiful plumage, and having been known to all our Indian ornithologists for over seventy years, that its breeding-grounds have remained, like those of many of its congeners, undiscovered; we therefore still have to record the structure and position of its nest and the details of its eggs.

Mr. A. Leith-Adams (P. Z. S. 1858) tells us it is "confined to the Himalaya ranges. Never seen in the plains of India. By no means common anywhere. Its habits exactly similar to the *Pyrrhula vulgaris*; but its call-note is not so loud. Frequents dense jungle. The *P. erythrocephala* was not seen during my visit to Cashmere, although frequently observed on the ranges near Simla."

In the 'Birds of India,' vol. ii., published in 1863, Mr. Jerdon remarks: "This Bullfinch has much the form of the European bird, but the tail is slightly longer and more forked. It is found throughout the Himalayas, more common in the north-west, somewhat rare in the south-east. I procured it at Darjeeling, but it is rare there, and only a winter visitant; and Mr. Blyth had not previously seen specimens from Sikkim. At Mussooree, Hutton states it to be common in winter, feeding on the ground, as well as on berry-bearing bushes, and it perches high on the top of trees."

It has been procured at Spita, in Ladak, by Dr. A. Stoliczka; at Darjeeling by Captain Beavan; in Kotegurh, in Thibet, according to Herr A. v. Pelzeln; at Dangali by Mr. W. E. Brooks, who says: "This was the only Bullfinch I saw near Darjeeling, and on the Senchal hill a little beyond the grassy open, where I obtained *Anthus ludovicianus*." Major C. H. T. Marshall in his notes on the birds of Chamba says: " I met with a flock of ten or twelve Bullfinches early in April at Dalhousie; as I had no gun, I failed to secure a specimen. I watched them for some time, and believe they belonged to this species."

The only remaining notice of this bird is contained in Surgeon-General L. C. Stewart's ' Natural History and Sport in the Himalayas,' published in the ' Zoologist,' 1886, as follows: "Fagoo, October 14.—I had a very successful day, and might have obtained many more specimens, but, as it was, got more than enough for the stuffer to prepare properly. Starting at daylight, I strolled about for three hours in the beautiful 'hanging' woods; many of the shrubs and trees were assuming their autumnal tints. Wild fruits and berries were in abundance; raspberry, barberry, and others, affording ample food to hosts of birds of many kinds. I first secured a pair of Bullfinches, *Pyrrhula erythrocephala*, a pretty species which I had found at Kussowlie the previous spring, and I got three or four more before leaving Fagoo."

Specimens examined.

No.	Sex.	Mus.	Locality.	Length.	Wing.	Tail.	Tars.	Culm.
a.	♂ Imm.	E. B.	Kotekhaie (*Hume*).	5·5	3·1	2·7	0·65	0·35
b.	♂ Imm.	E. B.	Darjeeling (*Beavan*).	6·3	3·05	2·75	0·65	0·4
c.	♂ Imm.	E. B.	N. India (*Hodgson*).	4·9	3·0	2·6	0·65	0·4
d.	♂ Imm.	E. B.	Darjeeling (*Beavan*).	4·85	3·0	2·55	0·65	0·4
e.	♂	E. B.	India.	5·5	3·1	2·7	0·6	0·4
f.	♂	E. B.	Himalayas.	5·5	3·0	2·6	0.65	0·4
g.	♂	E. B.	Himalayas.	5·35	3·0	2·7	0·65	0·35
h.	♀	E. B.	Doon.	5·6	3·0	2·65	0·62	0·35
i.	♀	E. B.	Himalayas.	0·0	3·0	0·0	0·65	0·4

The figures (Plate III.) are taken from *f* and *h* in my own collection.

CARDINALIS PHŒNICEUS.
VENEZUELAN CARDINAL.
PLATE II.

Fringilla cardinalis, Licht. Verz. Doubl. Mus. Berl. p. 89 (1823).
Cardinalis phœniceus, Gould, MS.
Cardinalis phœniceus, Bonap. Proc. Zool. Soc. 1837, p. 111.
Cardinalis phœniceus, Gray et Mitch. Gen. Birds, ii. p. 358 (1844).
Cardinalis granadensis, Lafr. Rev. Zool. 1847, p. 74.
Cardinalis phœniceus, Bonap. Consp. Gen. Av. p. 501 (1850).
Cardinalis phœniceus, Licht. Nomencl. Av. Mus. Berol. p. 44 (1854).
Cardinalis phœniceus, Eyton, Cat. Birds, p. 266 (1856).
Cardinalis phœniceus, Sclater, Cat. of Amer. Birds, p. 100. 1862.
Cardinalis phœniceus, Taylor, Ibis, 1864, p 83.
Cardinalis phœniceus, Scl. et Salv. Exot. Ornith. p. 125, pl. 63 ♂ et ♀ (1868).
Cardinalis phœniceus, Scl. et Salv. Proc. Zool. Soc. 1868, pp. 167, 170.
Cardinalis phœniceus, Scl. et Salv. Proc. Zool. Soc. 1869, p. 251.
Cardinalis phœniceus, Finsch, Proc. Zool. Soc. 1870, p. 553.
Cardinalis phœniceus, Gray, Hand-List Birds, ii. p. 102 (1870).
Cardinalis phœniceus, Scl. et Salv. Nomencl. Av. Neotr. p. 27 (1873).
Coccothraustes phœniceus, Russ, Stubenvögel, p. 540 (1879).
Cardinalis phœniceus, Sharpe, Cat. Birds Brit. Mus. xii. p. 116 (1888).

Figure. Scl. et Salv. Exot. Ornith. pl. 63.

English. *Venezuelan Cardinal. Colombian Cardinal.*

French. *Le Cardinal de Vénézuela.*

German. *Der purpurrothe Kardinal.*

Habitat. Colombia, Venezuela, and Trinidad.

Male. Bright vermilion red, clearer on the head, crest, rump, and under parts; mantle, scapulars, and lower back rosy brick-red; wings and coverts pale brown, more or less edged with rosy brick-red; tail brick-red, tinged with bright vermilion on the outer webs; frontal band extremely narrow, not uniting on the culmen, and chin black; axillaries, under surface of wings, and coverts vermilion, tinged with pink; "iris reddish-brown" (*Goering*); bill whitish horn at the base, brown on the culmen and tip: length 6·45, wing 3·2, tail 3·3, tars. 0·85, culm. 0·65.

Female. Above ashy-brown, tinged with rufous on the rump; narrow frontal band whitish, intermixed with blackish bristles; crest-feathers dull vermilion; wing-coverts and secondaries like the back, faintly tinged with brick red; primaries dull brown, outer webs brick-red; tail dull brick-red, with dusky edges; moustachial line and chin blackish; throat and abdomen ashy-white; breast, sides, and flanks dull rufous-brown; axillaries, under wing-coverts, edges of inner webs rosy-red; bill darker than in the male.

Young. Similar to the female, but rather more ashy on the mantle and scapulars.

Observ. The brilliant colour of the male is gradually assumed in patches, variously and unequally distributed over the body.

THE first notice of a species of Cardinal corresponding to the present bird, which I have been able to discover, is *Fringilla cardinalis* (n. *Lax. card.* Lin. Cayana), in a supplementary list of birds added by Dr. H. Lichtenstein to his 'Verzeichniss der Doubletten des Zoologischen Museums, Berlin,' p. 89 (1823), which I presume refers to this Venezuelan Cardinal, although I am unable to find any reference to its having been brought from Cayenne; but Lichtenstein's examples were possibly conveyed from Venezuela, and accidentally mixed with a collection of Cayenne skins.

I transcribe the following remarks respecting this species from Messrs. Sclater and Salvin's 'Exotic Ornithology,' published in 1868. They say: "The Venezuelan Cardinal is a beautiful representative of the well-known northern species, the 'Red Bird' or 'Virginian Cardinal, of the United States. It is of nearly the same form, but is readily distinguished by its smaller size, longer crest, and the absence of the black band on the forehead.

"This bird was first described by the late Prince Bonaparte in a paper published in the 'Zoological Society's Proceedings' for 1837, under the

MS. name applied to it by Mr. John Gould in his collection. The habitat there given is somewhat vague, being described as 'the country southward of the Bay of Honduras.' We are, however, enabled to state with certainty that its true *patria* is the littoral of Venezuela."

In the 'Revue Zoologique' for 1847, M. Lafresnaye described and renamed the present species *Cardinalis granadensis*; this being the only other synonym which this fortunate bird possesses.

In the 'Ibis' for 1864, Mr. E. C. Taylor says: "The low sandy coast near the town of Barcelona in Venezuela, covered with dense bush and low trees, is the only locality where I met with this beautiful species; there, however, it was tolerably plentiful. I do not believe it ever occurs in Trinidad." But Dr. O. Finsch has, since Mr. Taylor wrote the above, received specimens which confirm its existence in that island.

Mr. A. Goering procured this bird at Carúpano, and states that it is "found only on the coast, and not met with a few leagues in the interior. San Esteban is situated about six English miles inland from Puerto Cabello, in a valley, through which runs a small river. Most of the birds obtained here are different from those found in Eastern Venezuela, where my first collections were formed. It is singular that *Cardinalis phœniceus*, so common near Carúpano, is very rare here. I have never seen this bird on the hills, but only on the plains near the coast, which are covered with a simple vegetation of *Mimosa, Cactus*, &c."

On the authority of Dr. O. Finsch this species was received in a collection of birds sent to Mr. Kohlmann from the island of Trinidad.

The specimen *a* in my own collection is one of the types described by Bonaparte in the P. Z. S. 1837; the other is now in the British Museum.

Specimens examined.

No.	Sex.	Mus.	Locality.	Length.	Wing.	Tail.	Tars.	Culm.
a.	♂	E. B.	Honduras ? (*Bonaparte*).	6·35	3·25	3·3	0·9	0·7
b.	♂	E. B.	Cumana (*Bridges*).	6·15	3·2	3·3	0·85	0·65
c.	♂ imm.	E. B.	Cumana (*Bridges*).	6·1	3·1	3·05	0·9	0·65
d.	♂	A. Boucard.	Carúpano, Venezuela (*Goering*).	7.1	3·15	3·4	0·9	0·75

The figures (Plate II.) are taken from *b* in my own collection; that of the female from a specimen in the British Museum.

PHRYGILUS ALAUDINUS.
THE ALAUDINE FINCH.
PLATE II.

Fringilla alaudina, Kittl. Kupf. Vög. p. 18, pl. 23, fig. 2 (1832).
Fringilla alaudina, Gould, Darw. Zool. Beagle, p. 94 (1841).
Fringilla alaudina, Fraser, Proc. Zool. Soc. 1843, p. 113.
Fringilla alaudina, Russ, Stubenvögel, p. 476 (1879).
Emberiza guttata, Meyen, Nova Acta Acad. Leop. xvi. Suppl. p. 85, pl. 12, fig. 1 (1834).
Emberiza guttata, D'Orb. et Lafr. Mag. de Zool. 1837, p. 78.
Passerina guttata, Eydoux et Gerv. Mag. de Zool. 1836, p. 22, pl. 70.
Euspiza alaudina, Gray et Mitch. Gen. Birds, ii. p. 376 (1844).
Chlorospiza alaudina, Gay, Fauna Chilena, Zool. p. 357 (1847).
Chlorospiza alaudina, Phil. An. Univ. de Chile, xxxi. 1868, p. 265.
Fringilla (Niphœa) laciniata, Peale, United S. Expl. Exped. viii. p. 121 (1848).
Phrygilus guttatus, Licht. Nomencl. Av. Mus. Berol. p. 43 (1854).
Corydospiza alaudina, Sundev. Av. Disp. Tent. p. 33 (1872).
Phrygilus alaudinus, Bonap. Consp. Gen. Av. p. 476 (1850); Cab. Mus. Hein. i. p. 135 (1851); Burm. Syst. Ueber. Th. Bras. iii. p. 233 (1856); Eyton, Cat. Birds, p. 251 (1856); Cassin, United Stat. Expl. Exped. p. 136 (1858); Scl. Proc. Zool. Soc. 1858, p. 552, 1860, p. 87, Cat. Amer. Birds, p. 111 (1862); Scl. Proc. Zool. Soc. 1867, p. 322; Scl. et Salv. Proc. Zool. Soc. 1867, p. 985, 1868, pp. 568, 569; Gray, Hand-List Birds, ii. p. 89 (1870); Scl. Proc. Zool. Soc. 1871, p. 496; Scl. et Salv. Nomencl. Av. Neotr. p. 31 (1873); Tacz. Proc. Zool. Soc. 1874, p. 521; Salv. Proc. Zool. Soc. 1883, p. 421; Scl. Vert. Anim. Gard. Zool. Soc. p. 249 (1883); Berl. et Tacz. Proc. Zool. Soc. 1884, p. 294, 1885, p. 85; Tacz.

Ornith. Pérou, iii. p. 35 (1886); Sharpe, Cat. Birds Brit. Mus. xii. p. 793 (1888).

Figures. Kittl. Kupf. Vög. pl. 23, fig. 2. Meyen, Nova Acta Acad. Leop. pl. 12, fig. 1. Eydoux et Gerv. Mag. de Zool. pl. 70.

English. *Alaudine Finch,* or *Lark Finch.*
French. *Pinson-Alouette.*
German. *Der Lerchen-Ammersperling.*
Chilian. *Pichiquina. Platero.*
Ecuadorian. *Trigo.*

Habitat. Chili, Bolivia, and High Peru, extending its range into Ecuador.

Male. Head, whole of back, chin, throat, chest, and sides of body nearly uniform slaty-grey; lores slaty-black; mantle and scapulars broadly striated with brownish-black; rump and upper tail-coverts a little paler than the back; primaries, secondaries, greater and median wing-coverts dull black, edged with silvery-grey, browner on the secondaries; lesser wing-coverts, axillaries, and under wing-coverts bright slaty-grey; tail dull black, with an elongated white patch on the inner webs of all the feathers, except the two centre ones, which are dull brown; basal half of the outer webs of the first rectrices white; belly, flanks, thighs, and under tail-coverts white; "iris dark brown; legs and feet light chrome-yellow" (*H. Whitely*): length 5·65, wing 3·05, tail 2·5, tars. 0·85, culm. 0·5.

Female. Above pale earthy-brown, greyish on the hind neck, rump, and upper tail-coverts, each feather more or less narrowly and broadly streaked with dull brown; primaries pale brown, slightly edged with greyish-white on the outer webs; secondaries, greater and median wing-coverts darker brown, broadly edged with buff and pale reddish-brown; lesser coverts pale slaty-grey; tail as in the male, but narrowly edged, and tipped with silvery-grey; cheeks, sides of neck, and breast pale buff, narrowly striated with brown; lores, chin, and throat buffish-white; sides of body like the back; belly, flanks, thighs, and under tail-coverts white; under surface of wing and axillaries silvery-grey; bill yellowish-brown; feet yellow: length 5·45, wing 2·85, tail 2·25, tars. 0·8, culm. 0·45.

Young. Above earthy brown, centre of each feather very broadly marked with dark dull brown; wings, coverts, and tail dull brown, with very faint buff edges; median coverts edged with white; sides of face, neck, and breast dirty white, streaked with ashy-brown; sides darker; lores, chin, and throat dirty white; belly, flanks, thighs, and under tail-coverts white; the white patches on the inner webs of rectrices very small; under surface of wing and axillaries silvery-grey; bill and feet yellowish-brown: length 5·7, wing 2·85, tail 2·35, tars. 0·85, culm. 0·5.

Observ. From a series of thirty specimens of both sexes in my own collection, I am enabled to form a continuous series of phases in the plumage of this beautiful bird. The very old males become pure slaty-grey on the back, throat, and breast, with black centres to the feathers of the mantle and scapulars; some have blackish tips to the feathers of the nape and hind neck, while others have a patch of buffish-red, faintly striated with brown on the nape, the inner secondaries being broadly edged with reddish-brown. The young males are greatly varied with slaty-grey, with the whole of the upper parts striated with dark brown. The lesser wing-coverts of the adult male, female, and young are remarkable for their uniform slaty-grey.

The Alaudine Finch was first described by F. H. von Kittlitz in his 'Kupfertafeln zur Naturgeschichte der Vögel,' in 1832, under the name of *Fringilla alaudina*; in 1834 Meyen redescribed it under the name of *Emberiza guttata*, having a female or immature specimen for his type. Mr. G. Gray in 1844 placed the species under the genus *Euspiza*; C. Gay in his 'Fauna Chilena,' 1847, selected *Chlorospiza* for the generic term. It was not until 1850 that Bonaparte in his 'Conspectus Generum Avium' restored it to the genus *Phrygilus*, and in 1872 Sundevall created a new generic appellation (*Corydospiza*) for it.

This beautiful delicate grey bird is an inhabitant of the mountainous regions of Chili, Bolivia, Peru, and Ecuador; and from the number of localities in which it has been procured, and the various seasons of its capture, I was led to suppose that it migrated into the two latter places. However, I have come to the conclusion that it is a permanent resident throughout the year. The climate of these countries at the altitudes in which it is found varies but little; probably the great snowstorms during the winter season may drive it down from the higher ranges of the Andes to the warmer and more sheltered valleys and plains of the coast.

In Chili, however, it appears to be more abundant than in any other part of the western slopes of the Cordillera. M. A. D'Orbigny collected his specimens at Sicasica in Bolivia. Mr. Charles Darwin "obtained it in the neighbourhood of Valparaiso." Mr. Bridges says: "This little bird makes its appearance in the summer months; inhabits corn-fields; builds its nest on the ground, and lays from four to five whitish eggs with brown spots. The native name is *Pichiquina*." Mr. Peale " obtained it in the vicinity of Valparaiso, Chili, in the month of May, at which season it is not common ; it frequents low bushes, and is much on the ground. Its general habits and appearance resemble those of the Snow-bird of North America (*Niphæa hyemalis*); the tail, however, appears bordered with black while the birds are flying, instead of having the white margin of the northern species."

It was procured by Mr. L. Fraser above Punin, near Riobamba in Ecuador, at an elevation of nearly 10,000 feet above the sea-level, where he says it is found "on the small bushes and stones, taking flight like a Flycatcher or Humming-bird, although no insects were found in the stomach." He also sent home examples of this bird from Calacali, which is situated at a height of 8,000 feet above the sea-level, where he remarks it was " not uncommon ; food, small seeds and grubs ; lives entirely on the ground amongst the heather ; when disturbed, takes an undulating flight for about sixty or eighty yards."

Among the collections made during Mr. H. Whitely's travels in West Peru, many examples of this species in all phases of plumage were procured ; he first met with it at Islay, a seaport town below Arequipa ; in this latter locality, at an elevation of 7,800 feet above the sea-level, the bird was more abundant. " A nest of this species, taken near Arequipa in March 1868, is in Mr. Whitely's collection ; it is described as made of coarse grass, lined with finer grass and placed on the ground in fields of lucerne. The eggs are very like those of our Yellow-hammer (*Emberiza citrinella*)."

Professor W. Nation says : " In 1867 I discovered this beautiful bird on a large plain, covered with low bushes, a few miles from Lima. It was feeding on the ground, after the manner of a *Zonotrichia*. Subsequently I have made hundreds of visits to this plain, and have shown the examples to many sportsmen, but have neither seen it again myself nor been able to obtain any information respecting it. I am therefore of opinion that its occurrence in this plain was accidental, and hope to discover its true abode in some of the valleys of the Andes."

M. Jelski found it plentiful near Lima and Haunta in W. Peru. Capt. A. H. Markham sent it from Coquimbo, and from the volcanic region of Chimborazo, in Ecuador ; M. Stolzmann has sent examples, which were collected in April.

Specimens examined.

No.	Sex.	Mus.	Locality.	Length.	Wing.	Tail.	Tars.	Culm.
a.	♂	E. Bartlett.	Arequipa, Peru (*H. Whitely*).	5·65	3·05	2·5	0·85	0·5
b.	♂	,,	Arequipa, Peru (*H. Whitely*).	5·75	2·95	2·4	0·85	0·5
c.	♂	,,	Arequipa, Peru (*H. Whitely*).	5·9	3·05	2·5	0·9	0·5
d.	♂	,,	Arequipa, Peru (*H. Whitely*).	5·45	2·9	2·35	0·85	0·5
e.	♂	,,	Arequipa, Peru (*H. Whitely*).	5·75	3·0	2·45	0·9	0·5
f.	♀	,,	Arequipa, Peru (*H. Whitely*).	5·7	2·85	2·35	0·85	0·5
g.	♂	,,	Tinta, Peru (*H. Whitely*).	5·9	3·1	2·6	0·9	0·5
h.	♂	,,	Chili (*Reed*).	5·75	3·1	2·6	0·85	0·5
i.	♂	,,	Chili (*Reed*).	6·05	3·05	2·5	0·85	0·5
j.	? imm.	,,	Chili (*Reed*).	5·6	3·05	2·45	0·85	0·5
k.	♂	,,	Chili (*Reed*).	5·6	3·05	2·4	0·85	0·5
l.	♀	,,	Chili (*Reed*).	5·5	2·95	2·30	0·8	0·45
m.	♂	,,	Santiago, Chili (*Weisshaupt*).	5·55	3·05	2·5	0·8	0·5
n.	♀	,,	Santiago, Chili (*Weisshaupt*).	5·05	2·75	2·2	0·8	0·45
o.	♀	,,	Chili (*Reed*).	5·3	2·95	2·1	0·8	0·45
p.	♀	,,	Chili (*Reed*).	5·45	2·85	2·25	0·8	0·45
q.	♂	,,	Chili (*Reed*).	5·35	3·0	2·4	0·8	0·5
r.	♀	,,	Santiago, Chili (*Weisshaupt*).	5·15	2·95	2·3	0·8	0·45
s.	♀	,,	Santiago, Chili (*Weisshaupt*).	5·8	2·95	2·45	0·8	0·5
t.	♂	,,	Chivinda, Ecuador (*Buckley*).	5·0	3·0	2·35	0·8	0·5
u.	jun.	,,	Chivinda, Ecuador (*Buckley*).	4·7	2·7	2·0	0·85	0·45
v, w. adult.		,,	Chili (*Bridges*).					

The figures (Plate II.) are taken from *g* and *p* in my own collection.

PLOCEUS NIGERRIMUS.
THE SMALL BLACK WEAVER.
PLATE I. (Figs. 1, 2).

Le Républicain à capuchon écarlate, Temm. Cat. Cab. Ornith. p. 234, ♀ (1807).
Ploceus nigerrimus, Vieill. Nouv. Dict. xxxiv. p. 130 (1819); Vieill. Tabl. Encycl. Méth. ii. p. 700 (1823); Griff. Cuv. Anim. Kingd. ii. p. 134 (1829); Russ, Stubenvögel, p. 304 (1879); Shelley, Ibis, 1887, p. 38.
Ploceus niger, Swains. Classif. Birds, p. 279 (1837); Swains. Anim. in Menag. p. 306 (1837).
Ploceus (Melanopteryx) nigerrimus, Reichn. Zool. Jahrb. Jena, i. 1886, p. 125.
Sycobius nigerrimus, Gray et Mitch. Gen. Birds, ii. p. 352 (1849); Bonap. Consp. Gen. Av. p. 439 (1850); Hartl. Journ. für Orn. 1854, pp. 106, 411; Müller, Journ. für Orn. 1855, p. 461; Cassin, Proc. Acad. N. S. Philad. 1856 p. 318, 1859 p. 136; Hartl. Ornith. W. Afr. pp. 133, 274 (1857); Heine, Journ. für Ornith. 1860, p. 143; Reichb. Singvögel, p. 90 (1861); Bocage, Ornith. d'Angola, p. 333 (1877–81).
Malimbus nigerrimus, Gray, Hand-List Birds, ii. p. 43 (1870); Sharpe, Proc. Zool. Soc. 1871, pp. 612, 615; Sharpe, Cat. Afr. Birds, p. 60 (1871); Sharpe, Ibis, 1872, p. 72; Ussher, Ibis, 1874, p. 68; Elliot, Ibis, 1876, pp. 458, 464; Sharpe et Bouv. Bull. Soc. Zool. France, i. 1876, p. 47.
Hyphantornis nigerrimus, Reichn. Journ. für Ornith. 1873, pp. 448, 450; 1875, p. 39; 1877, p. 26; id. Gesellsch. 1874, p. 181.

English. *The Wholly-black Malimbus. The Small black Weaver. The White-naped Weaver-bird.*

French. *Le Malimbe tout-noir. Le Tisserin Noir.*

German. *Der ganz schwarze Malimbus. Der schwarze Webervogel.*

Habitat. West Africa ; extending its range from Fantee to Angola.

Localities. Fantee and Denkera (*Ussher*) ; Cameroon Mountains and Bimbia (*Reichenow*) ; Gaboon (*Du Chaillu* and *Reichenow*) ; Cape Lopez (*Verreaux*) ; River Camma and Moonda (*Du Chaillu*); Chinchosho (*Petit* and *Falkenstein*); Cabinda, Loango (*Petit, Perrein,* and *Falkenstein*) ; River Congo and Angola (*Perrein*).

Male. Black ; primaries and tail slightly tinged with brown, quills white along the edges, below the outer web ; axillaries and under wing-coverts black ; under surface of wing and tail dull black, bases of body-feathers dark slaty-grey ; iris straw-yellow ; bill black ; feet dark brown : length 6·05, wing 3·3, tail 2·35, tarsus 0·85, culmen 0·75. No. 1.

Female. Above olive-green, centre of each feather dark-brown, broadest on the mantle, and edged with yellowish-olive ; rump and upper tail-coverts yellowish-brown ; eyebrow greyish-green ; primaries and secondaries brownish-black, edged with pale yellowish-brown, broader and paler on the inner secondaries and greater wing-coverts; tail-feathers brownish-black ; under surface of body pale greyish-green, centre of belly pale yellow ; sides and flanks brownish ; under tail-coverts pale reddish-brown ; axillaries and under wing-coverts grey edged with yellow ; iris pale brown ; bill greyish-brown ; feet dirty flesh colour.

Young. "Upper parts dark green with longitudinal stripes of brown and black, under parts dull yellow darker on the sides ; wings and tail in some specimens brown, in others black. Bill lighter coloured than in the adult, under mandible nearly white."— (*Cassin*).

Juv. "Supra obscure viridis, fusco et nigricante striatus ; subtus obsolete flavidus, lateribus obscurioribus ; alis et cauda in nonnullis fuscis, in aliis nigris ; rostro pallidiore, mandibula fere albida " (*Hartlaub*).

Young. "Head and back dark olive-brown, each feather with a central line of black ; rump rufous brown ; cheeks, throat, and upper part of breast and flanks olive-yellow ; rest of under parts bright yellow ; under tail-coverts dark buff; wings and tail dark purplish-brown ; edges of secondaries yellow : length $6\frac{1}{2}$ inches, wing $3\frac{1}{4}$, tail $3\frac{1}{2}$, culmen $\frac{3}{4}$" (*D. G. Elliot*).

Observe. After a very careful comparison of a series of thirteen specimens of the true *Ploceus nigerrimus*, and *Ploceus albinucha*, and before reading Dr. Reichenow's description of the female of the former bird, I hurriedly came to the conclusion that the individual now described by me (see No. 2) was the true female of *Ploceus nigerrimus* (see No. 1), and the example described by Professor Barboza du Bocage as *Sycobius albinucha* I considered to be the young bird, which I figured as such in Plate 1, but the characters given by Cassin, Hartlaub, Elliot and Reichenow of the adult female and young of *Pl. nigerrimus*, with the details of the specimens in the British Museum, kindly sent to me by Mr. F. W. Frohawk, exclude all doubts as to the sexes of this species; but we must regard *Ploceus albinucha*, Bocage, as a distinct species, the synonymy of which, with descriptions, I have given below.

The earliest description of an entirely brownish-black Weaver-bird, which apparently refers to the present species, is given by Temminck in his 'Catalogue Systématique du Cabinet d'Ornithologie,' published in 1807, where he calls it the female of "*Le Républicain à capuchon écarlate*," and describes it as follows : "*La femelle est entièrement d'un noir rembruni*."

In 1819, Vieillot, in his 'Nouvelle Dictionnaire,' recognised the species as being distinct from its allies, and characterised it under the appellation of *Ploceus nigerrimus*.

Mr. J. Cassin, whose valuable observations on birds are well known throughout the Ornithological world, published an account of the birds collected by M. du Chaillu, in the 'Proceedings of the Academy of Natural Sciences' for 1856, in which our attention is called for the first time to the different stages of plumage of this peculiar form of Weaverbird, viz. :—"The specimens labelled by M. du Chaillu as both sexes of this little-known species are entirely black, and differ only slightly in size and lustre of plumage. The young are, however, very different, having the upper parts dark green with longitudinal stripes of brown and black ; under parts dull yellow, darker on the sides ; wings and tail in some specimens brown, in others black. Bill lighter coloured than in the adult ; under mandible nearly white. In young plumage this bird might readily be mistaken for a distinct species."

In the same 'Proceedings' for 1860, Mr. Cassin, although retaining this species under the generic name of *Sycobius*, remarks that it is "perhaps not properly referrible to this genus ; the green colour of the young approximating it to *Ploceus* and *Hyphantornis*."

Capt. G. E. Shelley, in the 'Ibis' for 1887, points out that "The Gold

Coast specimens are apparently always rather small, and have occasionally, but not always, white bases to the feathers of the hind neck; when these feathers are worn, a white collar at the back of the neck may sometimes be traced. One of these specimens formed the type of *Sycobius albinucha*, Bocage."

Dr. A. Reichenow, who has devoted much time and labour in working out the Weaver-birds of the genus *Ploceus*, which he published in the 'Zoologische Jahrbücher' for 1886, tells us that the Black Weaver-bird " inhabits Lower Guinea from the Cameroon River to Angola. In Upper Guinea its appearance seems to be only sporadic, until lately it has only been collected by Ussher in Denkera on the Gold Coast. In Lower Guinea, however, from the Cameroon onwards, it is very common, in some places the commonest Weaver-bird. Its special resorts are: the Cameroon wastes, Wuri, the Cameroon Mountains to the height of 3,000 feet. In its habits it very much resembles *Pl. cucullatus*, and where both species are found near together, it forms the constant, faithful companion of the latter. The nests of both species often hang mixed together on the same cocoa-nut palm, and not the slightest jealousy or unfriendliness can be detected between them. *Pl. nigerrimus* is fond of building on palms in the negro villages, or in plantations of Bananas, where it hangs its nests on the tips of Banana-leaves at no great height from the ground; however, where opportunity offers on the branches of trees overhanging the banks of rivers, and always in colonies of considerable size. The rounded nest is composed of fresh, wide grasses, runs up at the top into a point, by which it is fastened to the tree. The entrance has no tube-like appendage. The width always amounts to 12 cent., the length to 15 cent., of which six are covered by the mouth of the entrance. The well of the nest is frequently lined with flowering maize stalks. As a rule the nests hang quite independently on separate branches; still it may happen that a neighbouring shoot is twined in between. In large colonies two or three nests are often found close together, fastened on to the same branch, which is then likewise entwined by the building materials. The eggs are bright blue, and vary in length from 22 to 25 mm., in breadth from 15 to 16·5 mm. Two or three eggs form a clutch."

Specimens examined.

No.	Sex.	Mus.	Locality.	Length.	Wing.	Tail.	Tars.	Culm.
a.	♂	E. B.	West Africa (*Du Chaillu*)	6·05	3·3	2·35	0·85	0·75
b.	♀	E. B.	West Africa	5·45	3·1	1·95	0·75	0·73
c.	♂	E. B.	Gaboon	6·4	3·35	2·25	0·85	0·75
d.	♀	G. E. Shelley	Congo (*Dr. A. Lucan*)	6·3	3·4	2·3	0·9	0·8
e.	♀	G. E. Shelley	Gaboon (*Ansell*)	6·5	3·4	2·35	0·85	0·75
f.	♀	G. E. Shelley	Gold Coast	5·45	3·25	2·2	0·85	0·75
g.	♂	A. Boucard	Gaboon	6·0	3·3	2·35	0·9	0·75

PLOCEUS ALBINUCHA.

THE WHITE-NAPED WEAVER.

PLATE I. (Upper figure jun.)

Sycobius albinucha, Bocage, Jorn. Lisboa, 1876, p. 247.
Ploceus (Melanopteryx) nigerrimus (part), Reichen. Zool. Jahrb. Jena, i. 1886, p. 125.
Ploceus nigerrimus (pt.), Shelley, Ibis, 1887, p. 38.

"*S. albinucha*: S. nigerrimo *similis, sed minor; nitide niger; torque occipitali albo-vario; rostro graciliori nigro; pedibus fuscis*" (Bocage).

Male? Similar to *Ploceus nigerrimus* but much smaller, bill slighter, culmen straighter, or less curved; not so black, strongly tinged with dull brown on the primaries and tail; no nuchal patch, axillaries and under wing-coverts slaty grey; under surface of primaries ashy-grey; quills of wings and tail black above and white below (in *Pl. nigerrimus* they are black above and brown below); abdomen, flanks, thighs and under tail-coverts dull slaty-brown; bill black; feet brown: length 5·45, wing 3·1, tail 1·95, tarsus 0·75, culmen 0·73. No. 2. Probably the male.

Young? Similar, much smaller; tinged with brown above; nuchal patch greyish-white; primaries and tail-feathers edged with dull brown; throat and breast nearly black; belly, flanks, thighs and under tail-coverts dull slaty-brown; bill brownish-black, paler at the base of the lower mandible; feet pale brown: length 4·8, wing 3·05, tail 1·9, tarsus 0·65, culmen 0·65. Fig. Jun. Plate I. No. 3. Probably the female.

Observ. This *Sycobius albinucha*, Bocage, I shall consider a distinct species. The under tail-coverts of the young bird (No. 3) above described are tipped with red, indicating a different stage of plumage in the nestling.

In separating this bird from the preceding species, I am doubtful whether it should be placed under the genus *Malimbus* or *Ploceus*. I figured the bird and coloured all the plates, before I had completed the material now before me, hence the mistake in the word *juv.*, which should be fig. 2. *Jun.*

I HERE point out that all the specimens of *Pl. albinucha* examined are from the Gold Coast; they have the lower half of the under parts, or abdomen, dull slaty-brown; some are paler than others, which are apparently of different ages; one I possess is entirely black on the head, neck and back without the nuchal patch, but still retains the slaty-brown abdomen; they are all comparatively much smaller than *Pl. nigerrimus*, the bill much slighter and straighter, especially on the culmen.

Ploceus albinucha.

No.	Sex.	Mus.	Locality.	Length.	Wing.	Tail.	Tars.	Culm.
h.	?	G. E. Shelley	Gold Coast	5·4	3·15	2·05	0·75	0·75
i.	?	G. E. Shelley	Gold Coast (*Ussher*)	4·85	2·9	1·85	0·65	0·65
j	?	G. E. Shelley	Gold Coast	5·35	2·95	1·8	0·7	0·7
k	? jun.	E. B.	Fantee, W. Africa	5·35	3·15	2·0	0·7	0·7
l	? jun.	E. B.	Fantee, W. Africa	4·8	3·05	1·9	0·65	0·65
m.	?	A. Boucard	Fantee, W. Africa	5·3	3·15	2·0	0·75	0·7

The figures (Plate I.) are taken from *a* and *l* in my own collection, and figured for the first time.

PLOCEUS CASTANEOFUSCUS.
THE CHESTNUT-BACKED WEAVER-BIRD.

PLATE XI. (Figs. 1, 2).

Ploceus castaneo-fuscus, Less. Rev. Zool. 1840, p. 99.
Ploceus castaneofuscus, Reichb. Singvögel, p. 83 (1861); Russ, Stubenvögel, p. 301, pl. x. fig. 51 (1879); Shelley, Ibis, 1887, p. 38.
Ploceus isabellinus? Less. Rev. Zool. 1840, p. 226, ♀? Reichb. Singvögel, p. 83 (1861).
Hyphantornis isabellina, Gray et Mitch. Genera Birds, ii. p. 351 (1844).
Hyphantornis castaneofusca, Gray et Mitch. Genera Birds, ii. p. 351 (1844); Hartl. Journ. für Ornith. 1854, pp. 110, 219. Müll. Journ. für Ornith. 1855, p. 464; Scl. Proc. Zool. Soc. 1859, p. 433; Sharpe, Cat. Afr. Birds, p. 59 (1871); Scl. Vert. Anim. Gard. Zool. Soc. p. 246 (1883).
Hyphantornis castaneofuscus, Hartl. Ornith. Westafr. p. 126 (1857); Sharpe, Ibis, 1869, p. 191; Shelley et Buckl. Ibis, 1872, p. 289; Garrod, Proc. Zool. Soc. 1873, p. 462; Ussher, Ibis, 1874, p. 67; Reichnw. Journ. für Ornith. 1875, p. 39; Shelley, Ibis, 1883, p. 552; Rocheb. Faun. Sénég. Ois. p. 240 (1884); Shelley, Johnston's River Congo, p. 365 (1884).
Textor castaneo-fuscus, Bonap. Consp. Gen. Av. p. 442 (1850).
Ploceus (*Cinnamopteryx*) *Castaneofuscus*, Reichnw. Zool. Jahrb. Jena, i. 1886, p. 126.

Figure. Russ, Stubenvögel, pl. x. fig. 51.

Dutch. *Kastanjebruin Wever.*

English. *Chestnut-backed Weaver-bird. Chestnut-fuscus Weaver. Yellow-dun Weaver. Chestnut Weaver-bird. Isabelline Weaver.*

French. *Le Tisserin couleur de Châtaigne brun. Le Tisserin brun noir. Le Tisserin isabelle.*

German. *Der Kastanienbraune Weber. Der Isabell-Weber. Der Kastanienbraune Webervogel.*

Habitat. West Africa : " from the Congo to Senegambia " (*Shelley*).

Localities. Bathurst, Senegambia (*Rochebrune*) ; Casamauze, Senegambia (*Lesson*) ; St. Paul's River, Sierra Leone (*MacDowell*) ; St. Paul's River and Robertsport, Liberia (*Buttikofer*) ; Ashantee (*Berlin Mus.*); Fantee (*Ussher, Blissett, Kirby, Shelley* and *Buckley*); River Volta (*Ussher*); Cape Coast (*Higgins*); Cape Coast Castle (*Kirby*); Abouri (*Shelley*); Accra (*Haynes*); Abokobi (*Reichenow*); Rio Boutry (*Pel*); Ornitschi, River Niger (*Forbes*); Gaboon (*.l. Lecomte*) ; Congo (*Leyden Mus.*).

Male. Black ; mantle and scapulars dark cinnamon-brown ; rump, basal portion of upper tail-coverts, sides, abdomen, thighs and under tail-coverts chestnut-brown, brightest on the rump ; iris straw-yellow ; bill black ; legs and feet dark brown : length 6·1, wing 3·1, tail 2·15, tarsus 0·9, culmen 0·75 (*a*).

Young Male changing Plumage. Similar to female and young, but with brighter reddish-brown on sides, flanks and under tail-coverts ; interspersed with black and chestnut all over ; wings and tail black ; secondaries black with bright bullish outer margins : bill black ; feet brown ; length 6·05, wing 3·15, tail 2·4, tarsus 0·9, culmen 0·75 (*y*).

Female. Crown and hind neck dark greyish-olive, streaked with dull brown ; back brownish-olive, centre of each feather brownish-black edged with pale olive ; lower part of back, rump and upper tail coverts reddish-brown ; primaries dull black, edged with olive-green ; secondaries brownish-black broadly margined with yellowish-buff, like the median and greater wing-coverts ; lesser wing-coverts faintly edged with greyish-olive ; tail dull black faintly edged with greenish-olive ; cheeks, sides of head and neck greyish-olive ; chin and throat pale yellowish buff; breast, sides, flanks and under tail-coverts olive-brown, strongly tinged with rufous on the flanks and under tail-coverts ; centre of belly bright sulphur-yellow ; axillaries and under wing-coverts brownish-buff ; under surface of wing-feathers grey ; iris brown ; bill dark brown, paler on the under mandible ; feet brown : length 5·85, wing 3·05, tail 2·2, tarsus 0·8, culmen 0·75 (*j*).

Young Female. Crown olive-brown, not tinged with grey, and only faintly streaked with brown ; brown centres of feathers of mantle and scapulars not so large or decided as in the adult female; outer margins of inner secondaries broader and paler yellowish-buff; under parts much paler; centre of abdomen brighter sulphur-yellow; bill and legs paler brown: length 5·0, wing 2·9, tail 2·1, tarsus 0·8, culmen 0·7 (*h*).

The Chestnut-backed Weaver-bird, although described by Lesson in the 'Revue Zoologique par la Société Cuvierienne' for 1840, remained unfigured until now, with the exception of a small chromo portrait of it in Carl Russ's 'Stubenvögel,' published in 1879.

The distribution of this species resembles that of the preceding, with which it associates, occupying as it does the whole of the forest-bound coast of West Africa, from Senegambia in the north to the River Congo in the south, but it does not appear to penetrate far into the interior. The species, according to the little knowledge we possess of its habits, is extremely abundant in its native haunts, breeding in large colonies in the great palm and bamboo swamps bordering the rivers, where it suspends its nest from every available branch or frond, in common with a host of its congeners.

During Messrs. Shelley and Buckley's two months' Bird-collecting at Fantee on the Gold Coast, they found that *Hyphantornis castaneofuscus* "generally frequented the more wooded districts, where it is very common: the irides are yellow in the male, and brown in the female and young."

According to Governor H. T. Ussher, the Chestnut-back Weaver is "very common in Fantee, especially round Cape Coast. They are invariably found in grassy swampy places, and are particularly fond of the bamboos or canes, whence their nests may be seen depending in hundreds. They are very sociable, and are occasionally captured as cage-birds."

Dr. A. Reichnow says: "According to my observations, the Fox-weaver avoids the localities, or at any rate does not build in places frequented by *P. cucullatus* and *nigerrimus*. It does not hang its net on cocoa-nut palms or other high trees, but rather on low bushes. It prefers open ground which is strewn here and there with single bushes and trees, and likes to build on the waving reeds of the papyrus. The nest resembles in form that of *Pl. cucullatus*, but has no tube-like appendage at the entrance-hole, and is somewhat more loosely built than the latter. The eggs are bright blue, 23—24·5 mm. in length, and 15·5—16 mm. in breadth. I always found only two in a brood. Büttekofer also confirms the preference of this species for thickets of reeds wherein to place its nest, but found the bird, however, building on low bushes, in community with *Ploceus cucullatus*. This traveller mentions the number of eggs in a brood to be two or three."

This Weaver-bird is often brought to England alive, and appears to thrive on the ordinary food supplied to most finches; there is no doubt it does best in large aviaries where its liberty is not too confined. The large centre dome of the southern aviary in the Zoological Gardens is apparently suited to this species, in which I find it has bred several times; but those who are accustomed like myself to the notes and voices of these wild birds cannot fail to observe this extraordinary bird as it flies from one branch to another, raising all its feathers and uttering its prolonged *zwitz-zee-ee-ee* just as though it was scolding all the other inhabitants of its castle for their bad behaviour. During the summer it is always busily engaged weaving its nest, which is often destroyed before completion. I have examined nineteen specimens of this species, many of which were very obligingly lent to me by Capt. G. E. Shelley, Canon H. B. Tristram, and M. A. Boucard.

Specimens examined.

No.	Sex.	Mus.	Localities.	Length.	Wing.	Tail.	Tarsus.	Cul.
a.	♂	E. B.	W. Africa	6·1	3·1	2·15	0·9	0·75
b.	♂	E. B.	W. Africa	5·75	3·25	2·45	0·85	0·75
c.	♂	E. B.	Fantee, W. Africa (*Ussher*)	6·0	3·25	2·45	0·85	0·75
d.	♂	E. B.	Fantee, W. Africa (*Ussher*)	6·1	3·25	2·4	0·9	0·8
e.	♂	E. B.	Gaboon, W. Africa	6·0	3·15	2·35	0·9	0·75
f.	♂	E. B.	Fantee, W. Africa (*Kirby*)	6·15	3·05	2·2	0·85	0·7
g.	♂ imm.	G. E. Shelley	Gold Coast, W. Africa (*Kirby*)	6·05	3·15	2·4	0·9	0·75
h.	♀	G. E. Shelley	Abouri, W. Africa (*Shelley*)	5·0	2·9	2·1	0·8	0·7
i.	♀	G. E. Shelley	Abrobouko, Fantee (*Shelley*)	5·5	2·85	2·1	0·75	0·7
j.	♀	E. B.	Fantee, W. Africa (*Ussher*)	5·85	3·05	2·2	0·8	0·75

The figures (Plate II.) are taken from (fig. 1) *a*, the male in my own collection; and (fig. 2) *i*, a female kindly lent to me by Capt. G. E. Shelley.

PAROARIA DOMINICANA.
THE DOMINICAN CARDINAL.
PLATE XI. (FIGS. 1, 2).

Rubicilla americana, Ray, Syn. Meth. Avium, p. 86 (1713).
Tije-guacu Paroara, Ray, Syn. Meth. Avium, p. 89 (1713).
The Dominican Cardinal, Edw. Nat. Hist. Birds, iii. p. 127, pl. 127 (1750).
Loxia dominicana, Linn. Amœn. Acad. iv. p. 242 (1759); Linn. Syst. Nat. i. p. 301 (1766); Forst. Cat. Anim. N. Amer. p. 11 (1771); P. L. S. Müll. Vollst. Natursyst. iii. p. 548 (1773); Gmel. Syst. Nat. i. p. 848 (1788); Lath. Ind. Ornith. i. p. 377 (1790); Licht. Cat. Rer. Nat. Rar. p. 43 (1793); Daud. Traité d'Ornith. ii. p. 380 (1800); Vieill. Ois. Chant. p. 104, pl. lxix. (1805); Temm. Cat. Syst. Cab. d'Ornith. p. 99 (1807); Shaw, Gen. Zool. ix. p. 276 (1815); Griff. edit. Cuv. Anim. Kingd. Aves, ii. 137 (1829); Teget. edit. Licht. Cat. Rer. Nat. Rar. p. 43 (1880).
Cardinalis dominicanus, Briss. Ornith. iii. p. 116, pl. vi. fig. 4 (1760).
Cardinalis dominicanus, Briss. Syn. Meth. i. p. 339 (1763).
Cardinalis dominicana, Blyth, Cat. Birds, Mus. As. Soc. Beng. p. 126 (1849).
Coccothraustes brasiliensis, Briss. Ornith. iii. p. 246 (1760); Briss. Syn. Meth. i. p. 377 (1763).
Le Paroare, Buff. Hist. Nat. Ois. iii. p. 500 (1775); Sonn. edit. Buff. xlvii. p. 188, pl. 106, fig. 2 (1801); Buff. Nat. Hist. Birds, iv. p. 52, pl. 87, Engl. edit. (1812).
Cardinal dominiquain, Daub. Pl. Enl. 55, fig. 2 (1777)

Dominican Grosbeak, Lath. Gen. Syn. Birds, iii. p. 123 (1783) ; Lath. Gen. Syn. Suppl. i. p. 151 (1787) ; Gmel. Syst. Nat. Hist. vii. p. 123, Engl. edit. (1801) ; Bechst. Cage and Chamber Birds, p. 201, 4th edit. (1856).
Pope Grosbeak, Lath. Gen. Syn. Birds, iii. p. 124, var. B (1783).
Fringilla larvata, Bodd. Tab. des Pl. Enl. p. 4 (1783).
Le Capito, Azara, Voy. Amér. Mérid. iii. p. 300 (1809).
Fringilla dominicana, Vieill. Nouv. Dict. xii. p. 129 (1817) ; Vieill. Tabl. Encycl. Méth. iii. p. 952 (1823) ; Licht. Verz. Doubl. Mus. Berl. p. 22 (1823) ; Max. Beitr. Brasil. iii. p. 594, pl. i. (1830-1) ; Cab. Journ. für Ornith. 1854, p. 475 ; Gundl Ornit. Cubana, pp. 12, 15 (1876).
Spiza larvata, Gray et Mitch. Gen. Birds, ii. p. 375 (1849).
Spiza dominicana, Gray et Mitch. Gen. Birds, ii. p. 375 (1849) ; Eyton, Cat. Birds, p. 248 (1856).
Paroaria dominicana, Bonap. Consp. Gen. Av. p. 471 (1850) ; Burm. Syst. Uebers. Th. Bras. p. 211 (1856) ; Bolle, Journ. für Ornith. 1856, p. 169 ; Schmidt, Proc. Zool. Soc. 1880, p. 313 ; Salv. Cat. Coll. Strickl. p. 225 (1882).
Paroaria larvata, Sclater, Cat. Amer. Birds, p. 108 (1862) ; Scl. et Salv. Nomencl. Av. Neotr. p. 30 (1873) ; Forbes, Ibis, 1881, p. 337 ; Scl. Vert. Anim. Gard. Zool. Soc. p. 248 (1883) ; Sharpe, Cat. Birds Brit. Mus. xii. p. 811, pl. xvi., head only (1888).
Calyptrophorus dominicanus, Cab. Mus. Hein. p. 145 (1851) ; Licht. Nomencl. Avium Mus. Berol. p. 44 (1854) ; Gundl. Journ. für Ornith. 1862, p. 187.
Passerina dominicana, Gray, Hand-List Birds, ii. p. 97 (1870).
Coccothraustes dominicanus, Russ, Stubenvögel, p. 541, pl. xiii. fig. 65 (1879).

Figures. Edwards, Nat. Hist. Birds, pl. 127. Briss. Ornith. iii. pl. vi. fig. 4. Daub. Pl. Enl. 55, fig. 2. Sonn. Hist. Nat. pl. 106, fig. 2. Vieill. Ois. Chant. pl. lxix. Buff. Nat Hist. pl. 87. Russ, Stubenvögel, pl. xiii. fig. 65.

English. *The Dominican Card'nal. Dominican Grosbeak. Pope Grosbeak* variety. *The Paroare. Red-headed Cardinal.*

French. *Le Paroare. Le Cardinal Dominicain. Le Cardinal Dominiquain Le Gros-bec du Brésil. Le Pinson Paroare.*

German. *Der Dominicaner-Cardinal. Der Dominikaner-Kardinal aus Luisiana. Dominikaner-Finken. Dominikaner-Cardinale.*

Native names. *Tije-Guacu Paroara, Guira-Tirica, Gallo da campina,* and *Cardinal.*

Habitat. Brazil; extending its range along the sea-border, from Rio Janeiro in the south, to the River Amazon in the north.

Adult. Crown, sides of face, ear-coverts, chin, and throat shining crimson; hind margin of ear-coverts black; hind neck white, each feather broadly edged with black; mantle, scapulars, back, rump, and upper tail-coverts ashy-grey; feathers of mantle narrowly edged with black; wing- and primary-coverts black; primaries brownish-black, narrowly edged on the outer web with silvery-grey; secondaries black broadly edged with silvery-grey; tail blackish, fringed on the outer edges near the base with grey, like the upper tail-coverts, and tipped with white; outer rectrices brown; sides of neck, entire under-parts, and under tail-coverts pure white; sides and flanks pale grey; axillaries, under wing-coverts, under surface of wings, and tail greyish white; iris hazel brown; bill dark brown, lower mandible orange-yellow, brown at the tip; feet slaty-black: length 6·45, wing 3·6, tail 2·95, tars. 0·9, culm. 0·6.

Female. Similar.

Young. Head, chin, and throat cinnamon-brown, centre of the crown and ear-coverts dark brown interspersed with a few crimson feathers; hind neck buffish-white, each feather broadly edged with brownish-black; mantle brownish-grey narrowly edged with black; back and rump dull grey; upper tail-coverts dull greyish-brown; lesser wing-coverts black; the rest dull brown faintly edged with buff; primaries and secondaries blackish-brown narrowly edged with greyish-white, forming a white patch under the primary-coverts; first quill brown; tail blackish-brown, the first rectrices edged and tipped with dirty white; under parts white, very slightly tinged with buff.

Very Young. Similar, but the brown patch on the crown and ear-coverts, and the cinnamon of the face and throat much paler; primaries and secondaries very broadly edged with rufous-brown.

Observ. The males and females in all stages of plumage are alike. The bills of the young are brown, with a less tinge of yellow on the lower mandible.

In confinement these birds are apt to become quite black, excepting the head.

This very pretty Cardinal is one of the most abundant and best known species of the group to which it belongs, and from a very early date it has been brought to Europe alive and in skin from Brazil, but more plentifully from Bahia. The latter locality appears to be its true home, although its distribution is very extensive, inhabiting as it does the whole of the great forest-bound coast of Brazil, extending its range into the interior as far south-west as Paraguay.

The bright plumage, its attractive liveliness and sharp call-notes (although destitute of a song), will always recommend it to lovers of cage-birds. It is a hardy bird, and easily kept on various seeds.

Maximilian Prinz zu Wied tells us in his ' Beiträge zur Naturgeschichte von Brasilien ' : " This beautiful bird is very well known and is often kept in cages. Among the many specimens I saw, I found very few irregularities, whilst, according to the age of the bird, the red on the head is sometimes more pure, beautiful, and extensive, sometimes less so ; the back more or less spotted with black, and the underside and edges of the wings, which were pure and shining white in old birds, were of an impure or yellowish tint in the young ones.

" I observed this bird first in the open part of the town of Bahia ; it is met with, however, in the central regions of Brazil down to Paraguay, according to Azara.

" These birds are not rare at Bahia ; they are simple, quiet creatures, with a clear call-note and a little twittering song. In that region they are often kept in cages, wherein they thrive, the food being ground rice and maize. At Bahia, and also among the Spaniards in Paraguay, the name is *Cardinal*."

Mr. W. A. Forbes, who devoted much time to the birds of North-eastern Brazil, says :—" I found the Red-headed Cardinal common at Parahyba, and again saw it in the neighbourhood of Garanhuns, so that it occurs all over the district I traversed. It is usually seen singly or in pairs in the more or less cleared and open ground near cultivation. Many dozens are brought into the market at Recife to sell as cage-birds. The Brazilians call it ' *Gallo da campina*.' "

According to Dr. Max Schmidt, this bird has been known to live thirteen to fourteen years in confinement.

Although my researches for details respecting these birds extend over nineteen years, I have been unable to find any reliable information concerning the nidification of this species in a wild state.

Specimens examined.

No.	Sex.	Mus.	Locality.	Length.	Wing.	Tail.	Tars.	Culm.
a.	adult	E. B.	Brazil.	6·45	3·6	2·95	0·9	0·6
b.	jun.	E. B.	Brazil.	6·5	3·6	3·25	0·95	0·6
c.	jun.	E. B.	Brazil.	6·0	3·45	3·15	0·9	0·55
d.	adult	E. B.	Brazil.	0·0	0·0	0·0	0·9	0·6
e.	adult	E. B.	Brazil.	7·1	3·6	3·25	0·95	0·6
f.	adult	E. B.	Brazil.	7·3	3·45	3·2	0·95	0·6
g.	juv.	E. B.	Brazil.	6·4	3·4	2·9	0·95	0·55
h.	adult	E. B.	Brazil.	7·55	3·8	3·35	0·95	0·6
i.	adult	H. B. Tristram.	Brazil.	6·75	3·6	3·2	0·95	0·6

The figures (Plate II.) are taken from (fig. 1) a, and (fig. 2) e, which are in my own collection.

MUNIA MINUTA.
THE PHILIPPINE MUNIA.
PLATE VI. (Fig. 1).

Fringilla minuta, Meyen, Nov. Act. Nat. Cur. Bonn. xvi. 1834, Suppl. p. 86, t. 12, fig. 2 jun.
Amadina minuta, Gray et Mitch. Gen. Birds, ii. p. 370 (1849).
Munia minuta, Bonap. Consp. Gen. Av. p. 452 (1850).
Munia minuta, Reichb. Singvögel, p. 39, Note (1861).
Munia (Dermophrys) jagori, Cab. v. Martens, Journ. für Ornith. 1866, p. 14, No. 60.
Munia (Dermophrys) minuta, v. Martens, Journ. für Ornithologie, 1866, p. 14, No. 61.
Amadina minuta, Gray, Hand-List Birds, ii. p. 55, No. 6761 (1870).
Dermophrys jagori, Cab. Journ. für Ornith. 1872, p. 316, No. 6.
Munia minuta, Walden, Trans. Zool. Soc. ix. 1875, p. 208, No. 133.
Munia jagori, Wald. et Layard, Ibis, 1872, p. 106 ; Walden, Trans. Zool. Soc. ix. 1875, p. 207 ; Salvad. Ann. Mus. Civ. Gen. vii. 1875, p. 667 ; Sharpe, Trans. Linn. Soc. i. 1876, p. 353 ; Tweedd. Proc. Zool. Soc. 1877, pp. 538, 549, 699, 764, 832 ; 1878, pp. 287, 343, 710, 951 ; Salvad. Ann. Mus. Civ. Gen. xvi. 1880, p. 192 ; Scl. Voy. H.M.S. 'Challenger,' ii. pp. 6, 8, 22 (1881) ; Salvad. Ornit. Papuasia, p. 437 (1881) ; Guill. Proc. Zool. Soc. 1885, pp. 250, 268 ; Guill. Cruise of Marchesa, ii. Append. i. p. 361 (1886).

Figure. Meyen, Nov. Act. Nat. Cur. Bonn. xvi. Suppl. t. 12, fig. 2 jun.

English. *Little Munia. Jagor's Munia. Philippine Munia.*

French. *Le Petit Jacobin.*

German. *Der kleine Munia.*

Habitat. Philippine Archipelago. Luzon (*Meyen* et *Jagor*); Zebu and Halmahera (*Meyer*); Mindanao (*Challenger Expedition*); Amparo, S. Leyte, N. Bohol, Zamboanga, Valencia, Dumaquete, Butuan, Placer, San Mateo and Island of Negros (*Everett*); Sulu Island (*Guillemard*).

Male. Crown of head, nape, and cheeks black-brownish; chin, throat, mesial stripe, thighs, and under tail-coverts black; mesial stripe united to the black of the breast, and gradually expanding on the belly; back, wings and sides of body chestnut-brown; lower part of rump and upper tail-coverts glistening maroon; centre tail-feathers and outer edges of the rest glistening ferruginous; axillaries and under wing-coverts yellowish-buff; under surface of wing brownish-buff; iris reddish-brown; "bill ash-blue; legs slate colour: length 11·0 cent., wing 5·0 cent." (*Guillemard*).

Female. Similar, but with the black mesial stripe slightly divided on the breast by a narrow chestnut band, as in *Munia atricapilla*, but less decided.

Young. Similar in every particular to that of *Munia atricapilla*, but smaller.

Observ. This species has been separated from the rest on very trifling differences, which I think are insufficient to divide it from the Celebean form, although I have retained the synonymy and figured it.

The head in both sexes is brownish-black; the black mesial stripe in the male is very broad, covers the whole of the abdomen, and is united to the black of the breast. In the female a narrow band of chestnut divides the mesial stripe from the black of the breast.

"The male is larger than the female, and of richer colouring, the head being very nearly black, and the brown of the body a deeper chestnut. The union of the abdominal dark line with the same colour of the throat does not appear to be of any value as a characteristic of the sex" (*Guillemard*).

This Philippine form is much smaller than *Munia atricapilla*.

SOME doubt exists as to whether *Fringilla minuta*, which was described and figured by Meyen in 1834, is referable to the bird described by Dr. Cabanis in 1872, under the name *Dermophrys jagori*. Having closely examined and compared specimens of this group of *Munias* in my own collection with Meyen's figure, I am convinced that it is only the young of Dr. Cabanis's *Dermophrys jagori*, from the Philippine Islands.

Dr. Cabanis has already described a small species of the Nutmeg group as *Oxycerca jagori*, which must not be confused with the present species, for which I shall retain the earlier specific appellation, *minuta*.

From an elaborate paper on the 'Birds of the Philippine Archipelago,' published in the 'Transactions of the Zoological Society' for 1875, by the Marquis of Tweeddale, I have been enabled to confirm my views from his remarks on "two examples (♂ and ♀) of an almost black-headed *Munia*, which were obtained in Zebu by Dr. A. B. Meyer. Both have the upper tail-coverts glistening dark chestnut, and the middle pair of rectrices rich glistening ferruginous. In the male the black extends from the breast to the under tail-coverts, forming a broad, mesial black, continuous band. In the female this black mesial band is interrupted by a chestnut band crossing the breast. In examples of *M. rubronigra* from the Deyra Doon, Bengal, Tippera, Mymensing, and Tongoo, as well as of *M. formosana* from Formosa, and *M. brunneiceps* from Celebes and Banjarmassing, the black mesial band is not continuous, nor is it so broadly developed on the abdomen. In *M. rubronigra* the whole head is intensely black. In *Munia formosana* the occiput and nape are faded brown; and Mr. Swinhoe has established that this is normal in the adult bird. The Philippine, Celebean, and South-Bornean forms do not appear to have the head so intensely black as in *M. rubronigra*, although darker than *M. formosana*.

"In the Philippine examples the head and nape are not of a true black, but rather of a dark brown. This has also been pointed out by Dr. Cabanis. In *M. brunneiceps* of Celebes the head is still less black, and the black abdominal band is interrupted.

"May not Meyen's *Fringilla minuta* be *M. jagori* in first plumage, before the black feathers come in? Otherwise it is remarkable that a species stated by Meyen to occur in numberless troops in the Luzon sugar-plantations has not since he wrote (1834) been recognised.

"Eggs of a little amadavad (from the Island of Negros), with red body and black head, are probably the eggs of the little *Munia jagori*, which accord with this description. They are pure white. Axis 7''', diam. 5'''."

The nest has not yet been described.

According to Dr. F. H. H. Guillemard " this little species was abundant in Sulu, collected in flocks of from ten to thirty individuals, and feeding in the grass. Their habits and note reminded me strongly of the African *Estrelda astrild*."

The species has been procured in many of the smaller islands of the Philippine Archipelago which I have placed under the habitat.

I am indebted to Canon H. B. Tristram for the loan of the specimen procured by Mr. A. H. Everett in Cebu, one of the Philippine Islands.

The adult bird has not hitherto been figured.

Specimens examined.

No.	Sex.	Mus.	Locality.	Length.	Wing.	Tail.	Tars.	Culm.
a.	♂	E. B.	Philippines.	3·95	1·95	1·5	0·6	0·4
b.	♀	E. B.	Philippines.	3·45	1·95	1·2	0·6	0·5
c.	♀	H. B. Tristram.	Cebu, Philippines (*Everett*).	4·05	1·95	1·05	0·55	0·4

The figure (Plate VI. fig. 1) is taken from the male in my own collection.

MUNIA BRUNNEICEPS.
THE CELEBEAN MUNIA.

PLATE VI. (Fig. 2).

Donacola atricapilla, pt., Blyth, Ibis, 1870, p. 171.
Munia brunneiceps, Walden, Trans. Zool. Soc. viii. 1872, p. 73, pl. ix. fig. 1.
Munia jagori, Meyer, Journ. für Ornith. 1873, p. 405.
Munia brunneiceps, Walden, Trans. Zool. Soc. ix. 1875, p. 207.
Munia brunneiceps, Salvad. Ann. Mus. Civ. Gen. vii. 1875, pp. 666, 667.
Munia jagori, Meyer, Ibis, 1879, p. 132.
Munia brunneiceps, Salvad. Ornit. Papuasia, p. 438 (1881).
Munia brunneiceps, Blasius, Journ. für Ornith. 1883, p. 138.

Figure. Walden, Trans. Zool. Soc. 1872, pl. ix. fig. 1.

Habitat. Celebes.

Male. "Head, chin, throat, and breast brown; abdominal stripe, vent, and under tail-coverts black; remainder of plumage dark chestnut; wing two inches" (*Tweeddale*).

Female. "Head and nape of a lighter and less decided shade of brown" (*Tweeddale*).

Young. Similar to those of *Munia atricapilla*, but smaller

Observ. The black mesial stripe in this species forms an almost unbroken narrow line, from the upper part of the breast to the under tail-coverts.

In 'The Ibis' for 1870, Mr. E. Blyth called attention to various forms of the Black-headed Munias, which he found in the Leyden Museum and elsewhere, remarking that "Bornean specimens are similar to Indian, with belly and lower tail-coverts black; in the Sumatran this black is almost obsolete; and in those from Macassar the black beneath is well developed, while that of the head and neck is much imbrowned. It is quite arbitrary where to draw the line as to what are to be considered species, races, or varieties, in the genus *Munia*, at least in not a few instances."

Upon the above remarks the Marquis of Tweeddale separated the Celebean form from the Philippine and Formosan birds in the 'Transactions of the Zoological Society' for 1875, under the name of *Munia brunneiceps*; "from a Macassar example of a male collected by Mr. A. R. Wallace, and another from the same locality marked a female." "Were it not (he says) that Mr. E. Blyth had already remarked the imbrowned colouring of the head and neck in examples from Celebes, contained in the Leyden Museum, I should have felt less confidence in considering these Macassar individuals distinct from *Munia rubronigra*, Hodgs."

This Celebean Munia is closely allied in every respect to the Philippine bird above described, and almost identical with the Formosan species, which are all insular races of the true Indian form, *Munia atricapilla*, very difficult to separate, and should in my opinion be united under one name, *Munia minuta*, Meyen.

Dr. A. B. Meyer tells us in his 'Field-Notes on the Birds of Celebes,' that *Munia brunneiceps* is found "in flocks in March, near Menado, and in Macassar in January. According to age and sex, vary very much in the intensity of its brown and black colours.

"Iris brown; bill bluish; feet and claws light greyish-blue."

No.	Sex.	Mus.	Locality.	Length.	Wing.	Tail.	Tars.	Culm.
a.	♂	F. B.	South Celebes (*Dr. Platen*)	3·65	1·95	1·35	0·55	0·4
b.	adult.	Boucard.	Celebes.	3·3	2·0	1·2	0·55	0·45
c.	adult.	Boucard.	Celebes.	3·5	1·95	1·35	0·6	0·45

The figure (Plate VI. fig. 2) is taken from the specimen *a* procured by Dr. Platen in South Celebes.

MUNIA FORMOSANA.
THE FORMOSAN MUNIA.

PLATE VI. (FIGS. 3, 4).

Munia formosana, Swinh. Ibis, 1865, p. 356.
Amadina formosana, Gray, Hand-List Birds, ii. p. 55 (1870).
Munia formosana, Swinh. Proc. Zool. Soc. 1871, p. 385.
Munia formosana, Elwes, Proc. Zool. Soc. 1873, p. 667.
Munia formosana, Walden, Trans. Zool. Soc. 1875, p. 207.
Munia formosana, David et Oust. Ois. Chine, p. 342 (1877).
Munia formosana, Salvad. Ornit. Papuasia, p. 438 (1881).

Habitat. Island of Formosa.

" Similis *M. rubronigræ*, sed occipite nuchaque fuscis nec nigris "
(*Swinhoe*).

Male. "Above, sides of the breast and flanks chestnut; forehead, face, and under-parts deep black, the former fading into brown on the occiput and nape; lower rump deep glossy maroon; upper tail-coverts and two central tail-feathers flammeous, remaining tail-feathers light hair-brown, washed and edged with chestnut; axillaries and basal edge of under-quills pale buff, the under-stems white; edges of carpus beneath chestnut, marked with black; the chestnut on the breast forms a narrow belt; irides deep rich brown; bill cobalt-blue, deeper on the culmen and gonys; legs and claws plumbeous, with light yellowish soles and bases: length 4·25, wing 2·12, tail 1·5 inches" (*Swinhoe*).

Female. Similar, but rather paler.

Immature. "Above light yellowish-brown, washed with chestnut on every part except the head; under-parts pale dingy buff" (*Swinhoe*).

Observ. "Some of the specimens are entirely in the young plumage, others show every step of maturity. The moult is probably completed before the bird begins to breed, and those in the youngest garb are doubtless the produce of late nests last year" (*Swinhoe*).

The black mesial stripe gradually expands on the lower part of the chest, and is scarcely united to the black of the breast.

This interesting little Munia was discovered by Mr. R. Swinhoe during his sojourn in the Island of Formosa in 1865, and in a letter to the 'Ibis' (p. 356) of the same year he described it, adding the following remarks:—

"On the 26th of March my hunter returned from the hills (Takow, Formosa). He had penetrated no great distance, as his collection, consisting chiefly of birds of the plain, and containing no *Accipitres*, plainly showed. He brought, however, an extremely interesting species from the lower range. This was a *Munia* of which there were several specimens both in young and old plumage, dead and alive. It is a new species, closely allied to *M. rubronigra* of Hodgson, but singularly differing from it in the occiput and nape being brown instead of a rich black, as are the other dark parts. This bird supplies another curious confirmation of what I have before stated as to the affinities of the fauna of this island with that of the Himalaya, rather than with that of China. It has the black ventral stripe of *M. rubronigra* which is wanting in *M. sinensis*. I propose to call it *Munia formosana*."

The four specimens in my own collection were procured by Mr. R. Swinhoe in 1865, two adults and two young ones, these latter birds are in an intermediate and curious change of plumage.

I have transcribed Mr. Swinhoe's descriptions, which were taken from fresh individuals, and correspond exactly with those I possess; two of which are now figured for the first time.

Nothing is known with regard to the extent of country inhabited by this bird in the Island of Formosa, or its nest and eggs.

Canon H. B. Tristram kindly lent me two specimens which were collected in Formosa by Mr. R. Swinhoe.

Specimens examined.

No.	Sex.	Mus.	Locality.	Length.	Wing.	Tail.	Tars.	Culm.
a.	♂	E. B.	Fungshan (*Swinhoe*)	3·8	2·2	1·55	0·6	0·45
b.	♂ imm.	E. B.	Takow (*Swinhoe*).	3·15	2·2	1·15	0·6	0.4
c.	♀	E. B.	Takow (*Swinhoe*).	3·75	2·0	1·53	0·6	0·45
d.	♀ imm.	E. B.	Takow (*Swinhoe*).	3·4	2·1	1·5	0·6	0·4
e.	♂	H. B. Tristram.	Formosa (*Swinhoe*)	4·1	2·2	1·6	0·6	0·45
f.	♀	H. B. Tristram.	Formosa (*Swinhoe*)	3·9	2·15	1·45	0·6	0·45

The figures (Plate VI.) are taken from (fig. 3) *a* and (fig. 4) *d*, specimens in my own collection, procured by Mr. R. Swinhoe.

MUNIA FERRUGINOSA.
THE FERRUGINOUS MUNIA.
PLATE VII. (Figs. 1, 2).

Loxia ferruginosa, Sparrm. Mus. Carls. pl. 90, 91, ♂ et jun. (1789).
Loxia ferruginosa, Lath. Gen. Syn. suppl. ii. p. 196 (1801); Lath. Ind. Ornith. Suppl. ii. p. xiv. (1801); Shaw, Gen. Zoology, ix. p. 327 (1815).
Coccothraustes ferruginosa, Vieill. Nouv. Dict. xiii. p. 541 (1817); Vieill. Tabl. Encycl. Méth. iii. p. 1012 (1823).
Ferruginous Grosbeak, Lath. Gen. Hist. Birds, v. p. 265 (1822).
Fringilla majanoïdes, Temm. Pl. Col. 500, fig. 3 (1838).
Munia ferruginosa, Blyth, Cat. Birds Mus. A. S. B. p. 116 (1849); Reichb. Singvögel, p. 41, pl. xv. figs. 134, 135 (1861); Wald. Ibis, 1871, p. 177.
Amadina ferruginea, Gray et Mitch. Gen. Birds, ii. p. 370 (1849).
Munia ferruginea, Bp. Consp. Gen. Av. i. p. 451 (1850); Bernst. Journ. für Ornith. 1861, p. 180; Wallace, Proc. Zool. Soc. 1863, p. 486; Sclater, Vert. Anim. Gard. Zool. Soc. p. 239 (1883).
Dermophrys ferruginea, Cab. Mus. Hein. i. p. 174, Note (1851).
Amadina ferruginosa, Gray, Hand-List Birds, ii. p. 54 (1870).
Spermestes ferruginosa, Russ, Stubenvögel, p. 166, pl. vi. fig. 29 (1879).

Figures. Sparrm. Mus. Carls. pl. 90, 91. Temm. Pl. Col. 500, fig. 3. Reichb. Singvögel, pl. xv. figs. 134, 135. Russ, Stubenvögel, pl. vi. fig. 29.

Dutch. *Zwartkeel-Nonnetje.*

English. The *Black-breasted Maja. Javan Maja-Finch. Black-throated Nun. Black-throated white-headed Nun. Javan Nun. Ferruginous Grosbeak. Ferruginous Munia. Ferruginous Finch.*

French. *Le Majan à poitrine noire. Gros-bec Majanoïde. La Nonnette à tête blanche et à poitrine noire.*

German. *Die schwarzbrüstige Maja oder Nonne. Die schwarzbrüstige Nonnen-Amadine.*

Sundanese. *Bondol.*

Habitat. Java. Flores (*Wallace*).

Male. Crown, sides of head, and hind neck white; back, wings, and sides of body dark chestnut brown; rump and upper tail-coverts glistening dark maroon; centre tail-feathers and outer edges of the rest glistening dark ferruginous; chin, throat, breast, mesial stripe, flank, thighs, and under tail-coverts black; axillaries, under wing-coverts, and inner edges of wing-feathers yellowish-buff; iris reddish-brown; bill plumbeous, whitish at the tip; legs slaty-black : length 4·1, wing 2·05, tail 1·5, tarsus 0·6, culmen 0·45.

Female. Similar, with a slight tinge of yellowish-buff on the crown and nape.

Young. Above dark rufous brown; primaries, secondaries, and tail-feathers brown, edged with pale rufous brown; chin and throat buffish-white; under parts fulvous, palest on abdomen and under tail-coverts; iris dark hazel brown; bill and legs dull slaty-brown : length 3·85, wing 2·0, tail 1·5, tarsus 0·6, culmen 0·45.

The little Munias which form the present group, although possessing white or pale-coloured heads, still retain the black mesial stripe, which is more or less developed on the abdomen, but in the last one (*Munia pallida*) it is obsolete. These pale-headed birds hold, in my opinion, the closest relationship to the former five black-and-brown-headed species.

The Ferruginous Munia was first described and figured by Sparrman in his 'Museum Carlsonianum,' published between the years 1786–89. The figure in plate 90 represents an adult bird, which he says is a male, but whether this is so is difficult to decide, the two sexes being alike. In plate 91 is depicted what Sparrman calls the female; this is a representation of a young bird (and not the female) in its fulvous brown plumage, a characteristic of the whole of the young birds of this peculiar form of Weaver.

The distribution of this very pretty species is apparently restricted to the islands of Java and Flores.

"This bird," Bernstein tells us, "is, like *Munia oryzivora*, a well-known frequenter of the inhabited regions of Java. The two sexes cannot be distinguished from one another in anything save that the old males have a darker and more pronounced colouring. When Bonaparte described the plumage of the female as differing from that of the male, this statement was founded on a mistake, and the description of the female given has reference to the plumage of the young. During the months when the rice fields are flooded and under cultivation, *Munia ferruginea*, like the rice-bird, inhabits small woods, thickets and hedges along the roads, or between fields and meadows : sometimes, also, it lives in little wildernesses formed by Alang Alang and low bushes, which latter it seems to prefer, as I never yet found it missing in such places. As soon, however, as the rice begins to ripen, it betakes itself to the fields, and by its numbers not unfrequently works considerable damage. Smaller and quicker in its movements than the rice-bird, it is quite as easily kept in captivity on rice and other species of grain ; it is also sociable towards other small birds and companions, with whom it is accustomed to sleep close together on the same perch. Its call-note which one frequently hears is a clear *wit–wit–wit*. I have never heard its song, but on the other hand have often found its nest. The latter is always placed in a low position, a few inches, at most half a foot, above the ground ; sometimes in a small shrub standing between the Alang-Alangs ; sometimes it is built among this grass and supported by its blades, but never immediately upon the ground. It is round in shape, with the entrance at the side, and is of considerable extent in proportion to the size of the bird, as its diameter usually amounts to 6 inches.

"All the nests which I have found belonging to this species were composed exclusively of blades and fibres of various grasses, more especially of wool-bearing ones, which materials were only loosely woven together on the outside, and were also mixed with larger leaves and those of the Alang which gave to the whole structure a somewhat dishevelled appearance ; while inside they were carefully and more finely entwined, and well mixed with soft grass wool. The pure white, rather long-shaped eggs, of which usually six or seven, and but rarely four, are found in one nest, measure 16–17 mm. in diameter, in a few cases only 15 mm., while their greatest transverse diameter amounts to 11–12 mm."

Specimens examined.

No.	Sex.	Mus.	Locality.	Length.	Wing.	Tail.	Tars.	Culm.
a.	♂	E. B.	Java.	3·0	2·0	1·35	0·65	0·45
b.	♂	E. B.	Java (H. Blyth).	4·1	2·05	1·5	0·6	0·45
c.	♀	E. B.	Java.	3·85	2·0	1·45	0·6	0·5
d.	♂	E. B.	Java.	4·25	2·0	1·5	0·65	0·45
e.	jun.	E. B.	Java.	3·85	2·0	1.5	0·6	0·45

The figures (Plate VII.) are taken from the male (fig. 1) *b*, and the young bird (fig. 2) *e*, both in my own collection.

MUNIA MAJA.
THE WHITE-HEADED MUNIA.

PLATE VII. (Fig. 3).

The Malacca Grosbeak, Edwards, Gleanings, ii. p. 202, pl. 306, fig. 1 (1760).
Maia sinensis, Briss. Ornith. iii. p. 212, pl. ix. fig. 2 (1760).
La Maia de la Chine, Briss. Ornith. vi. suppl. p. 76 (1760).
Maia sinensis, Briss. Syn. Méth. i. p. 365 (1763).
White-headed Grosbeak, Lath. Gen. Syn. iii. p. 151 (1783).
White-headed Grosbeak, Lath. Gen. Hist. Birds, v. p. 264 (1822).
Majan, Bodd, Tabl. d. pl. Enl. 109, 1 (1783).
La Maja de la Chine, Buff. Pl. Enl. 109, fig. 1 (1777).
Majan, Buff. Hist. Nat. Ois. iv. p. 107, pl. 3, l. f. (1778).
Le Majan, Vieill. Ois. Chant. p. 87, pl. lvi. (1805).
Loxia maja, Linn. Syst. Nat. i. p. 301 (1766); Müll. Vollst. Natursyst. iii. p. 549 (1773); Gmel. Syst. Nat. ii. p. 849 (1788); Lath. Ind. Ornith. i. p. 391 (1790); Daud. Traité d'Ornith. ii. p. 441 (1800); Shaw, Gen. Zool. ix. p. 301 (1815); Vieill. Nouv. Dict. xii. p. 236 (1817); Griff. Cuv. Anim. Kingd. ii. p. 152 (1829).
Fringilla maja, Horsf. Trans. Linn. Soc. xiii. 1822, p. 162; Vieill. Tabl. Encycl. Méth. iii. p. 975 (1823); Licht. Doubl. Mus. Berol. pp. 26, 89 (1823).
Loxia leucocephala, Raffles, Trans. Linn. Soc. xiii. 1822, p. 314.
Coccothraustes major, Steph. Gen. Zool. xiv. p. 87 (1824).
Amadina maja, Blyth, Journ. As. Soc. Beng. xiii. 1844, p. 949, xiv. 1845, p. 554, xv. 1846, pp. 36, 285; Gray et Mitch. Gen. Birds, ii. p. 370 (1849); Eyton, Cat. Birds, p. 253 (1856); Gray, Hand-List Birds, ii. p. 54 (1870).

Amadina leucocephala, Gray et Mitch. Gen. Birds, ii. p. 370 (1849).
Munia maja, Blyth, Cat. Birds Mus. A. S. B. p. 116 (1849) ; Bonap.
Consp. Gen. Av. i. p. 451 (1851) ; Horsf. et Moore, Cat. Birds Mus.
E. Ind. Comp. ii. p. 505 (1856–8) ; Moore, Proc. Zool. Soc. 1859,
p. 444 ; Reichb. Singvögel, p. 40, pl. xiv. fig. 130, pl. xv. figs. 131,
132 (1861) ; Walden, Ibis, 1871, p. 177 ; Salvadori, Uccelli di
Borneo, p. 264 (1874) ; Tweedd. Ibis, 1877, p. 318 ; Salvadori, Ann.
Mus. Civ. Gen. xiv. 1879, p. 73 ; Salvin, Cat. Coll. Birds Strickl.
p. 251 (1882) ; Scl. Vert. Anim. Gard. Zool. Soc. p. 239 (1883).
Dermophrys maja, Cab. Mus. Hein. i. p. 174 (1851).
Munia major, Garrod, Proc. Zool. Soc. 1873, p. 462.
Spermestes maja, Russ, Stubenvögel, p. 163 (1879).

> *Figures.* Edwards, Gleanings, ii. pl. 306, fig. 1. Brisson,
> Ornith. iii. pl. ix. fig. 2. Buffon, Pl. Enl. 109, fig. 1. Vieill.
> Ois. Chant. pl. lvi. Reichb. Singvögel, pl. xiv. fig. 130, pl.
> xv. figs. 131, 132.

Dutch. *Nonnetje.*

English. *Malacca Grosbeak. White-headed Grosbeak.* The *Majan* or *Maja Finch. White-headed Finch. Nun. White-headed Nun.*

French. *Le Majan. La Maja de la Chine. Le Gros-bec à tête blanche. La Nonnette à tête blanche. Capucin à tête blanche. Mahian à tête blanche. Le Gros-bec de Malacca.*

German. *Die weissköpfige Maja. Nonne. Nonnenvogel. Nonnenfink. Nonnenweberfink. Der Weisskopf. Die weissköpfige Nonnen-Amadine.*

Native Names. *Pipit,* Sumatra (*Raffles*). *Petap Whobun,* Malay (*Blyth*).

Habitat. Malacca and Sumatra. No doubt introduced into India, China, and many of the islands in the Malayan Archipelago.

Male. Head creamy white, tinged with buff on the nape and throat ; back and wings dark cinnamon-brown ; primaries, secondaries, and tail-feathers dark brown on the inner webs ; rump and upper tail-coverts glistening deep red-brown ; centre tail-feathers and outer edges of the rest glistening dark ferruginous; lower part of throat and chest ashy-brown, tinged with buff; sides like the back; belly, flanks, thighs, and under tail-coverts black; axillaries and under surface of wing yellowish-buff; iris dark brown; bill plumbeous; legs slaty black: length 4·1, wing 2·1, tail 1·45, tarsus 0·6, culmen 0·45.

Female. Similar, but much paler; the creamy white of the hind neck gradually forms a pale greyish band, which blends on to the mantle; the black mesial stripe much more restricted than in the male.

Young. Similar to that of *Munia ferruginosa*, but paler, especially on the under-parts.

Observ. In the adult male the crown of the head and cheeks become almost white; the black mesial band expands on the chest, and gradually decreases towards the middle of the abdomen. The female is generally more ashy-brown on the hind neck; the black mesial stripe restricted to the centre of the abdomen, and scarcely reaches to the chest, which is rather more ashy than that of the male.

The moulting in the young is gradual and gives it a mottled appearance; the mesial stripe being dull blackish-brown, interspersed with buffish-white feathers.

THE White-headed Munia, or so-called Maja Finch, appears to be one of the earliest and best known species of this insular group of Asiatic Weaverbirds, and from a very remote period it has been brought to Europe in great numbers by trading and other vessels which touch annually at many of the islands in the Straits of Malacca, or Malayan Peninsula, where this bird abounds, especially in those islands where rice and smaller cereals are cultivated to any great extent.

This bird, like all its congeners, is exclusively a dry seed eater, and congregates in enormous flocks on the paddy-fields when the seed is ripe, and after the harvest season, when the wild seeds have attained maturity, it finds subsistence until the following harvest. It is at this period of its existence (and after the breeding season) that it is procured in vast numbers and shipped to various parts of the globe; the greater number come to Europe, although the natives retain them as cage pets among many others of the same family.

Lieut. H. R. Kelham tells us: "This little White-headed Munia is very common throughout the west of the peninsula, including the islands of Penang and Singapore. When the grain is ripe it is to be seen in countless numbers in the paddy-fields. On being disturbed, it rises with a feeble, twittering cry, the flocks whirling and twirling over the top of the paddy like clouds of dust on a road when the wind is blowing. It is commonly known in the Straits as the 'cigar bird'—a capital name; for when flying, its white head, brown body, and small size give it very much the appearance of a cigar with the white ash on it."

Reichenbach remarks in his 'Singvögel,' published in 1861, that "these birds have often been brought to us in modern times from East and South India, more especially from Sumatra and Borneo. They are great favourites, more for their gentleness and pretty manners than for their weak voice. I received lately from Sumatra four little pairs with their nests and eggs, and a fifth nest was already to be found in Thienemann's collections. The long melon-shaped nest is built between reeds and sedges ; it has an oval opening of 5 cents. in diameter. It is composed of grasses of the millet species, loosely and untidily woven together and wound round outside with a quantity of narrow and broad blades of grass, and thickly lined again inside with very fine silky-haired grasses twined together. The two or three eggs are dull white."

Specimens examined.

No.	Sex.	Mus.	Locality	Length	Wing.	Tail.	Tars.	Culm.
a.	♂	E. B.	Singapore (*Armstrong*).	4·1	2·1	1·45	0·6	0·45
b.	♀	E. B.	Malacca.	3·65	2·0	1·45	0·6	0·45
c.	imm.	E. B.	Malacca.	4·15	2·05	1·35	0·6	0·45
d.	jun.	E. B.	Malacca.	4·05	2·1	1·35	0·6	0·45
e.	jun.	E. B.	Malacca.	3·9	2·1	1·35	0·6	0·4
f.	?	E. B.	Malacca.	3·9	2·05	1·4	0·6	0·45
g.	♀	E. B.	Malacca.	3·75	2·2	1·45	0·6	0·45
h.	?	F.W.Frohawk.	Malacca.	4·0	2·15	1·45	0·6	0·45
i.	imm.	A. Boucard.	Malacca.	4·15	2·05	1·4	0·6	0·45
j.	jun.	E. B.	Malacca.	4·0	2·05	1·3	0·6	0·45

The figure (Plate VII.) is taken from a male (fig. 3) *a*, in my own collection.

MUNIA PALLIDA.
THE PALLID MUNIA.

PLATE VII. (FIG. 4).

Munia pallida, Wallace, Proc. Zool. Soc. 1863, pp. 486, 495.
Amadina pallida, Gray, Hand-List Birds, ii. p. 54 (1870).
Amadina pallida, Blasius, Journ. für Ornith. 1883, p. 125.

English. *The Pallid* or *Celebean White-headed Munia*.

Habitat. Celebes. Lombok and Flores (*Wallace*).

"Rufo-cinerea, subtus pallide rufa ; capite colloque albis, pectore albescente, crisso caudaque rufo-castaneis, uropygio et caudæ tectricibus superioribus intense sericeo-castaneis " (*Wallace*).

Adult. "Above rufous ash ; beneath pale rufous ; head and neck white ; breast tinged with rosy ash ; tail and under tail-coverts dark rufous ; rump and upper tail-coverts glossy chestnut brown ; bill and feet blue-lead ; iris dark : length 4½ inches, wing 2¼ inches " (*Wallace*).

Female. Similar.

Observ. Mr. Wallace states that this bird is "very near *Munia maja* (L.), but differs in the much paler colouring of both the upper and under surface."

THE Pallid Munia is an insular form which so closely resembles the White-headed Munia, that I doubt whether it can really be separated, although I give it as distinct, on the authority of Mr. A. R. Wallace who discovered it in Celebes.

The three pale-headed birds here described verge one into the other in the same manner as the three last Black-headed Munias ; therefore it is somewhat difficult to say which is the older form, although I am inclined to regard the Javan or Black-throated bird as the type. This bird appears to be extremely rare in collections, and according to Mr. Wallace is very local, and almost exclusively confined to Lombok and Flores. I am unable at present to give any details of its habits or nidification. It is now figured for the first time, from the specimen procured by Mr. A. R. Wallace, which is in the British Museum.

MUNIA MELÆNA.
THE DUKE-OF-YORK ISLAND MUNIA.

PLATE VIII. (Fig. 1).

Munia melœna, Sclater, Proc. Zool. Soc. 1880, p. 66, pl. vii. fig. 2.
Munia hemimelœna (err. ?), Sclater, Proc. Zool. Soc. 1880, p. 66.
Munia melœna, Reichnw. et Schal., Journ. für Ornith. 1880, p. 322.
Munia melœna, Salvadori, Ann. Mus. Civ. Gen. xvi. 1880, p. 192.
Munia melœna, Salvadori, Ornit. Papuasia, p. 439 (1881).

Figure. Sclater, Proc. Zool. Soc. 1880, pl. vii. fig. 2.

Habitat. New Britain. Duke of York Island (*Brown*).

"Nigra; uropygio, caudæ tectricibus superioribus et rectricum marginibus externis castaneis; cauda acuminata, rectricibus duabus mediis quam cæteræ longioribus; ventre medio rufo, hypochondriis nigro variegatis, crisso nigro; alis extus et dorso postico fuscescenti-nigris, subalaribus rufescentibus; rostro crasso et pedibus nigris. Long. tota 4·3, alæ 2, caudæ 1·3" (*P. L. Sclater*).

Male. Head and back dull black; rump and upper tail-coverts glistening ferruginous; centre tail-feathers and outer edges of the rest glistening pale ferruginous; primaries and secondaries dull blackish-brown; chin, sides of head, breast, sides, flanks, latter part of abdomen, and under tail-coverts black; side feathers irregularly barred with pale rufous like the belly; axillaries and under wing-coverts pale fulvous; iris blackish: bill and feet slaty-black: "length 4·3, wing 2·0, tail 1·3" (*P. L. Sclater*).

Female. Similar, but not so black, rump and upper tail-coverts paler glistening ferruginous; abdomen pale fulvous; bill and feet slaty-black: length 3·85, wing 2·1, tail 1·4, tarsus 0·65, culmen 0·6.

For the knowledge of the existence of this new and very peculiar black form of *Munia*, we are indebted to the Rev. G. Brown, who procured it at Kabakadai on the coast of New Britain.

It was described and figured in the 'Proceedings of the Zoological Society' for 1880, by Mr. P. L. Sclater, who says :—

" This species is remarkable for its general black colouring, varied only by the chestnut upper tail-coverts and the broad rufous patch on the belly. Its bill is stronger even than *M. forbesi*.

" Besides the skins, Mr. Brown sends a small collection of birds in spirit, of which the exact localities are not stated. It contains a second example of *Munia hemimelæna*, also *Donacicola spectabilis*."

At present no particulars have come to my knowledge respecting the differences of the adult and young, or the habits and nidification.

The only specimen of *Munia melæna* which I have had an opportunity of seeing is that of a female collected by the Rev. G. Brown at Kabais, New Britain, now in the collection of Canon H. B. Tristram, who very kindly lent it to me for the purposes of this work.

The figure (Plate VIII. fig. 1) is taken from a male in the British Museum.

MUNIA FORBESI.
FORBES'S MUNIA.

PLATE VIII. (FIG. 2).

Munia forbesi, Sclater, Proc. Zool. Soc. 1879, pp. 447, 449, pl. xxxvii. fig. 3.
Munia forbesi, Reichnw. et Schal. Journ. für Ornith. 1880, p. 203.
Munia forbesi, Salvadori, Ann. Mus. Civ. Gen. xvi. 1880, p. 192.
Munia forbesi, Salvadori, Ornit. Papuasia, p. 438 (1881).

Figure. Sclater, Proc. Zool. Soc. 1879, pl. xxxvii. fig. 3.

Habitat. New Ireland.

" Testaceo-rufa, subtus paulo dilutior ; capite undique cum gula, hypochondriis et ventre imo cum femoribus et caudæ tectricibus productis nigris ; rostro et pedibus nigris. Long. tota 4, alæ 2, caudæ acuminatæ 1·5 ; rostro crassiusculo " (*P. L. Sclater*).

Male. Head and chin black ; back, wings, and tail-feathers chestnut-brown, darkest on the primaries ; rump and upper tail-coverts glistening ferruginous, centre tail-feathers and outer edges of the rest glistening pale ferruginous ; throat and under-parts bright rufous ; ventral patch and under tail-coverts black ; axillaries and under surface of wing pale fulvous ; iris hazel brown ; bill and feet slaty-black : "length 4·0, wing 2·0, tail 1·5 " (*P. L. Sclater*).

FORBES'S MUNIA is another well-marked species of this group of thick-billed Weavers, and was discovered in New Ireland by the Rev. G. Brown, who has not given us any details respecting the habits and nidification.

Mr. P. L. Sclater described and figured the species in the ' Proceedings of the Zoological Society' for 1879, and remarks that "a single example of this Finch, obtained in the Topaia district of New Ireland in September 1878, is in the collection. It is a rather thick-billed species, belonging to the group of *M. malacca*. I propose to name it *Munia forbesi* in compliment to Mr. W. A. Forbes, F.Z.S."

The figure (Plate VIII. fig. 2) is from a specimen in the British Museum.

MUNIA SPECTABILIS.
THE BLANCHE BAY MUNIA.

PLATE VIII. (FIG. 3).

Donacicola spectabilis, Sclater, Proc. Zool. Soc. 1879, pp. 447, 449, pl. xxxvii. fig. 2.
Donacicola spectabilis, Layard, Ibis, 1880, p. 297.
Donacicola spectabilis, Reichnw. et Schal. Journ. für Ornith. 1880, p. 203.
Donacicola spectabilis, Salvad. Ann. Mus. Civ. Gen. xvi. 1880, p. 192.
Donacicola spectabilis, Salvad. Ornit. Papuasia, p. 441, 1881.

Figure. Sclater, Proc. Zool. Soc. 1879, pl. xxxvii. fig. 2.

Habitat. New Britain.

"Brunnea; pileo, nucha et capitis lateribus nigris; tectricibus caudæ superioribus et rectricum mediarum marginibus pallide castaneis; subtus alba; gula, ventre imo, et crisso cum femoribus nigris; subalaribus ochraceo-albis; rostro et pedibus nigris. Long. tota 3·4, alæ 1·8, caudæ 1·2" (*P. L. Sclater*).

Male. Crown of head, hind neck, cheeks, chin, and throat black, washed with grey; mantle, scapulars, and wings blackish-brown, edges of feathers brighter; rump, upper tail-coverts, centre tail-feathers, and outer edges of the rest glistening ochraceous brown, shaft-stripes brown; breast, sides, and belly white, tinged with buff in the centre; axillaries, under wing-coverts, and inner edges of primaries and secondaries buff; under tail-coverts black; "iris deep brown; bill and feet black" (*Layard*): length 3·6, wing 1·95, tail 1·45, tarsus 0·6, culmen 0·45.

Female. Similar, but the back is not so dark as in the male; the breast and belly are strongly tinged with yellowish-buff; bill and feet black : length 3·7, wing 1·85, tail 1·55, tarsus 0·6, culmen 0·4.

The Rev. G. Brown during his residence in the Duke of York Island, New Britain, prepared several collections of bird-skins which he transmitted to Mr. P. L. Sclater for determination ; among them were the three species figured and described above (Plate VIII.).

We are now in possession of four very remarkable species, viz. *Munia melæna*, *forbesi*, *spectabilis*, and *flaviprymna*, all of which are modifications of one type, and are easily distinguished from the other members of this large group by the ventral patch and under tail-coverts being black, and by the absence of the black mesial stripe which is so conspicuous in the *Munia malacca* form.

Mr. P. L. Sclater points out that " this Finch, of which there is a single skin, is perhaps not very far from *Donacicola flaviprymna*, Gould, B. Austr. iii. pl. 96, but is immediately recognizable by its black head and neck."

Mr. E. L. C. Layard, in notes of a collecting trip in New Britain, says :—" This little Finch was found only in Blanche Bay. It was in large flocks, diligently hunting for grass-seeds on the ground in the banana and cocoanut plantations, very easy to approach. I killed seven at one shot."

The male and female above described were procured by Mr. C. L. Layard in Blanche Bay, New Britain, in 1879, and are now in the collection of Canon H. B. Tristram, who kindly lent them to me for examination.

The figure is taken from the male above referred to.

www.ingramcontent.com/pod-product-compliance
Lightning Source LLC
Chambersburg PA
CBHW032142230426
43672CB00011B/2422